UTOPIAN
DREAMS,
APOCALYPTIC
NIGHTMARES

Purdue Studies in Romance Literatures

PSRL volume 42

UTOPIAN DREAMS, APOCALYPTIC NIGHTMARES

Globalization in

Recent Mexican and

Chicano Narrative

Miguel López-Lozano

Purdue University Press
West Lafayette, Indiana

∞ The paper used in this book meets the minimum requirements of
American National Standard for Information Sciences—Permanence of
Paper for Printed Library Materials, ANSI Z39.48-1992.

Printed in the United States of America
Design by Anita Noble

Library of Congress Cataloging-in-Publication Data

López-Lozano, Miguel, 1961–
  Utopian dreams, apocalyptic nightmares: globalization in recent Mexican and Chicano narrative / Miguel López-Lozano.
       p.   cm. — (Purdue studies in Romance literatures ; v. 42)
  Includes bibliographical references and index.
  ISBN 978-1-55753-484-2 (alk. paper)
  1. Mexican fiction—20th century—History and criticism. 2. American
fiction—Mexican American authors—History and criticism. 3. Globalization in literature. I. Title. II. Series.
  PQ7207.G58L66 2007
  863'.6409972   2007043143

To the memory of Antony Higgins

Contents

Acknowledgments

This book is dedicated to the memory of Antony Higgins, who taught me about the academic profession and true friendship. I would like to thank him and all the people who have been key to the realization of this book. Gwen Kirkpatrick and Danny J. Anderson have been behind me every step of the way. I would like to thank my students, colleagues, chairs, and deans at the University of New Mexico for providing sound mentoring to start and finish this book and for support in the critical stages of the process. I would also like to extend my gratitude to Floyd Merrell and Susan Clawson for their editing expertise along with all the editors and staff at the Purdue Studies in Romance Literatures series.

I would like to express my thanks to those who helped me to see beyond the limits of the moment, Susan Dever, Melissa Axelrod, and Eleuterio Santiago-Díaz, as well as my fellow *mexicanistas* Ignacio Corona, Ignacio Sánchez Prado, and José Pablo Villalobos, whose dialogue and collaboration expedited the elaboration of this book. Thanks are due also to the folks in Interlibrary Loan at the University of New Mexico, who have searched far and wide to find me all the materials I needed. And finally I thank my wife, Kimberle López, for bearing with me through it all.

Permission has been granted by the journal *Aztlán: A Journal of Chicano Studies* to reprint portions of chapter 2 that appeared previously in an article entitled "The Politics of Blood: Miscegenation and Degeneration in Alejandro Morales's *The Rag Doll Plagues*," published in issue 28.1 (2003): 39–73.

Permission has also been granted to reprint the portions of chapter 4 on Homero Aridjis that were previously published under the title "Pensar la nación mexicana a través del apocalipsis ecológico en dos novelas distópicas de Homero Aridjis" in the volume *La luz queda en el aire: estudios internacionales en honor a Homero Aridjis*, edited by Thomas Stauder (Frankfurt: Universität Erlangen-Nürnberg Press, 2005), 173–86.

Introduction

Utopian Dreams,
Apocalyptic Nightmares:
Rewriting Mexican History
in the Times of NAFTA

> Who controls the present, controls the past
> Who controls the past, controls the future
> George Orwell
> *Nineteen Eighty-Four*

These words from George Orwell's *Nineteen Eighty-Four* (1949) contemplating the importance of history and its impact on the future reflect a critical paradigm for contemporary Latin American and US Latino writers as they confront the social and political changes accompanying rapid modernization and globalization. Through the depiction of a desolate future, *Nineteen Eighty-Four* inspires a re-examination of the implications of the manipulation of history by a dictatorial state interested in advancing technology and industrialization at any cost, thus revealing the perils and contradictions of modernity. As the epigraph from Orwell suggests, control over the interpretation of history can be a key instrument for legitimizing the state and its projects. Like Aldous Huxley's *Brave New World* (1932) and Ray Bradbury's later *Fahrenheit 451* (1953), Orwell's 1949 masterpiece suggests the potential of memory as a form of cultural resistance to a world devoid of individual identity in which citizens are overwhelmed by the automatized images disseminated by an overarching system of mass media. Just as European novelists in the late nineteenth and early twentieth centuries depicted the dystopian consequences of the industrial revolution, Mexican and Chicano writers at the turn of the millennium employ science fiction techniques to engage the questions of industrial development, urbanization, and environmental damage brought to the foreground by the signing of the North American Free Trade Agreement (NAFTA) in 1992,

1

coincidentally the same year as the quincentenary of the initial encounter between Europe and the Americas.

The apocalyptic futures portrayed in science fiction works like those of Huxley, Orwell, and Bradbury stress the alienation of the individual in a world beset by conformity and consumerism. Latin American and US Latino authors also employ apocalyptic motifs to highlight the homogenizing effects of globalization and concomitant marginalization of difference. Because Latin America's official history legitimizes projects of development that erase indigenous peoples, women, and nature from the discourse of modernity, presenting them as merely the backdrop of efforts toward progress, contemporary writers excavate the past in order to revisit some of the discourses that generated this marginalization. It is through this re-examination of history and, in particular, the history of the colonial encounter, that Mexican and Chicano novelists of the late 1980s and 1990s establish a connection between the past, present, and future consequences of the material and human exploitation conducted in the name of economic progress and industrial development.

Europe's problematic encounter with the Americas fueled the imagination of sixteenth-century explorers and thinkers, giving birth to the concept of the modern literary utopia that envisioned the New World as the earthly paradise. Paradoxically, the encounter with the Amerindians contributed to the emergence of the Western notion of modernity, which in the context of Latin American societies led to a cultural homogenization that excluded the Other from participating in the creation of the new societies. Supremacy over the recently conquered peoples of America became the foundation of modernity, an enterprise defined in terms of control over native peoples, women, and nature. Since the early exploration of the New World, America has been construed as different from Europe and specifically "otherized" in exotic and feminine terms. In order to facilitate their subordination to colonial rule, the Europeans feminized and "otherized" the Amerindians either as barbaric cannibals or noble savages who presumably lacked the intellectual depth to govern themselves or others. Following independence, the founding fathers of the new Latin American nations continued to consider women and native peoples as closer to nature. These strategies of domination thus converged in the colonies and later in the independent republics, forming a base for the inequities of contemporary societies.

Following the colonization of the Americas, the Industrial Revolution brought a change of perspective regarding the location of utopia. In the Golden Age, utopia was imagined as a pastoral Arcadia or the biblical Garden of Eden, a natural paradise from which mankind was expelled. With the dawn of industrial capitalism, nature came to be considered as an endless reserve of raw materials available for exploitation as science and technology were developed to meet the needs of Europe's growing population. While in the early modern age the territories of the Americas had provided both material and imaginary resources for the emergence of capitalism, in the industrial age, images of technology displaced the pastoral utopia, thus negating the Golden Age dreams of a return to nature as a pristine state.

While the pastoral was the frame for utopian visions from their classical origins through the early modern period, by the Enlightenment, utopia had found a favorable location in the city, which united nature's resources and humanity's wise utilization of raw materials, technological knowledge, and political savvy. This interest in representing the city as the ultimate expression of modernity is reflected in developing countries such as those of Latin America in the form of rapidly expanding capitals where elites follow Western patterns of social, economic, and cultural organization. With this in mind, by the late twentieth century, images of gargantuan cities, vexed by an antagonistic relationship between humankind and machine, had become the focal point for the discussion of the apocalyptic futures in Latin American dystopian literary production.

At the turn of the millennium, Latin American and US Latino authors draw on the disturbing images first depicted in science fiction novels in order to criticize the imposition of a notion of modernity emanating from hegemonic centers in Europe and the United States, proposing alternative models of development and social organization.[1] Dystopian fiction provides the means for Mexican and Chicano authors to question fundamental tenets of Latin American culture such as the Western model of industrialized capitalism as the only possible pattern for the economic development of the hemisphere. Mexico's entrance into a global economy and the concurrent socioeconomic and political crisis of the 1980s and 1990s provoked intellectuals to challenge the value of this model of development for a society that even into the twenty-first century remains divided along racial, class, and gender lines.

The literary dystopias produced in this context are negative representations of imagined future worlds in which the by-products of industrial consumerism have destroyed the dreams of harmonious progress. As in classic science fiction, social problems are shown to be related to a perversion of the goals of modernity represented by mechanization and authoritarianism, encompassing the lack of economic opportunities for already marginalized sectors of Latin American society. These issues, added to the ecological damage wrought by industrialism, form a volatile mix underscoring the conditions for the end of humanity as we know it. This link between narrative dystopia and the socially exclusionary aspect of modernity is the core of the present study. The novels studied here present a problematic view of the project of modernity in the New World and the project of modernization begun in the 1950s in Mexico. They represent a nostalgic view of the location of national culture and the sites where it used to be articulated.

Through the use of dystopian tropes, turn-of-the-millennium Mexican and Chicano writers address the potential effects of globalization—the latest phase of modern development—on the landscape and cultures of Mexico and the borderland. This theme forms a common thread among the narratives examined in the following chapters: Carlos Fuentes's *Cristóbal Nonato (Christopher Unborn,* 1987); Alejandro Morales's *The Rag Doll Plagues* (1992); Carmen Boullosa's *Cielos de la tierra* (Heavens on Earth, 1997); and Homero Aridjis's *La leyenda de los soles* (The Legend of the Suns, 1993) and *¿En quién piensas cuando haces el amor?* (Who Do You Think of When Making Love?, 1996). Written under the shadow of NAFTA, these dystopian novels engage the theme of Mexico's pattern of development, revisiting images of science fiction to depict the potentially disastrous impact of globalization on the environment and on the indigenous peoples of the Americas.

These novels reposition the meaning of modernity and its liberating potential, beginning by promoting an examination of its origins from the encounter with the Other and the domination of nature. As suggested by the above epigraph from *Nineteen Eighty-Four*, it is only through the excavation of the history of exclusion that the present problems of Latin America can be addressed. Likewise, through the study of cautionary tales of ecoapocalypses, a more beneficial conceptualization of the relationship between humankind and the natural environment can be envisioned. These Mexican and Chicano novels produced during a crucial period in the history of both nations ultimately point to the potential for local responses to global problems—for example, in the form of grassroots movements, Non-Governmental Organizations, and alternative development—to contribute to the creation of a more equitable and self-sustaining society in the northern American hemisphere.

Utopia, the "Discovery of America" and the Enlightenment Project

The association between the literary and philosophical discourse of utopia and the discovery of America is not merely coincidental, since not only did the first images of utopia initially inspire the exploration of new territories, but, significantly, the lands discovered in 1492 provided a space for concretizing dreams of ideal societies in paradisiacal locations that enticed the European imagination for centuries to come.[2] The emergence of the modern literary utopia coincides with the dramatic changes of the sixteenth century: the period of flourishing of arts and sciences known as the Renaissance; the Protestant Reformation, which questioned the univocal interpretation of life according to Catholicism; and the exploration and colonization of the Americas, which brought to reality a territory until then only imagined in Western myths such as the Garden of Eden, the lost continent of Atlantis, and the ideal city.[3] Beginning with Columbus's depiction of the New World as the earthly paradise, the theme of utopia has been a constant throughout the history of Latin America: first in the colonial period, as the Europeans projected images of the earthly paradise upon the New World; and later, after independence, when Latin American elites began to conceptualize modernization as a new kind of utopia, one that encapsulates the desire to achieve the levels of productivity, comfort, and consumption associated with the nations and economies of the First World. Thus, utopia is first used to project the European imagination onto the American landscape and its peoples, and later used to embody Latin American dreams of prosperity.

Although notions of an ideally perfect society have been present in scholastic sources since classical Greco-Roman times,[4] it is only with Thomas More's publication of *Utopia* in 1516 that we begin to see outlined the main characteristics of what would become the modern literary utopia.[5] Beginning with More's work, this literary genre typically describes an ideal commonwealth situated in an idyllic geographic setting, adopting as a sign of its modernity a rational perspective of world affairs. The impact of the discovery of America on the evolution of utopian narrative is immediately apparent, given that More's own fictional protagonist, a member of Amerigo Vespucci's expeditions, stumbles upon the island of Utopia during his travels in the New World.[6] America served as an inspiration for European writers because of its vast territories, abundant flora and fauna, and the infinite potential of seemingly deserted spaces in which no trace of "civilization" had left its mark. The discovery of the Americas afforded Europe a space upon which to project images of its own myths and dreams in a domain outside the confines of the Old World, igniting the promise of a moldable future and the possibility of escaping the restrictions of European societies of the time. The connection between the practical and the imaginary is paramount, as Peter J. Taylor concludes that the effect of the discovery of the New World "destroyed classical cosmology and stimulated both the factual study of new worlds in geography and the new fictional genre of utopias in which new worlds were invented" (80–81). The evolution of literary utopias is thus linked to the search for a vision of the world beyond the narrow margins of the European imagination of the late sixteenth century and the will and desire to bring to fruition an ideal society.

Resisting the Eurocentric notion of the "discovery of America," historian Edmundo O'Gorman in the *Invention of America* focuses on how through the process of conquest and colonization we witness an arduous quest to pursue the goal of constructing a perfect society. This connection between the discovery of the Americas and the development of utopian narrative has caught the attention of several literary critics, among them science fiction scholar Tom Moylan. As Moylan points out, the impact of the New World on the utopian imagination is paramount:

> The discovery of the non-European continents and islands provided visionaries of the fifteenth and sixteenth century with actual and imaginary space in which to create both practical and literary experiments. The new space in the world reinforced the sensibility found in the landscape painting and pastoral poetry of the time that effused the presence of an Arcadian locale in which dreams could be lived. The newly explored and reported-upon lands gave an air of possibility to dreams which had until then been restricted to the frame of the painting or the end of the poem. (*Demand the Impossible* 3–4)

The discovery of the Americas thus provided Europe with a locus upon which to project its own preconceived myths and desires.

Latin American critic Beatriz Pastor underscores how the European dreams of realizing utopia through the construction of something resembling the Greek *polis* or the Christian earthly paradise were reinvigorated with the discovery of new territories after 1492. Coinciding with the enterprising spirit of the Renaissance, the exploration of the new lands created the opportunity to bring to life the dormant desires of a perfect society. The allegedly "deserted" lands of the New World thus represented the possibility of escaping an oppressive Europe awakening from the Middle Ages and creating a better society in the Americas. Pastor points to how explorers and settlers projected fantasies of utopia upon the recently found territories of the New World, which revealed new possibilities beyond the European imagination, as well as providing the raw materials for realizing those dreams.[7]

Pastor identifies utopia as an expression of alternative European belief systems for the materialization of which America provided an optimum location. Immediately following the first explorations, the search for utopia became the instrumental core of settlement and organization of the recently founded missions and colonial societies.[8] According to Pastor, embedded in these utopian dreams we also find the impulse to dominate the newly found lands, "a través del deseo de poseer, la necesidad de conocer, la determinación de controlar" (27). Thus utopian ideals go hand in hand with the subordination of the Other and of nature through this will to know and resolve to control. Whereas in Europe, beginning with More's *Utopia*, the age of discovery represented the possibility of creating a perfect society through literary depictions of unspoiled nature, just governments, and architectural splendor, in the New World the palpable side effects of utopian desire manifest themselves in the violent encounter between European dreams and Amerindian reality.

The discovery of America not only exercised a compelling effect on the European mentality in the expansion of their imaginary; concretely, through colonization it also provided the material and economic conditions that made possible the development of epistemic models resulting in what we now regard, in the words of German philosopher Jürgen Habermas, as the "project of modernity." Responding to Habermas's assertion that modernity had its birth in Europe's cities, several scholars ranging from Tzvetan Todorov, to Enrique Dussel, and Aníbal Quijano identify the discovery of the American territories and their native populations as the key moment for the development of Western modernity. In Todorov's *The Conquest of America*, this critic writes:

> First of all, the discovery of America, or of the Americans, is certainly the most astonishing encounter of our history. We do not have the same sense of *radical difference* in the discovery of other continents and of other peoples: Europeans have never been altogether ignorant of the existence of Africa, India, or China; some memory of these places was always there already—from the beginning. (4; emphasis mine)

While Europeans had previous knowledge of Asia and Africa, the discovery of the Americas occurred as a completely unexpected event, yielding a new geographical and cultural dimension to the Western world.[9]

As Dussel proposes, however, the encounter also produced an "eclipsing" of Amerindian cultures, subjectivities, and projects of social organization: "Whereas modernity gestated in the free, creative medieval European cities, it came to birth in

Europe's confrontation with the Other. By controlling, conquering, and violating the Other, Europe defined itself as discoverer, conquistador, and colonizer of an alterity likewise constitutive of modernity" (12). The Western understanding of indigenous cultural practices became a point of comparison for Old World conquistadors, a yardstick against which they measured their own civilization in a dense process of self-fashioning. Through colonization, Europe imposed its own perception of otherness upon indigenous societies, while simultaneously impeding native systems of knowledge and collective memory from developing their own critical understanding of the encounter. Echoing Jacques Lacan's notion of otherness, both Todorov and Dussel highlight the importance of the creation of the concept of the primitive as a complementary counterpart to the civilized modern self. Significantly, these scholars emphasize how both halves of this equation—European self and Amerindian Other—are essential to the formation of the modern psyche.[10] Thus the cultural construction of "race" contributed to the marginalization of those aspects of human nature that are seen as irrational and pernicious for the realization of the ideal society. Through the collaboration of science, Western thinkers utilized the "primitive" Other as a symbol of untamed energies over which they presumably needed to exert control.[11]

The need to communicate and disseminate the new entities and cultural frameworks entering the European imaginary, however, contributed to the secularization of knowledge, which was until then a privilege of a religious hierarchy and the monarchy that did not allow the common citizen to partake. As Quijano points out, the need to communicate the newness of the recently discovered territories led to the formation of a scientific and critical spirit, announcing the dawn of the age of discovery ("Modernity" 202–03). Hence the encounter facilitated the development of sciences in order to communicate, translate, and later classify and systematize human experience. This secularization of knowledge also had a secondary effect in which hope was displaced from a nostalgic return to the Golden Age toward possible worlds located in the future and within the reach of all individuals through rationality.

Critics such as David Harvey underscore how one of the main goals of the project of the Enlightenment—the main motor of modern thought—justified humanity's control over nature: "[T]he scientific domination of nature promised freedom from scarcity, want, and the arbitrariness of natural calamity" (12). Hence, the domination of nature not only promised the means to improve human life but also implied the use of reason to safeguard the administration of natural resources. This scientific approach to all aspects of human existence equaled a new form of utopia: "The development of rational forms of social organization and rational modes of thought promised liberation from the irrationalities of myth, religion, superstition, release from the arbitrary use of power as well as from the dark side of our own human natures" (D. Harvey 12). Therefore the Enlightenment aimed to control both human nature and natural world for the benefit of humanity. The most promising contribution from the Enlightenment was in terms of the democratization of society and the empowerment of the individual as the subject of history, replacing the dictates of the church and the monarchy.

In similar terms, the imposition of a Western concept of humanity also had a dramatic effect on the natural habitat, as Europe justified its hegemony over America in terms of the domination of culture over nature. Through this domination, Europe created material and intellectual tools to assure the satisfaction of human needs. Parallel to the evolution of the sense of history, whose ultimate subject was Western man, the ideology of modernity upheld a hierarchical binary structure that excluded from society whatever was perceived as close to nature, utilizing the rationalizations that patriarchal culture had long used to position women as inferior to men.

Woman, Nature, and Other

In the early European documents on the New World, we find the descriptions of utopia meshed with the image of America as a desirable young woman, representing an extension of the Western perception of nature as feminine. As early as Columbus's third voyage, European explorers began to describe the New World as the mythical Garden of Eden, signifying a projection of humankind's desire to exert control over nature. In Columbus's 1498 letter to the Spanish monarchs written when he reached the mouth of the Orinoco River, we see his utopian belief of having discovered the earthly paradise as well as one of the earliest representations of America in feminine terms. In the Admiral's words: "But as for this other hemisphere I maintain that it is like a half of a very round pear which had a long stem, as I have said, or like a woman's teat on a round ball. [. . .] I am completely persuaded in my own mind that the Terrestrial Paradise is in the place I have described" (Morison 286–87). In Columbus's missive, heaven on earth is described as a female body inviting the gaze of the colonizer which is soon translated into terms of military, political, and cultural domination.

Scholar Louis Montrose notes that the basic ingredients of a colonialist ideology such as the representation of alleged indigenous savagery, deceit, and cannibalism, blended with a "crude and anxious misogynistic fantasy," resulted in a genderization of the New World landscape as feminine, while that terrain and its people were sexualized in masculine terms (181). For instance, in Jan van der Straet's paintings, America is depicted as an Amazonlike young woman who warmly welcomes Amerigo Vespucci while "awakening" into history.[12] Early imaginations of America present her as naked and void of cultural acumen. Montrose suggests that the conflation between male desire and fears and fantasies of castration operates in the description of Amazons as wild and ungovernable. In a 1504 letter, Vespucci himself claims that Amazon women collect the virile members of their companions, and there is no man to be seen in a situation of control. Montrose concludes that, "The matriarchal, gynocratic Amazons are the radical Other figured but not fully contained by the collective imagination of European patriarchy" (201). The existence of this myth calls attention to colonial operations of signification and the symbolic violence to which Amerindians were subjected, while it sheds light on the mechanisms of marginalization of the Other that coincided with the rise of modernity.

The connection between the domination of nature and the Western construction of the Other, then, are a result of early European encounters with the unknown. In order to rationalize the conquest of the New World, colonizers established dichotomies such as civilized/savage; European/Amerindian; civilization/nature; man/woman; and sexually normative/sodomite. The criteria of difference were based on practices that the European colonizers denominated as aberrant, as exemplified in the hundreds of references to alleged native sodomy, cannibalism, and human sacrifice compiled in Francisco Guerra's *The Pre-Columbian Mind*.[13] In *The Man-Eating Myth*, anthropologist William Arens has observed that following Queen Isabella's 1503 edict regarding the treatment of her new subjects, the Spanish crown did not permit the enslavement of Amerindians but it did condone the subjugation of "rebellious" sodomites, cannibals, and idolaters, epithets that were routinely evoked in reference to the native tribes as means of justifying the imposition of Catholicism and culture (58). This operation thus served as a thinly disguised rationalization of a colonialist discourse that established a view of modern identity in juxtaposition to different attitudes and customs regarding sexuality and gender. As scholars such as Richard Trexler, Rudi Bleys, and José Piedra have asserted, the conquistadors imposed a gendered hierarchy in which the Amerindian symbolically—and at times literally—is feminized and raped. As early as 1950, Mexican poet and Nobel Prize winner Octavio Paz had observed that the conquest of Mexico can be thought of in terms of a sexual violence in which the colonizer imposes his force upon the colonized. In this way, America is transformed into the location of radical otherness, establishing a polarity between European identity/indigenous alterity and reason/nature.

As a part of the broader process that Dussel refers to as the "eclipse of the Other," with the European exploration and settlement of the Americas we also witness a marginalization of nature deeply inscribed in the colonizing project. Not only did the encounter between Old and New Worlds lead to the subjugation of indigenous societies, in parallel fashion it also led to the exploitation of nature for the purposes of developing a capitalist system. Along with the subordination of native cultures, the contact between Europe and America also brought the reinforcement of the long-standing binary opposition between male and female and culture and nature. This hierarchy was validated by the encounter with the Other, as the perceived radical cultural difference of the Amerindian led European thinkers to reinforce the boundaries between humanity and nature through the use of reason as exclusionary practice. As observed above, the Other serves as a frame of reference for the construction of a modern subjectivity, which defines the European self as rational while oppressing women and Amerindians by associating them with nature and unreason.

In recent decades feminist studies have developed a scholarly current that examines the presumptions and implications of patriarchal culture's association of women with nature. In her 1974 essay "Is Female to Male as Nature Is to Culture?" Sherry Ortner asserts that in cultures around the world women tend to be restricted to a secondary status because of their presumed proximity to nature in comparison with men, who are associated with culture and civilization. Because of women's ability to procreate and nourish their progeny, males see them as natural, while males have to manifest their power through artificial means such as the elaboration of social structures. Ortner underscores that because culture is male dominated and oriented toward exerting control over nature, it is only logical to assume that women as part of nature should be subordinated to men: "Since it is always culture's project to subsume and transcend nature, if women were considered part of nature, then culture would find it 'natural' to subordinate, not to say oppress, them" (Ortner 73). At the core of this discussion is the notion that oppressed groups are the objects of similar strategies of subordination by patriarchal culture. Therefore, colonizers justify the subordination of women and indigenous groups on the basis of their apparent proximity to nature.

The notion that culture is destined to dominate nature and all associated with it has inspired feminist critics to scrutinize this perceived link as a key component in the formation of a feminist project of liberation. The parallel strategies of othering have led ecofeminist critics to address the relation of indigenous peoples and women to nature. According to Val Plumwood's analysis of the cultural construction of nature:

> The category of nature is a field of multiple exclusion and control, not only of non-humans, but of various groups of humans and aspects of human life which are cast as nature. Thus racism, colonialism and sexism have drawn their conceptual strength from casting sexual, racial and ethnic difference as closer to the animal and the body construed as a sphere of inferiority, as a lesser form of humanity lacking the full measure of rationality or culture. (4)

13

By discussing the colonization of the natural environment from a feminist point of view, scholars like Plumwood call attention to the comparable ways in which women, nature, and native peoples have been similarly marginalized from modernizing agendas.

In a similar vein, Carolyn Merchant explains that in the early modern age there were two components of the image of nature based on antagonistic terms: nature as creator represented by the idea of mother earth, "a kindly beneficent female who provided for the needs of mankind in an ordered, planned universe" and contrarily, "as wild and uncontrollable [nature] that could render violence, storms, droughts, and general chaos" (2). This second image inspired the development of industry, technology, and scientific inquiry in the name of power over nature, which became a core concept for the Enlightenment. Merchant describes how as a result of the Industrial Revolution, the representation of nature as a nurturing mother was slowly replaced by the image of nature as a source of disorder and violence, hence in need of the intervention of rationality, in the form of mechanical and technological advances.[14] As Merchant observes, "As Western culture became increasingly mechanized [. . .], the female earth and virgin earth spirit were subdued by the machine" (2). In this way, then, it became seen as necessary to control nature and all related to it through the hegemonic notion of reason.

Scholar Frances Bartkowski in *Feminist Utopias* has pointed out that although traditionally women writers have not cultivated genres such as the literary utopia/dystopia, beginning in the 1970s as a result of the women's movement in Europe and the United States there has been a solid production and distribution that locates women in the forefront of utopian and dystopian creativity. Ecofeminism is a practical movement for social change arising out of struggles of women to sustain themselves, their families, and their communities.[15] These struggles are waged against the "maldevelopment" and environmental degradation caused by patriarchal societies, multinational corporations, and global capitalism (Bartkowski 2). Thus the ecofeminist movement emerges from the deep contradictions in contemporary society regarding the use and abuse of nature by a logic of exploitation and consumerism.

As we have seen, the exploitation of nature encompasses a human dimension, as Amerindians and women have long been considered to be extensions of nature whose subordination is a fundamental element for the propagation of modernity. While some feminist scholars reject the association with nature as demeaning to women, those followers of ecofeminism opt to build on this connection in order to address the ecological problems that have emerged as a result of industrialization. As a response to the feminist discussions of the domination of nature by mankind, ecofeminism problematizes the relationship between women and nature and points to the need for women to participate in the efforts to preserve the environment not only as mediators but as active agents of social change. By examining this association with nature constructed through the colonizing optic, the novels discussed here address the potential alliances between those groups displaced by the conquest, namely, women and Amerindians, and their collective efforts to protect the environment.

From the Garden of Eden to the End of History

Since the first expressions of European modernity, literary utopias have been used to present a counterpoint to a real society that fails to recognize such principles as the pursuit of perfection through the aid of reason and the struggle against the abuse of power on behalf of hegemonic elites. Visions of utopia have long had a direct connection to the publication of scientific discoveries and the construction of an objective framework from which to trace the relationship between humankind and nature. As discussed above, early utopian literature described the natural state of the New World by combining the Christian notion of the Garden of Eden with myths of America as a feminine locus, presenting overlapping images of mother nature and the earthly paradise (Ben-Tov 19). The blending of these two icons underlies the notion of a home away from Europe, an "elsewhere" with the potential for realizing Western dreams of religious, political, and economic freedom. In Renaissance representations of nature, "she" is described in benevolent tones as a provider, a nurturing and organic persona. However, with the advent of the scientific revolution, utopian narratives such as Sir Francis Bacon's *New Atlantis* (1626) replaced the image of nature as an animate entity with the concept of the earth as an inextinguishable source of raw materials for human use, giving birth to the

15

scientific utopia. Bacon's protagonist, for example, subverts the anthropomorphic image of nature by locating a scientific laboratory in the interior of a mountain (Ben-Tov 17). Hence the subordination of nature to science and industry represented a new form of utopian narrative that promoted a systematic exploitation of the natural world in the name of progress.

In Europe in the seventeenth and eighteenth centuries, there occurred a broad transformation in the perception of the relation of humans to their environment. As a result of philosophical and scientific inquiries such as those of Galileo, René Descartes, Isaac Newton, and Francis Bacon, there arose the scientific method with its focus on objectivity and empirical verification and, ultimately, with the Enlightenment, the division of human knowledge into separate categories. This new epistemological framework replaced the view of the world as an organic being with the image of the earth functioning like a machine. Thus, the study and manipulation of nature began to be systematized: "As new technologies started exploiting the environment on a large scale, they were supported by a scientific ideology that called for appropriating nature's powers while reducing the figure of Mother Nature to dead, passive matter, the 'natural resources' of man's creation" (Ben-Tov 22).

In Europe, as a result of the scientific revolution and later the industrial revolution, there was not only an increased reliance on machinery but also an evolution toward more "modern" ways of thinking about social reality. The application of machinery for increasing both agricultural and industrial production renewed the optimism of utopian thinking. According to Lyman Tower Sargent and Gregory Claeys, "[S]cientific discovery and technological innovation from the seventeenth century on began to hold out the promise of an indefinite progress of the human species toward better health, a longer life, and the domination of nature in the interests of humankind" (3). Thus progress becomes the new utopia as the goal of human improvement replaces the wonder and mystery of mother nature with the modern notion of the environment as a mere stockpile of resources for the construction of a man-made paradise.

By the late nineteenth and early twentieth centuries, the specific form of science fiction as a literary means of expressing both utopian and dystopian visions of modernity had evolved in the writings of Jules Verne and H. G. Wells.[16] Their early works manifest faith in science as a facilitator of human happiness but also evidence concern about the potential effects of the abuse of technology by unscrupulous scientists and capitalists. This positive vision of industry and science changed as pollution brought by industrialization and growing doubts about their methods darkened the literary assessment. The most famous promoters of this literary genre are Edward Bulwer-Lytton's *The Coming Race* (1871), and H. G. Wells's works *The Time Machine* (1885) and *When the Sleeper Awakes* (1899). Literary dystopias are negative representations of imagined future societies where the abuse of technology, authoritarianism, dehumanization, and the uncertainty of earth's future have created the conditions for the end of humanity as we know it. From the dawn of the industrial revolution until it reached its peak in the late nineteenth century, throughout the Western world there was a growing belief in the advantages of technology for the satisfaction of human needs. This initial confidence rapidly waned in the early twentieth century when science and technology came to be employed against humanity in the two world wars, as machine guns, tanks, and poison gas annihilated large numbers of soldiers on the battlefields of Europe, and as a result both the goals and means of industrialization came to be challenged.

As a response to developments in scientific inquiry, by the early twentieth century there had emerged a new literary genre, the industrial dystopia grounded in futuristic depictions of the potentially pernicious effects of technology and mechanization. While utopian dreams were projected to geographic locations such as the New World, the dystopian visions of science fiction were displaced chronologically, projecting the apocalyptic nightmares of modernity toward the future. Whereas the genre of the literary utopia had been revitalized by the discovery of the Americas and the rise of modernity, its antipode the dystopia emerges under the particular historical circumstances of a turn-of-the-century crisis of faith in the possibility of unlimited progress.

Literary dystopias are defined as negative representations of imagined future societies where the abuse of technology, authoritarianism, and the overall dehumanization of society have created the conditions for the end of humanity as we know it. In the major works of dystopian science fiction, an imaginary society is described in terms of its highly mechanized organization resulting in the loss of mankind's individuality and freedom of choice. Dystopian novels describe a desolate future, the denial of human history, and the end of democracy, as members of the futuristic society are forbidden to engage in any form of coherent political project.

According to critics there are different currents of anti-utopian writing: on the one hand, there are narratives that express a belief that utopia is unattainable; and on the other, there are those that maintain that if achieved, a utopian vision would have undesirable by-products. Gary Saul Morson defines dystopia within this latter category as "a type of anti-utopia that discredits utopias by portraying the likely effects of their realization" (116). The dystopia implies in its ideological perspective a spirit of reform, based on an underlying utopian dream whose fulfillment has unforeseen consequences. As critic Dragan Klaic writes: "Dystopia is [. . .] an unexpected and aborted outcome of utopian strivings" (3). Dystopias are thus the negative complement of utopias, representing the dark mirror of endeavors to achieve perfection in an imperfect world.

As the centerpiece of their critical agenda, dystopian fictions such as Yevgeny Zamyatin's *We* (1924), Huxley's *Brave New World* (1932), Orwell's *Nineteen Eighty-Four* (1949), and Bradbury's *Fahrenheit 451* (1953) have scrutinized the utopian rhetoric of autocratic regimes that eschew democracy in the name of lofty ideals:

> [A]s the socialist state or the consumer society claimed to have achieved utopia, the more radical critique that the genre [of utopian narrative] is capable of escaped into the mountains of negativity and re-emerged as the dystopia, [. . .] [in which] utopian figures of hope were transmuted into an attack on present social systems which claim to be already existing utopias. (Moylan, *Demand the Impossible* 8–9)

In effect, societies claiming to have attained utopia represent a diverse spectrum of ideologies, be they the goal of improving the species through genetic enhancement, the collective ideal of socialism, or the notion of the satisfaction of all human needs through abundant consumer goods. Notably, for every state-sponsored utopia there exists a contrary vision of the potential negative effects of the realization of its goals. Hence dystopias are clearly related to the utopian dreams that generated them.

Dystopia represents a despairing view of the future with particular attention to the consequences of an uncritical belief in technology as the cornerstone of the rhetoric of progress. In *The Scientific World View in Dystopia,* Alexandra Aldridge writes that dystopia "always aims to critique and ridicule that world view [of the industrialist utopia] for its adherence to instrumental values, its elevation of functional and collective ends over the humanistic and individual" (ix). Hence dystopian writers are critically aware of the degeneration of the dream of modernity and how it has been corrupted by societies that have become detached from the ostensible goal of progress to achieve improved conditions for humanity. The previous faith in mankind's benevolent relationship with industry is thus transformed into foreboding of a dehumanized world where the machine replaces humankind altogether.

In its exposé of the indiscriminate acceptance of modernity's artifacts, the dystopia expresses a disdain for technology by transporting its reader to a future time where there is little hope for mankind. In spite of its severe criticism of the widespread adoption of technology in all areas of human life:

> The dystopian novel is not literally anti-scientific or anti-technological in the sense that it represents machine phobia. Instead, its authors [. . .] have been watchful over the intrusion of scientific values—objectivity, neutrality, instrumentalism—into the social imagination. They have criticized the replacement of a humanistic ethos with a scientific technological one. (Aldridge ix)

In dystopian novels the enemy is not the machine itself but rather the regimes that have mechanized society and instrumentalized humanity for the ends of the dictatorial state or the needs of the market. This tradition extends from Mary Shelley's *Frankenstein* (1818) to Fritz Lang's film *Metropolis* (1926), Ridley Scott's *Blade Runner* (1982), a film adaptation of Phillip Dick's *Do Androids Dream of Electric Sheep?* to Margaret Atwood's *The Handmaid's Tale* (1986). A new generation of science fiction films, heralded by Andy and Larry Wachowski's *The Matrix* (1999),

Steven Spielberg's *A. I. Artificial Intelligence* (2001), and Alex Proyas's *I, Robot* (2004), marks the vibrant resurgence of this genre. Dystopian narratives build on our dread of dehumanization as they depict "[i]mages of massification, identity by number, bureaucratic and technocratic control of behavior and desire, portrayal of daily life in a lustreless collectivity or in endless consumption" (Moylan, *Demand the Impossible* 9). Hence many dystopias represent the fear of forsaking the uniqueness of individuality as human beings are replaced by artificial intelligence.

Yevgeny Zamyatin's *We* (1920) is widely recognized as the first modern dystopia, setting its basic themes: mistrust of an autocratic government; the use of technology for the purpose of surveillance; and an apathetic citizenry that values comfort and mediocrity over free will. *We* is set in a distant future, in a postapocalyptic society ruled by order to an extreme that human beings have their names replaced by numbers, perform daily routines regulated with mathematical precision, and have no sense of individuality. Even sexuality is regulated by the Table of Hours, anticipating the politics of reproduction that will later become a key part of the science fiction repertoire.[17] Significantly, all walls in this society are transparent, which allows the Guardians—spies for the Benefactor—to supervise the activities of the citizenry, predating Orwell's Big Brother.

The One State has eliminated world hunger and most diseases but technological might now transcends the natural environment, which is kept at bay outside the Green Wall. As in the novels examined in the following chapters, the inhabitants of the One State are represented as utterly alienated from nature: "Personally, I see nothing beautiful in flowers, or in anything belonging to the primitive world long exiled beyond the Green Wall. Only the rational is beautiful: machines, boots, formulas, food, and so on" (48).

Zamyatin's narrator is a rocket scientist who labors in the construction of a space ship designed to conquer other planets. In this dystopia, reason becomes the new god and people follow it without questioning its ultimate consequences:

> Our gods are here, below, with us—in the office, the kitchen, the workshop, the toilet; the gods have become like us. *Ergo, we have become as gods.* And we shall come to you, my

> unknown readers on the distant planet, to make your life as
> divinely rational and precise as ours. (69; emphasis mine)

Reason and technology thus become the new utopias this dictatorial regime aims to spread all over the galaxy, as the official
One State Gazette claims: "You will subjugate the unknown
beings on other planets, who may still be living in the primitive
conditions of freedom, to the beneficent yoke of reason" (1).
Pointedly, Zamyatin underscores the interconnection of utopia
with the purpose of empire, as reason becomes the dominant
paradigm for the subordination of other species.

Setting the tone for the manipulation of literature as sup-
portive of the state in later dystopian fiction, in Zamyatin's One
State the arts must suppress creativity in the name of unques-
tioning support of the official ideology: "Everyone who feels
capable of doing so must compose tracts, odes, manifestoes, poems, or other works extolling the beauty and the grandeur of the
One State" (1–2).[18] The theme of revisionist history that will be
crucial to the novels examined below is also present in *We*. For
example, the narrator describes the "free" elections of the One
State's Benefactor, in which several citizens vote against the
leader but their resistance is erased by an article appearing in
the next day's newspaper: "Yesterday we celebrated Unanim-
ity Day, which everyone has long waited with impatience. For
the forty-eighth time, the Benefactor, who has demonstrated his
steadfast wisdom on so many past occasions, was elected by a
unanimous vote" (148–49).

As do later science fiction novels like Orwell's *Nineteen
Eighty-Four*, *We* represents a resistance movement whose plans
are thwarted by the Guardians who round up the population
to undergo the Great Operation, reducing citizens to living
automatons. Nevertheless, several rebels, including a woman
pregnant with the narrator's child, manage to escape to the
natural world outside the Green Wall. In the midst of the return to normality after the Great Operation, there are signs of
alternative possibilities, as fighting still goes on in some parts
of the city: "In the western parts of the city there is still chaos,
roaring, corpses, beasts, and—unfortunately—a considerable
group of numbers have betrayed Reason" (232). In the last
scene of the novel, the narrator has been subjected to the Great
Operation but the continuing fighting as well as the escape of

the protagonist's companion with his child offers hope for the destiny of humanity.

One of the earlier English-language classics of science fiction, Huxley's *Brave New World,* poses as a central question the use of bio-medical technology to create a perfect race. In his dystopian view of the future, Huxley presents a society controlled by genetic manipulation, dramatizing in graphic detail the theory and methodology of artificial reproduction. Huxley's society is completely stratified by its use of eugenics, resulting in a human hierarchy of Alphas, Betas, Gammas, Deltas, and Epsilons, each of which is programmed to perform specific functions with no hope of ever transcending this designated role.[19] Hence Huxley's nightmare reverses the liberating dream of modernity by placing emphasis on the arrest of individuality and freedom of choice at the hands of a mentality of hyperconsumption. Notably, the classes who are not destined to leisure are programmed to become alienated from nature: "A love of nature keeps no factories busy. It was decided to abolish the love of nature, at any rate among the lower classes, but *not* the tendency to consume transport" (Huxley 22). Significantly, in *Brave New World*, time is referred to as Before or After Ford, fetishizing the assembly line that emblematizes factory workers' alienation from the fruits of their labor.

Like Zamyatin had done earlier, Huxley highlights the influence of propaganda as the state's prominently posted slogan, "Community, Identity, Stability," stands as an emblem of a doctrine that applies the principles of efficiency to society. *Brave New World* exemplifies a state that is antagonistic to the teachings of history, as Our Ford, the prophet of mass production and consumption, is repeatedly quoted as saying: "History is bunk." As indicated by this introduction's epigraph from Orwell, the issue of interpretation of the past is central to dystopian writing. In Huxley's brave new world, historical understanding is deemed as dangerous because it could lead to strengthened community bonds and potential resistance. Thus the erasure of history is "[a]ccompanied by a campaign against the Past; by the closing of museums, the blowing up of historical monuments [. . .]; by the suppression of all books published before A.F. 150" (51). Filling the vacuum created by the absence of museums and libraries, mass media is also in charge of disseminating official propaganda with the sole purpose of subduing individuality and dissension.

To signify the panoptical presence of power exercised by an omnipotent ruler, in Orwell's *Nineteen Eighty-Four* the ubiquitous but invisible Big Brother continuously monitors the activities of the residents of Oceania. The established system is upheld by agencies such as the Record Department and the Ministry of Truth, whose main role is the promotion of an official version of history and culture:

> And the Record Department, after all, was itself a single branch of the *Ministry of Truth, whose primary job was not to reconstruct the past but to supply the citizens of Oceania* with newspapers, films, textbooks, telescreen programs, plays, novels—*with every conceivable kind of information, instruction, or entertainment,* from a statue to a slogan, from a lyric poem to a biological treatise, and from a child's spelling book to a Newspeak dictionary. (Orwell 39; emphasis mine)

Significantly, Newspeak dictionaries are constantly being revised, pointing to language as a key means to control the citizenry. As an expression of the manipulation of technology, the state uses mass media to keep the citizenry in check:

> The invention of print [. . .] made it easier to manipulate public opinion, and the film and the radio carried the process further. With the development of television, and the technical advance which made it possible to receive and transmit simultaneously on the same instrument, *private life came to an end.* Every citizen [. . .] could be kept for twenty-four hours a day under the eyes of the police and in the sound of official propaganda, with all other channels of communication closed. *The possibility of enforcing not only complete obedience to the will of the State, but complete uniformity of opinion on all subjects, now existed for the first time.* (169; emphasis mine)

The apparatus of surveillance and the fear of an omnipresent governmental organism forestall any hope of escaping Big Brother's gaze.

Orwell's systematic view of the state as an all-powerful entity encompasses all aspects of human expression, penetrating the individual space of its denizens through diverse strategies:

> There was a whole chain of separate departments dealing
> with proletarian literature, music, drama and entertainment
> generally. Here we produced rubbishy newspapers, con-
> taining almost nothing except sport, crime, and astrology,
> sensational five-cent novelettes, films oozing with sex, and
> sentimental songs which were composed entirely by me-
> chanical means. (39)

Orwell makes a correlation between education and alienation
as the working classes are trained exclusively to be "productive members of society," that is, to keep the war machine and
the industrial apparatus in constant motion. Thus, the populist
stance of Oceania denies members of society any option apart
from bending to the demands of the "Party." Like Huxley,
Orwell points to how an autocratic state subjects knowledge,
history, and language to a constant revision in order to erase
community bonds that could lead to resistance.

In a similar fashion, Ray Bradbury's *Fahrenheit 451* depicts
a dystopian society in which censorship has escalated to the
point where books are prohibited altogether. The protagonist is a
fireman whose job is to burn books as well as to denounce those
who hold them. The title of the novel refers to the temperature at
which fire consumes paper, emblematic of the anti-intellectual-
ism of a society ruled by a dictatorial echelon. Like the citizens of
Huxley's brave new world and Orwell's Oceania, in Bradbury's
future, people are bombarded with mass media and engrossed in
interactive soap operas that anticipate today's reality shows.

Books are burned because they show the subtleties of life that
do not correspond to the state's intentions to control memory,
identity, and ultimately reality. In spite of the extreme censorship, dissidents in Bradbury's novel form utopian circles where
they read, share, and memorize the contents of diverse books.
Their communities are kept together because they leave the cities and escape to the wilderness in search of nature and history:
"Take it [knowledge] where you can find it, in old phonograph
records, old motion pictures, and in old friends; look for it in
nature and look for it in yourself. Books were only one type of
receptacle where we stored a lot of things we were afraid we
might forget" (82–83). Thus in the face of this society's anti-intellectual stance, resistance emerges in the form of preservation
of literary history and memory.

Mexican literature since its origins has engaged the utopian and dystopian modes. For example, Ross Larson refers to the work of colonial Mexican author Bernardo de Balbuena, *El siglo de oro en las tierras de Erífile*, as one of the first examples of the utopian genre in the New World. Gabriel Trujillo Muñoz also observes how realistic writers such as José Joaquín Fernández de Lizardi in his masterpiece *El Periquillo Sarniento* (1816) dedicates two chapters discussing the utopian kingdom of "Sauchoufú" as a critique of the stratification of colonial society. In addition, Miguel Angel Fernández Delgado cites the eighteenth-century religious figure don Antonio de Rivas as the first practitioner of "proto-science fiction narrative in Mexico" (Fernández Delgado 18). Still influenced by Enlightenment aims but now in the nineteenth century, we have the appearance of Pedro Castera (1846–1906) whose short story "Viaje celeste" and novel *Querens* anticipate twentieth-century science fiction works. By the beginning of the twentieth century under *modernismo* and predating famous writers such as Aldous Huxley and George Orwell and influenced by dystopian writer H. G. Wells's *Time Machine*, the famous Mexican poet Amado Nervo published the collection of stories entitled *Almas que pasan* (1906) in which "La última guerra" criticizes the dystopian use of technology.

After the violent events of the Mexican Revolution, several writers such as Martín Luis Guzmán, Julio Torri, José Martínez Sotomayor, and Francisco L. Urquizo employed the dystopian fantasy to address the changes in Mexican society. Francisco Urquizo's 1934 novel *El tío Juan* depicts a Quixotic figure five hundred feet tall who battles injustice, while Luis Guzmán's "Cómo acabó la Guerra en 1917" describes the invention of the computer and the control of information that George Orwell later will explore in his classic dystopia *Nineteen Eighty-Four*.

With the extended modernization of the country in the 1940s and 1950s occurred an explosion of themes and motifs of contemporary fantastic science fiction. In 1947, Rafael Bernal published *Su nombre era muerte*, in which insects rebel against humanity. Canonical writers such as Carlos Fuentes (*Los días enmascarados*, 1954) and Juan José Arreola (collection of short stories *Varia invención*, 1949, and *Confabulario*, 1952) also resorted to science fiction to engage contemporary issues.

During the 1960s and 1970s we saw a slow development of the genre and the appearance of the first journals dedicated solely to science fiction such as *Cromonauta*. Authors of this period include Carlos Olvera, *Mexicanos en el espacio* (1968); René Rebetez, *La nueva prehistoria* (1968); Menen Desleal, *La ilustre familia androide* (1968); and René Avilés Fávila, "Hacia el fin del mundo" (1970). This decade saw the emergence of science fiction works such as Tomás Mojarro's *Trasterra* (1973), Marcela del Río's *Proceso a Faubritten* (1976), José Emilio Pacheco's *Sangre de medusa* (1976), and Gustavo Sainz's *Fantasmas aztecas* (1979).

While the classic science fiction novels saw their initial publication in the years surrounding the two world wars, the genre continued to evolve in the second half of the twentieth century, and in particular since the 1960s, when a consumeristic ideology and the damaging effects of industrialism became reinvigorated targets of dystopian critique. In recent decades, both utopian and dystopian writing have come to focus on two main issues, the situation of women and the status of ecology. The feminist current criticizes the exclusion of women—and other sexual minorities—from the mainstream of society, while the ecocritical current addresses the effects of industrialization on the environment, proposing alternative worlds in which humankind lives in harmony with nature.[20]

Modernity and Modernization in Mexico

While European colonizers focused the flow of utopian images toward America, with the arrival to power of their American-born descendants known as criollos following their independence,[21] this stream reverts its course as modernity itself comes to represent a utopia for developing nations. During the seventeenth and eighteenth centuries, people on both sides of the Atlantic struggled against the conservative forces of religious obscurantism that forestalled the development of personal freedom, the acquisition of experimental knowledge, and the decline of feudal power. In Europe, the Enlightenment led to the formation of an independent modern subjectivity that sparked the spirit of industrialism; in Latin America, however, the ascent to power of conservative rural elites curtailed the development of social forces capable of participating in the industrial revolution, promoting instead a mode of production based on an agrarian society favorable for the perpetuation of feudalism in the hands of the church, the army, and individuals who possessed vast holdings of land. As Spanish American elites grew to be more dependent on European manufactured goods, modernity itself came to constitute a new form of utopian goal.

Significantly the ideas of the Enlightenment also had a positive influence in the Americas, as it would be impossible to speak about Latin American independence if the founding fathers of Latin American republics had not read the works of the European Enlightenment by authors such as Rousseau, Voltaire, and Robespierre and discovered the idea of the people as subject of history through the gaze of the French Revolution. The leading sectors of the newly born republics adopted many of the tenets of the Enlightenment such as the organization of societies around the idea of the nation-state and of representative democracy, departing from the authority of religion and monarchy that had predominated since the early sixteenth century. The fact was that one of the most important aspects of Enlightenment thought implied a break with the past and its traditions, which led Latin Americans to search for solutions in order to address the problems of their new societies.[22]

In this way, modernity gave birth to the concept of representative democracy that guarantees that each citizen has his/her own voice heard in the destiny of the republic. This translated in Latin America into the form of an affirmation of national identity in contrast to the European customs and increased conflict with traditional seats of power, including the church. The Enlightenment reshaped culture both in Europe and in the Americas during the eighteenth and the early nineteenth centuries through the consolidation of nonreligious knowledge as the base of authority; interest in scientific investigation of the laws of the universe and its resulting discoveries; the critique of existing social reality and order and the acceptance of the idea of change as an inherent part of modern society; and a clear determination to struggle against social prejudices and the use of arbitrary power (Quijano 203–04).

But as Aníbal Quijano points out, the project of the Enlightenment had its own contradictions:

> From its very beginnings, the European Enlightenment
> contained an unbridgeable split between tendencies that saw
> reason as the historical promise of liberation of humanity
> from its own ghosts, from social injustice and the prisons of
> power, and on the other hand, tendencies that saw rationality
> in instrumental terms, as a mechanism of power, of domina-
> tion. (206)

Thus Enlightenment thought fomented the fundamental contradictions of modernity that continue to plague Latin America:
the utopian desire for a democratic civil society paradoxically
contrives to dominate nature and all associated with it.

Through the years following the wars of independence,
then, Latin American political, economic, and cultural elites
began importing cognitive frameworks that further occlude the
presence of indigenous society. This not only contributed to
the problem of dependency but also added a positivistic view,
identifying certain elements of national culture that would be
considered as impediments for modernization, namely, the indigenous population that survived in Mexico, Central America,
and the Andean region.[23] As a result, the idea of the state as the
representative of an "imagined community" in Latin America
was initiated from the top down, favoring criollos, mestizos,
and urban middle classes.

Within the common parlance of the ruling elites entered
a new term: *progress*. The rhetoric of progress became an
exclusionary discourse tending to ignore issues such as even
development among different social groups, equal access to
education, sustainable economic growth, and the democratization of society. The sector most negatively affected by this
internally imposed notion of progress has been composed of the
rural peasantry and the indigenous communities who have seen
their lands taken away while being reduced to living in poverty
and isolation. This trend in Latin America was particularly evident in Mexico, which had a large indigenous and rural population. As Carlos Fuentes observes in reference to these patterns
of social stratification during the initial century of Mexico's
independence: "The dreams of Mexican modernity in the nineteenth century—liberalism and positivism—were achieved
only partially and always at the expense of the communitarian
bonds, the dignity, the rights, and the culture of the peasant and

indigenous peoples" (*A New Time for Mexico* 18).[24] Fuentes's comments refer specifically to Porfirio Díaz's positivist regime, which in the second half of the nineteenth century oversaw a dramatic push for "order and progress."[25] Díaz's administration transformed Mexico City into a modern capital and energized the country, building an infrastructure for transportation and economy. At the same time, Díaz—himself part Zapotec—forcibly ended the Caste War (1867–1901), pushing the Yaquis, Mayans, and other ethnic groups from their ancestral lands, as well as expanding the system of haciendas that concentrated agricultural commerce in the hands of a few rich landowners. Through a strong-arm policy, Díaz centralized power and imposed his iron will, silencing popular discontent. This climate of repression during the *Porfiriato* ultimately led to political unrest, reaching a climax in 1910 with the dawn of the Mexican Revolution, whose military phase lasted until 1917.

During the 1920s following the presidency of Alvaro Obregón (1920–24), there emerged a power structure that gave rise to the dominance of a single political party. At the end of his administration, Plutarco Elías Calles (1924–28) concentrated all the political and economic forces of the country—labor, farmers, capitalists, and the military—in order to secure the continuity of rule and elimination of dissension. In 1928, Obregón was re-elected through the use of force and fraud but was assassinated before taking office.[26] In 1929, during the presidency of Emilio Portes Gil (1928–32), Calles founded the Partido Nacional Revolutionario (PNR, National Revolutionary Party) whose name changed to the Partido Revolucionario Mexicano (PRM, Mexican Revolutionary Party) in 1938 under Lázaro Cárdenas, and finally in 1946 under Miguel Alemán Valdés acquired its present name of Partido Revolucionario Institucional (PRI, Institutional Revolutionary Party), which maintained a stronghold over Mexican politics for the remainder of the twentieth century.[27]

From the revolutionary period onwards, the Mexican administrations attempted to integrate indigenous societies through the image of the mestizo (the mixed-race product of Amerindian and European blood). With the influence of Porfirian positivism and the incorporation of the ideology of the Mexican Revolution, from Andrés Molina Enríquez's *Los grandes problemas nacionales* (1909), Manuel Gamio's *Forjando patria* (1916), José Vasconcelos's *La raza cósmica* (1925), and through the present day, Mexican nationalistic discourse has attempted to ambiguously resist the incorporation of the indigenous peoples by representing them as objects of study and not as citizens of the nation. The problem, as William Rowe and Vivian Schelling write, is that "[*m*]*estizaje*, a word denoting racial mixture, assumes a synthesis of cultures, where none is eradicated. The difficulty with the idea of *mestizaje* is that, without an analysis of power structures, it becomes an ideology of racial harmony which obscures the actual holding of power by a particular group" (18). Thus the concept of *mestizaje* conflated race and culture and failed to take into account the pivotal role of class issues.

Throughout the twentieth century, Mexican governments oriented their national projects through efforts of modernization. One of the primary goals of the Mexican Revolution was the redistribution of land to those groups, both mestizo and indigenous, dispossessed by a *latifundismo* ultimately rooted in the colonial *encomienda* system.[28] Historian Thomas Benjamin underscores how the project of nation emerging from the Revolution envisioned an agrarian utopia that aimed to reverse the exploitation of the indigenous and *campesino* communities through the creation of *ejidos*, or parcels of land, organized according to the indigenous structure of the *calpulli* (the Nahuatl word for neighborhood), which promoted crop sharing and cooperation in planting and harvesting. In a way, the *ejido* represented a return to a pre-Porfirian agricultural past in order to distinguish it from the pre-Revolutionary regime. Nevertheless, in spite of the efforts of several postrevolutionary administrations, notably that of Lázaro Cárdenas in the 1930s, the Revolution's promise of agrarian reform was never completely fulfilled.

The Revolution's attempt to serve the needs of beleaguered peasants encompassed endeavors to implement agrarian reform as well as the creation of programs aimed at incorporating indigenous communities. In contrast to other Latin American countries, the Mexican state created an official ideology of *indigenismo* to address, at least on the symbolic and theoretical levels, the problems of the native communities. State-sponsored *indigenismo* strove to aid the native peoples in combating centuries of economic and social disenfranchisement by including them in a modern national project. As part of this enterprise, the regimes following the Revolution supported the social sciences in their efforts to study the ancient cultures of Mesoamerica in order to establish an autochthonous foundation for Mexico following the revolutionary upheaval. Hence while images of pre-Columbian civilizations decorated the newly built official buildings following the Revolution, at the same time campaigns were launched by state agencies to re-educate indigenous communities and make them part of Westernized mestizo Mexico.

Significantly, postrevolutionary governments established official agencies devoted to the study of indigenous communities such as the Instituto Nacional Indigenista (INI, National Indigenist Institute) and the Instituto Nacional de Antropología e Historia (INAH, National Institute of Anthropology and History).[29] These state measures, however, were not effectively geared toward empowering the indigenous communities as such, but rather toward the conversion of Amerindians into modern subjects, that is, into Mexican citizens, a category officially defined as inherently mestizo. As Claudio Lomnitz points out: "[Mexican anthropology] was charged with the task of forging Mexican citizenship both by 'indigenizing' modernity and by modernizing the Indians, thus uniting all Mexicans into one mestizo community" (*Deep Mexico* 232). As a result of this endeavor to promote an official mestizo identity, those indigenous groups who resisted acculturation stood out in even starker contrast to the more Westernized mestizos. In effect, to be modern in postrevolutionary Mexico has implied negating the heterogeneous composition of the nation while adopting a cosmopolitan ideology that excludes indigenous cultures.

Both the official ideology promoting *mestizaje* as well as state-sponsored *indigenismo,* then, attempted to incorporate the indigenous communities within the nation but they did so in order to assimilate the native peoples as "Mexicans." Octavio Paz writes in his 1950 *Labyrinth of Solitude*: "The Mexican does not want to be either an Indian or a Spaniard. Nor does he want be descended from them. He denies them. And he does not affirm himself as a mixture, but rather as an abstraction: he is a man" (87). Thus, the utopia of a mestizo Mexico—ironically aided by *indigenismo*—had a dark side in that the goal of racial and cultural *mestizaje* ultimately entailed the disappearance of indigenous societies as such. Thus, both Europe's utopian images of the New World and Latin America's utopian dreams of modernity are ultimately founded upon the marginalization of the same native peoples.

The most significant changes in public policy toward the native peoples were enacted under the administration of Lázaro Cárdenas (1934–40), who attempted to implement agrarian reform through the creation of official agencies such as the Banco Nacional Agropecuario, which provided financial planning and support for farmers, and the aforementioned Instituto Nacional Indigenista, which organized aggressive educational campaigns to acculturate the indigenous communities.[30] The concerted effort to foster agrarian reform lasted from the end of the military phase of the revolution until the end of the Cárdenas regime when World War II brought significant changes to the role of the Mexican economy.[31]

During the 1940s, President Manuel Ávila Camacho (1940–46) transformed the economic base of the country from an agrarian orientation to a semi-industrial platform, a transition from Cárdenas's focus on social reform to a more conservative political program marking for some the end of the Revolution in Mexico. One of the most important modifications was the de-acceleration of land redistribution in favor of a shift toward the creation of large commercial farms.[32] In a series of initiatives known as the "Green Revolution," Ávila Camacho sponsored private ownership instead of the *ejido* and cooperatives, imitating the Western pattern of development with the goal of transforming agrarian production into a modern profitable business. The country's participation in World War II, during which Mexico controlled the price of certain metals needed for the construction of ships, planes, and weapons, resulted in an economic boom and improved relations with the United States. Better relations with its powerful northern neighbor helped Mexico to maintain a steady growth and prosperity that lasted for several decades (Meyer et al. 609).

As a result of the "Green Revolution" of the 1940s, Mexico's model of agriculture changed from that of small cooperatives to one based on assembly-line agribusiness. Thanks to bank loans and grants from the Rockefeller Foundation, Mexico's large farmers could afford modern machinery to improve the methods of irrigation and harvesting. Also this wave of modernization was able to improve the distribution of agricultural products to formerly isolated sections of the country, now connected by newly opened highways. But the dream of making the Mexican countryside productive also had a downside, since large-scale agro-industry benefited the most from these measures, which in turn negatively affected the communal land-owning *ejidos* and remaining indigenous communes. As the price of corn dropped because of increased production, small landowners were forced to abandon their communities in order to migrate to the cities or to the United States to work as itinerant laborers under the bracero program. Ironically, while there was more abundant food at lower prices, there were also more people unemployed and rural life began to deteriorate.

A period of time that economists have termed the "Mexican Miracle" began to develop following World War II during the administrations of Miguel Alemán Valdés (1946–52), Adolfo Ruiz Cortines (1952–58), Adolfo López Mateos (1958–64), and ending with Gustavo Díaz Ordaz (1964–70). The term "Mexican Miracle" refers to a series of measures that diversified the utilization of the natural and human resources of the country as well as consolidating the turn from an agrarian-based economy to industrialized capitalism. From the late 1940s through the 1960s, the Mexican economic system stabilized as a result of the strong hand of the government and sustained economic growth. In addition to the diversification of the economy, Alemán promoted the modernization of the country's infrastructure, constructing highways to facilitate transportation across the nation. In diminishing forms, each of the four administrations supported economic growth and political stability as well as acting to increase social programs. The narrowing of the country's agricultural base in the mid-century resulted in disaster by the 1970s, however, as Mexico had to import staples to meet the demands of an ever increasing population.[33] This in turn raised the need for subsidizing farmers with the profits of the growing oil industry.

Gustavo Díaz Ordaz (1964–70) was the president of Mexico during the 1960s, when world politics were experiencing one of the most dramatic changes in history. While students were protesting in France, the United States, and elsewhere, in Mexico on the eve of the 1968 Olympic Games students from the Universidad Nacional Autónoma de México and the Instituto Politécnico Nacional joined in protest of the government's repression, demanding the resignation of Mexico City's mayor and chief of police. In September 1968, several student organizations took over the installations of the UNAM but President Díaz Ordaz sent ten thousand troops and regained control of the university buildings. On October 2, 1968, students were marching in the Plaza de las Tres Culturas in Tlatelolco when the Army opened fire against the protesters, killing hundreds of men, women, and children.[34] In spite of maintaining economic growth, Díaz Ordaz's repressive regime and the student massacre of Tlatelolco marked the end of the "Mexican Miracle" and initiated the crisis of legitimacy of the Mexican state.

During the administrations of Luis Echeverría Álvarez (1970–76) and José López Portillo (1976–82), the country experienced continued economic growth thanks to the oil boom. The resulting resources, however, were used to increase the role of the state, with the government buying companies to create employment and diversify the economy. Thus the discovery of petroleum posed the possibility of a new utopia of industrialization. Echeverría's administration distinguished itself from earlier regimes in that he believed that the state needed to be involved in the exploitation of natural resources as well as in policies of investment. President Echeverría developed several areas of the Mexican economy, including tourism, the development of the maquiladora industry along the border with the United States, and the opening of industrial corridors in several parts of the country.

At the beginning of the 1970s, inflation accelerated dramatically. A belief in the dream of continued oil production led to a rise in levels of consumption, and imports from the United States radically transformed the standard of living in the cities. Reflecting the optimism of this period, Mexico's elite drove expensive cars and attained a level of affluence similar to that of the First World. External deficits associated with government borrowing and an increasingly overvalued exchange rate led to a large increase in Mexico's foreign debt. By the late 1970s, the failure of Echeverría's model of development was apparent, and large sums of investment funds had already migrated from the country.

In addition to an economic crisis, galloping inflation, and decreasing oil demands, when López Portillo took office, an agreement with the International Monetary Fund was in effect that called for a devaluation of the *peso*, as well as setting limits on borrowing and public expenditures, including social welfare projects and government subsidies in food and education (Meyer et al. 651–57). In spite of the signs of a decreasing need for oil, López Portillo continued the trend initiated by Echeverría's administration and increased public spending, borrowing heavily to invest in oil. López Portillo failed to reverse the downward course of the Mexican economy and in a serious mistake, he nationalized most of the banks, which ultimately had to be rescued with more loans from the International Monetary Fund. At the end of his presidency, it was made public that he and his family had amassed a large fortune through embezzlement. Furthermore, Mexico City's chief of police, Arturo "El negro" Durazo Moreno, was also found to have embezzled public funds, as well as to have created a culture of corruption within the police force. It was clear that López Portillo had damaged the credibility of the presidency irreparably, betraying the confidence of the citizenry and spending the earnings of the oil boom in extravagant luxury.

The presidency of Miguel de la Madrid Hurtado (1982–88) marks the beginning of the period, which continues today, of rule by what are called the "technocrats"—a term referring to public officials educated in universities in the United States. Upon taking office, De la Madrid found a government beleaguered by corruption and malfeasance and an economy in which the *peso* was struggling relative to the dollar. Rather than repudiate the external debt and face an economic embargo, De la Madrid opted for austerity, selling large numbers of the businesses that the two previous administrations had acquired. It is within this context that the country entered a new stage of its economic development, with NAFTA marking Mexico's entry into the global market.

Globalization and Transition to Democracy

Whereas De la Madrid began the de-centralization of the economic system, his successor, Carlos Salinas de Gortari (1988–94) steered Mexico into a new project of modernization through globalization. By the late 1980s, the state had absolute control of nearly one thousand companies, which it immediately began to sell to private investors both national and international. A law established in 1944 had stipulated that 51 percent of any enterprise on Mexican soil had to be owned by Mexicans.[35] Salinas reformed several policies to privatize industry and open the door for foreign capital, welcoming globalization. By globalization—following Arjun Appadurai—we mean the flow of capital, merchandise, communications, and imaginaries across the world. These flows modify the relationship between the local, the national, and the global, as communities that have access to global markets are capable of transcending the limitations—and corruption—of local networks (García Canclini, *Culturas híbridas*, *Consumidores y ciudadanos* and *La globalización imaginada*).[36] With recent advances in portable technology, corporations are able to seek both labor and facilities around the world. Thus developed economies do not produce in their own countries of origin but pursue business in locations where amicable states have opened their market in exchange for jobs in the manufacturing and processing of industrial goods. This new role for developing countries with a surplus of population and natural resources has led to the reduction of protectionist measures in order to attract capital and industry.

In 1992, the presidents of Mexico, the United States, and Canada signed the North American Free Trade Agreement, which opened exchange among these countries.[37] Although non-official talks can be dated as far back as 1988, President George Bush, Sr., signed the original agreements with Carlos Salinas de Gortari and Canada's Brian Mulroney on December 17, 1992. The treaty was revised and ratified by the three countries and re-signed by President Bill Clinton, who oversaw the final details in November and December of 1993. The accord officially entered into effect on January 1, 1994; it is not merely coincidental that on the very same day, the Zapatistas began their rebellion in Chiapas, since it was predicted that NAFTA would have a negative impact on indigenous peoples.

The signing of NAFTA theoretically represented the instantaneous arrival of Mexico's ruling classes to the promise of higher standards of living, comfort, and luxury, as cultural critic Carlos Monsiváis wrote in 1992:

> La formulación ensoñadora o utópica es, de hecho, la renuncia a cualquier problematización, es dar por sentado que el solo acto de la firma liquida los siglos de atraso y escasez. Mucho antes de que sepamos en qué consistirá el TLC, el sueño cultural le declara el fin de sitio arrinconado de la nación (leáse su clase dirigente) en el mundo, a la globalización, a la prosperidad, al Primer Mundo por vía del Tratado de Libre Comercio. ("De la cultura mexicana en vísperas del Tratado de Libre Comercio" 209)

With the signing of NAFTA, Mexico's political and economic elite thus enter by decree into modernity, magically bypassing prior stages of development. As Monsiváis further elaborates, the potential effects of the treaty were interpreted differently depending on the observer's perspective: by supporters it was interpreted as utopian, as the solution to past problems; and by detractors as dystopian, that is, as a loss of Mexico's sovereignty over resources and territory, and as a deferral of programs of social development. Significantly, Monsiváis observes that, "[t]he idea of Mexico belonging to the First World is, without a doubt, the most important utopia for bourgeois and middle-class sectors" (*Mexican Postcards* 136).

One of the basic tenets of neoliberal policies is the opening of the economy to allow for the flow of investors, materials, and merchandise, modifying the role of the state from being the promoting agent of modernity to instead being only a partner. Complying with the basic principles of NAFTA, Mexico deregulated investment, causing tariffs imposed on foreign goods to be lifted, in an attempt to bring more investors to the country and create more employment. Since there are no tariffs to be reinvested in Mexico, the possibility of furthering the development of a sound economy with a stable industry and accessible services is not guaranteed.

The Salinas administration adopted the treaty and its policies almost immediately. Within a few years, the Mexican state went from being the owner of the company to the provider of financial incentives for investment and the creator of basic infrastructure for the construction of factories. Some of Salinas's first actions included facilitating foreign investment by reversing agrarian reform, as he declared the *ejido* "unproductive" and ultimately concluded that it was a failure (Meyer et al. 670). Salinas ceased distributing land to indigenous and *campesino* communities, ending seventy years of a semi-effective reform movement.[38] Those marginalized by race and class have thus become more disenfranchised as social programs are cut and funding instead is directed to the development of international competition and a widening of the industrial base. As one of the conditions of NAFTA and the World Trade Organization, protections against the importation of goods are lifted; this affects national industry and commerce, as small and medium-sized nationally operated companies are unable to compete. The neoliberal policies are not entirely conducive to the development of an industrial core, since most of the *maquiladoras* are easily sent to other parts of the world if labor and environmental regulations make businesses less profitable. In spite of all the effort placed on developing the country's economic base since the 1940s, Mexico's second most abundant source of income for the year 2003 resides in the remittances sent home by immigrant workers in the United States, surpassed only by petroleum exports and exceeding those of tourism and foreign investment.[39]

Mexico's rapid entrance into the global economy did not pass without scrutiny. Indeed, the discussion surrounding the 1992–93 signing of NAFTA has precipitated a broad revision of notions of national identity in Mexico as well as a reconsideration of economic, political, and cultural relations with the United States. In particular, as mentioned above, NAFTA has been criticized for its negative impact on indigenous societies of Mexico, provoking protest and even the armed resistance of the Zapatista rebellion in Chiapas. Indigenous communities are the most affected by the project of globalization, as most of the resources once dedicated to social programs for their integration have been reallocated to the development of industry and technology. As Neil Harvey observes: "This decision particularly affected those maize producers who until the pact had managed to maintain productivity levels of the previous decade. New credit provided through PRONASOL (later known as Solidaridad) covered only half the production costs in this sector" (180). Furthermore, because they do not own their land and their methods of production are outdated, their isolated and poverty-stricken communities do not have the capability to compete with the agro-industry of the United States or Canada.[40] While postrevolutionary regimes had rendered services to the indigenous communities, albeit in meager form, the Salinas administration opted to end this tradition, shifting the focus to investing all the available resources of the nation toward attracting foreign capital.

The succession to Salinas's presidency was marred by violence, as the PRI's presidential candidate, Luis Donaldo Colosio, was murdered, and public opinion fingered Carlos Salinas as the mastermind behind this assassination. Colosio's replacement, Ernesto Zedillo, won the presidency and continued Salinas's neoliberal policies even when a severe economic and political crisis plagued the beginning of his service. Zedillo reformed Mexico's political culture, sharing power with the other branches of government and reversing sixty years of a presidential headlock on the decision-making process. In 1997, Zedillo cut the ties between the president and the PRI, ending de facto the favoritism of this party.

Since the 1920s when violence and fraud were employed to secure the continuity of the system, the party that later became the Partido Revolucionario Institucional won twelve consecutive presidential elections. Throughout its history, the PRI has been linked to political corruption, assassinations, and electoral fraud as well as representing a direct connection between the state and big business. As Brian Hamnett notes: "The Mexican party eventually became a vast organism, outside of which no access to political power or influence would be possible. At its core stood the *quid pro quo* between the state and organized labour" (236). For some seven decades, the PRI managed to maintain control over Mexico's public scene, continuing to win national elections even when its victory margins decreased in the 1980s and 1990s, as it began to lose state elections to its main opponents, the right-wing Partido de Acción Nacional (PAN, National Action Party) and the left-center Partido de la Revolución Democrática (PDR, Party of the Democratic Revolution). In the 1997 National Congress elections, the PRI lost its majority in the lower house, and finally, in 2000, ended its hegemony over the presidency with the election of the PAN's candidate, Vicente Fox Quesada; nevertheless, even during Fox's presidency (2000–06), the PRI continued to exercise considerable influence over public matters.

As Néstor García Canclini observes in *La globalización imaginada*, however, resistance is possible from many quarters since intellectuals can intervene from the margins to contest hegemonic projects:

> Los escritores y artistas no devorados por el establishment cultural, o que aun siendo recibidos por él rechazan la agenda única con que el mercado estructura la esfera pública, cumplen una función contrapública en tanto que introducen temas locales o formas de enunciarlos que parecen improductivos para la hegemonía mercantil. (199)

García Canclini thus points to art as a viable form of resistance to the rules of the market, since local artists can create awareness of social issues and problems, thereby forming a critical voice that questions the illusory logic of unlimited progress that supporters of neoliberalism propose.

Because globalization allows private industry to compete with the role of the state as regulator of projects of modernization, it is important to analyze how this change in the economic order is addressed in the novels under consideration here. While globalization ostensibly offers a "new world order," a world without borders featuring easy transit where merchandise and identities are able to flow without restriction between north and south, many Mexican and Chicano novelists problematize this, addressing the possibilities, limitations, and scope of this new rhetoric of development as they imagine the future of Mexico in the years surrounding the signing of NAFTA. In doing so, these narratives address also the "crisis of utopias" where new borders are drawn.

Dystopias hence are negative representations of imagined worlds where the purposes of modernity—the improvement of human existence through the use of reason, the accumulation of knowledge, and the wise urbanization of the land and its products—are juxtaposed with the decrepit image of societies beset by authoritarianism, dehumanization, and uncertainty regarding the future. Because dystopias express the desire for a better world while reflecting on the historical conditions that challenge present societies, in the final decades of the twentieth century Mexican and Chicano authors employ the genre of science fiction to address the problems plaguing Mexico and the borderlands.

The following chapters analyze specific examples of the representation of Mexico's utopian dreams and apocalyptic nightmares. Chapter 1, "The Brave New World of Carlos Fuentes's *Cristóbal Nonato*," examines how Fuentes's 1987 novel employs dystopian fiction to represent Mexico as a sick body struggling to survive in a globalized world market. This chapter discusses *Cristóbal Nonato's* portrayal of the challenges Mexico encounters as it attempts to create its own brand of modernity without first resolving problems ultimately stemming from colonization. Although he depicts Mexico in an acute crisis, suffering the effects of unregulated industrialization and bureaucratic corruption, Fuentes ends his novel on a positive note as his protagonists reject the opportunity to abandon their homeland for the utopia of Pacífica, opting instead to remain and work toward a more democratic future for Mexico.

The second chapter focuses on Chicano writer Alejandro Morales's *The Rag Doll Plagues* (1992), which thematizes the effects of globalization through the representation of a series of devastating epidemics in three historical contexts: colonial Mexico; contemporary Los Angeles; and an apocalyptic post-NAFTA future in which the political border between the United States and Mexico has been abolished, but cultural, racial, and class lines continue to divide communities. After dramatizing interethnic relations contributing to Mexican and Chicano identity over several centuries, Morales offers a cure for the plagues of the future that entails the formation of alliances among diverse social sectors in order to forge a new beginning based on a multicultural aesthetics.

Chapter 3, in turn, focuses on Carmen Boullosa's *Cielos de la tierra* (1997), which investigates Mexico's trajectory of development through the representation of three different failed utopian societies: a colonial scholastic institution that is destroyed by the greed of the colonizers; a contemporary Mexico City that contradicts the utopian myth of postrevolutionary

Mexico as a fully integrated mixed-race society; and a future world known as L'Atlàntide where language and history are banned, leading to the annihilation of humanity. Calling attention to the systematic erasure of marginalized communities in the name of progress, Boullosa suggests that we can avoid this ultimate crisis by embracing more holistic values characterized by a greater respect for the environment, indigenous communities, and individuals of both genders.

Finally, chapter 4 examines Mexican author and environmental activist Homero Aridjis's *La Leyenda de los soles* (1993) and its sequel *En quién piensas cuando haces el amor?* (1995), both set in the megalopolis of Mexico City in the year 2027. In these novels, Aridjis scrutinizes Mexico's project of modernity, highlighting how industrialization has destroyed the ecosystem while political corruption has hindered the emergence of a democratic society. Through his dystopian narratives, Aridjis proposes that a renewed link with the earth's ecology is necessary in order to escape the ecoapocalypse.

Utopian Dreams, Apocalyptic Nightmares concludes that Latin American and US Latino perspectives on the past and the future of their societies represent a key site for the analysis of the problems of underdevelopment, social injustice, and ecological decay that plague today's world. Whereas utopian discourse was once used to justify colonization, Mexican and Chicano writers now deploy dystopian rhetoric to interrogate projects of modernization, contributing to the current debate on the global expansion of capitalism. The narratives studied here coincide in expressing confidence in the ability of popular sectors to claim a decisive role in the implementation of more effective measures to guarantee an ecologically sound, ethnically diverse, and just society for the future of the Americas.

Chapter One

The Brave New World of
Carlos Fuentes's *Cristóbal Nonato*

A Critique of Mexican Modernity

> Every true poet is inevitably a Columbus. America
> existed for centuries before Columbus, but only
> Columbus succeeded in discovering. The multipli-
> cation table existed for centuries before R-13, yet
> it was only R-13 who found a new Eldorado in the
> virginal forest of figures.
>
> Yevgeny Zamyatin
> *We*

Since his monumental 1975 novel *Terra nostra*, the internation-
ally known Mexican writer Carlos Fuentes has evidenced a
particular concern with the implications of the 1492 Euro-American encounter for contemporary global culture and society.[1] A
dozen years later, and some half dozen years before the signing
of the North American Free Trade Agreement between Canada,
the United States, and Mexico, Fuentes's *Cristóbal Nonato*
(1987)[2] constitutes an early critical assessment of some of the
potential effects of globalization on the cultural and economic
makeup of both Mexico and the US border region. Fuentes
projects his dystopia five years into the future, setting his novel
in a historically symbolic 1992, that is, precisely five centuries
after the initial contact between America and Europe. *Cristóbal
Nonato*—along with several other Mexican and Chicano novels published during the decade of the 1990s—searches in the
periods of the conquest and the colony for the roots of social
and economic problems that have impeded the modernization
of Mexican society. This novel's originality resides in its use
of the literary dystopia to examine the historical conditions that
have hindered Latin American development in light of European and US-inspired efforts to implement Western modernity

in developing nations. The concurrence of the signing of the NAFTA treaty and the quincentenary of Columbus's first voyage presents a fruitful juncture for questioning the conditions of Mexican development both because of the importance of the discovery for the emergence of Western modernity and because of the evolution of globalization at the dawn of the new millennium.[3] In *Cristóbal Nonato*, Fuentes engages his reader in a serious reappraisal of the meaning of modernity and its application in postrevolutionary Mexico, posing crucial questions: What is Western modernity and why has it proven so difficult to implement in the two centuries since Mexico's independence from Spain? And, significantly, what are the possible effects that modernity's newest embodiment—globalization—might have on Mexico as a nation and on people living in the US-Mexican border region?

In order to scrutinize Mexico's project of modernity, Fuentes skillfully employs motifs, techniques, and themes associated with the literary dystopia—notably, the critique of the utopian image of the city as the ultimate representation of the national body and an examination of the deleterious effects of industrialization on the environment—and combines these with other concerns such as the role of indigenous communities in the modern nation. As do all the novels discussed in the present study, *Cristóbal Nonato* subscribes to the dystopian genre as it represents a reevaluation of the concepts of modernity, utopia, and nation as they have been applied to Latin America, depicting a futuristic society negatively affected by the pursuit of an industrial capitalism that ignores the unique historical and cultural composition of Mexico.

The rather intricate plot of *Cristóbal Nonato* begins with the young couple Ángel and Ángeles Palomar conceiving their son Cristóbal—who is also the main narrator of the novel—on the contaminated sands of Acapulco in order to win the fictitious Discovery of America contest that would confer unlimited lifelong power of governance over the crumbling nation to the male child born at midnight on October 12, 1992, that is, five hundred years to the day after Columbus's initial landing in the New World:[4]

> SEPAN CUANTOS: El niño de sexo masculino que nazca precisamente a las 0:00 horas del día 12 de octubre de 1992 y cuyo nombre de familia, aparte del nombre de pila

(seguramente, lo estimamos bien, Cristóbal) más semejan-
zas guarde con el Ilustre Navegante será proclamado HIJO
PRÓDIGO DE LA PATRIA, su educación será proveída por
la República y dentro de dieciocho años le serán entregadas
las LLAVES de la REPÚBLICA, proemio a su instalación,
al cumplir los veintiún años, como REGENTE DE LA
NACIÓN, con poderes de elección, sucesión y selección
prácticamente omnímodos. De manera CIUDADANOS que
si su apellido por pura casualidad es Colonia, Colombia,
Columbiario, Colombo, Colombiano o Columbus, para no
hablar de Colón, Colombo, o Palomo, Palomares, Palomar
o Santospirito, e incluso, ya de perdida, Genovese (¿quién
sabe? Quizás ninguno de los anteriores y entonces A USTED
YA SE LE HIZO) entonces óyeme MACHO MEXICANO,
EMBARAZA A TU SEÑORA, PERO YA! (13–14)

Cristóbal Nonato is divided into nine sections that trace each
month of the narrator's period of gestation;[5] following a cir-
cular structure, the novel ends on the same polluted beaches
of Acapulco with the birth of Cristóbal and his twin sister. Il-
lustrating the fragmenting effects of the national system that
ruled Mexico for more than seventy years, in his projected 1992
Fuentes presents us with a dystopic vision of how the country
suffers another crisis after the collapse of its economy during the fictitious "1990 disaster,"[6] as a consequence of which
certain territories have been granted to transnational corporations in order to pay some of the interest on the national debt,
which amounts in the novel to a symbolically charged 1492
billion dollars.[7] As a result, entire regions such as the Yucatán
Peninsula have been granted to Club Med, while the states
of Chiapas, Tabasco, and Campeche form part of a territory
named CHICATAM under the control of the US oil consortium
known in the novel as the Five Sisters. In addition, the intervention of US Marines compromises national sovereignty when
they occupy Veracruz and Puebla with the ostensible purpose
of suppressing a popular rebellion against the state under the
fictitious Modified and Reaffirmed Inter-American Rio Treaty
(MORE-RIOT).[8] At the center of the chaotic country remains
Mexico City where globalization in the form of products and
fashions associated with US popular culture flow and transform
the cultural composition of the nation, presenting a clear threat
to the post-revolutionary national identity that was predicated
on political, economic, and cultural autonomy.

Near the beginning of the novel, the unborn narrator introduces his father's uncle, Homero Fagoaga, representing an apt pupil of the Partido Revolucionario Institucional (PRI), the party that dominated Mexican politics for the larger part of the twentieth century. Ángel Palomar's other uncle, the anthropologist Fernando Benítez, serves as the counterpart to his conservative brother since he is a social scientist who documents the last indigenous tribe within the fragmenting nation that represents Mexico in a futuristic 1992. The disparity between these two uncles forms an ideological axis in which Homero Fagoaga represents the excesses of conservatism and corruption, in contrast to the concerned liberal humanitarianism of Fernando Benítez.

Along with Ángel's relatives, the narrator introduces a group of marginalized characters that compose a "Rock Aztec" band called the "Four Jodiditos"—translated as the Four Fuckups—whose members are: Orphan Huerta, a lumpen proletariat boy who has grown up on the streets of Mexico City; Hipi Toltec, a youth who believes that he is the reincarnation of the Aztec god of earth renewal Xipe Totec; Egg, a piano player; and an invisible female band member, Baby Ba, who at the end of the novel will turn out to be Cristóbal's twin sister.

In a parody of Columbus's notion of the New World as an earthly paradise, Fuentes describes Acapulco Bay as a highly polluted environment because of the dumped garbage of thousands of national and international tourists. The Four Jodiditos along with the Palomar couple plot to destroy Acapulco in order to avenge the ecological abuse of the formerly paradisiacal port, as environmental contamination threatens its once pristine waters and sands. They plan to achieve this goal by flooding hotel rooms with the waste produced in the resort and by training coyotes—once used for the repression of peasants—to attack the hordes of tourists that pollute the vacation spot. We assume that the Palomars and their crew have been successful when we observe that a tidal wave has flushed several tourists into the ocean, only to find out later that this ecoterrorism was really executed by the Mexican army in an effort to purge the port of drug traffickers, prostitutes, and political enemies who were threatening the secession of Acapulco from what remains of the Republic of Mexico.

After the destruction of Acapulco, Ángel and Ángeles Palomar and Ángel's uncles travel back to Mexico City, where Fuentes depicts a corrupt and decadent federal government that—unable to guarantee a safe and healthy modern life for its citizens—wields power through the manipulation of national symbols aided by mass media and ultimately by armed repression. Although in this fictional version of 1992 the Institutional Revolutionary Party has lost presidential elections to the conservative Partido de Acción Nacional (PAN), the PRI still holds the majority of seats in congress, maintaining the system virtually unchanged.[9] As do Fuentes's earlier works such as *La región más transparente* (1958), *Las buenas conciencias* (1959), and *La muerte de Artemio Cruz* (1962), this novel also calls the reader's attention to the corrupt habits of public functionaries who have contributed to the disintegration of the dream of transforming Mexico into a modern democratic nation.

In *Cristóbal Nonato*, "old boy"-style political decadence is represented by super-minister Ulises López, the incarnation of the unscrupulous and conniving politician who through treacherous means has forced his way to the highest echelons of the political system, betraying the ideals of the Revolution in his climb to the top. In order to emphasize how the political system has changed guards without an accompanying democratization of society, Fuentes introduces the younger generation of equally unethical politicians embodied by minister Federico Robles Chacón, who through the manipulation of mass media maintains control of the nation's citizens either by reducing a token democracy to the mindless participation of the people in nationally televised contests or by creating nationalistic symbols such as the cultural icon known as "Mamadoc."

On a more positive note, *Cristóbal Nonato* underscores potential manifestations of cultural resistance as marginalized sectors respond to the demands of the modern economy through what cultural critic Néstor García Canclini would term "cultural reconversion," where common folks combine tradition and technology to participate in the economy.[10] In order to illustrate how disenfranchised sectors adapt to the needs of the global marketplace, Fuentes focuses on the truck drivers of the fragmenting republic, who create alternative forms of economic organization by endeavoring to trade goods without money. These responses, however, are not idealized, as Fuentes also notes how subaltern resistance movements are rapidly suppressed, appropriated, or otherwise manipulated by the state. In the novel, the initial energy of the truckers' grassroots resistance is distorted as the nefarious personage known as the Ayatollah Moreno assumes leadership of the movement. The charismatic leader transforms the peaceful creativity of the popular rebellion into a fanatical expression of nationalistic fundamentalism, leading to a spectacle of gratuitous violence. The state in the figure of Minister Robles Chacón attempts to incorporate this movement into the system but after the Ayatollah refuses to acquiesce, the minister orders the violent repression of a massive demonstration marching on Mexico City.

After the massacre, a fire ignites in the capital that exhausts the already scarce supply of breathable air, forcing the unborn Cristóbal's parents to escape the city. Back again on the beaches of Acapulco, the Palomar couple meets two mysterious characters who invite Ángel and Ángeles to abandon the splintered Republic of Mexico for the harmonious utopia of Pacífica to begin a new future, just as Cristóbal is about to come into the world along with his twin sister, Baby Ba. Pacífica symbolizes an alternative to Western models of modernity in that it represents a Pacific Rim-inspired manifestation of utopia where the contradiction between technology and humanity has presumably been resolved; but significantly, Ángel and Ángeles reject this offer of paradise, electing instead to remain in their homeland to help create a new country, a post-nation emerging from the ruins of contemporary Mexico.

Ambitiously, Fuentes in *Cristóbal Nonato* scrutinizes how the fundamental goals of postrevolutionary Mexican modernity—the development of national resources, the democratization of society, and the participation of ethnic minorities in the construction of a truly modern society—have not yet been achieved.[11] The discussion in the following section will center on the analysis of Fuentes's literary dystopia by examining the role of modern institutions of knowledge in the formation of national identity, with a specific focus on anthropology and its ambiguous relation with the indigenous peoples of Mexico. The chapter will then turn to the effects of modernization on the environment of two key areas of the nation: Acapulco and

Mexico City. Finally, this chapter will conclude with a discussion of alternative possibilities for Mexico's future development and participation in the global market as projected by Fuentes in 1987, on the eve of the negotiations that ultimately led to the signing of the NAFTA treaty.

Anthropology and the Encounter with the Other

From his earlier works such as his first short stories contained in the collection *Los días enmascarados* (1954), the novel *Cambio de piel* (1967), and the essays in *Tiempo mexicano* (1971), and through his recent novellas compiled in *El naranjo* (1993), the role that anthropology plays in documenting the indigenous communities on the margin of the modern nation has been a frequent topic in Carlos Fuentes's literary production. Fuentes has been a stern critic of the failure of the state's attempts to integrate Amerindian groups into the modernizing process without truly understanding their cultures, which ultimately results in increasing their isolation and exclusion from the rest of Mexico. In *Cristóbal Nonato,* he appraises how colonization and its aftermath have caused the alienation of indigenous communities, taking them almost to the brink of extinction, while also pointing to the failure of postrevolutionary Mexico to successfully assist these groups in their struggle for survival against the backdrop of globalization.

As discussed above, a key component of the discourse of modernity has been the construction of the Amerindian communities as culturally different from the European, a process that Enrique Dussel, drawing on Edmundo O'Gorman's terminology, refers to as "the invention of the Other." Historian J. H. Elliot in *Spain and Its World* underscores the singularity of the discovery of the Americas for European self-discovery, observing how the interest in studying indigenous cultures has oscillated between representing them as a source of fascination or an object of loathing.[12] Beginning with the conquest of the territories of present-day Mexico and throughout the colonial period, ethnography functioned as a fundamental tool for accessing the culture of the colonized and using it to instruct the imperial authorities—both religious and civil—on ways to dominate the Amerindian culturally, spiritually, economically, and politically.

Hence sixteenth-century missionaries such as Bernardino de Sahagún, Andrés de Olmos, and Diego Durán studied indigenous societies with a practical aim in mind. As Elliot proposes: "[Ethnographic] inquiries were generally guided by considerations of utility. Crown officials needed precise information on Indian land tenure and inheritance patterns if they were to dispense justice according to custom [. . .]. Missionaries needed precise information on pagan superstitions if they were to cast down the idolaters" (44). In order to dismantle the religious and cultural apparatus of the indigenous societies by means of evangelization and acculturation, early ethnographers formulated extensive reports on native customs. Thus the victor's knowledge about the culture of the vanquished aided in the subjugation of conquered peoples; ironically, this same effort also succeeded in salvaging from oblivion the memory of the same customs that the missionaries were seeking to extirpate, ultimately resulting in the preservation of a record of pre-Columbian practices for posterity.

During the period of the conquest and colonization, through independence, and to the present day, indigenous peoples have remained marginalized while paradoxically at times serving as a symbolic representation of Mexican identity. As discussed above, the Mexican Revolution, at least ostensibly, aimed to improve the lot of the indigenous population, as one of its goals was the redistribution of land to those groups displaced by the landowning classes in a quasi-feudal system ultimately rooted in colonialism. Anthropology was key to the legitimization of the Revolution's nation-building discourse, as the state supported the work of professional anthropologists such as Manuel Gamio who in *Forjando patria* (1916) emphasized the need to include the culture of the native groups in the formation of Mexican identity in order to differentiate the revolutionary project from the Eurocentric models represented by former regimes such as that of turn-of-the-century dictator Porfirio Díaz.

As Roberto González Echevarría proposes, in the decades following independence, anthropology provided the emerging Latin American nations with an alternative origin distinct from that offered by the West (150–51). Anthropology thus paved the way for the inclusion of historically marginalized ethnic groups into the state's imaginary by adding an aura of scientific progress to the Revolution's effort to project a modern image of the nation. Commenting on the triumphant regime's attempts to include the marginalized communities, historian Alan Knight shrewdly observes: "The new [revolutionary] regime, raising the standard of the 1917 Constitution and consolidating itself through the 1920s, incorporated *indigenismo* into its official ideology. It claimed, in other words, to seek the emancipation and integration of Mexico's exploited Indian groups: emancipation from the old oppressions of landlord, cacique, and *cura* [priest]; integration into the new revolutionary state and nation" (80). In brief, state-sponsored *indigenismo* strove to aid the native communities in combating centuries of economic and social marginalization by including them in a modern national project.

Thereby the regimes following the Mexican Revolution supported the social sciences in their efforts to study the ancient cultures of Mexico in order to establish an autochthonous foundation for the new nation after the revolutionary upheaval. As mentioned above, the government established official agencies devoted to the study of indigenous communities such as the Instituto Nacional Indigenista (INI) and the Instituto Nacional de Antropología e Historia (INAH).[13] Hence, postrevolutionary state-sponsored anthropology, rather than aiding in the incorporation of indigenous peoples into the modern nation, ironically has contributed to the reinforcement of a hierarchy between a Westernized modernity and so-called backwardness, ultimately widening the chasm between modern Mexico and the indigenous communities.[14]

During the 1920s and 1930s, the state's interest in studying the cultural heritage of the indigenous communities paralleled the fascination of metropolitan travelers such as the French poet Antonin Artaud, and US and British novelists Graham Greene, D. H. Lawrence, and Malcolm Lowry, among others, who visited Mexico, evidencing a particular interest in Amerindian cultures. Literary critic Luis Mario Schneider explains how anthropology and avant-garde art coincided in the validation of indigenous cultures for different purposes. European intellectuals searched in the cultures of Africa, Asia, and Latin America for the "primitive," that is, for the essence of man, untouched by modernization and its dehumanizing effects. This endeavor, more than manifesting an inherent interest in the exploration of aboriginal cultures, served the purpose of providing the West with alternative ways of comprehending the unbalance created by modernization, and ended up mystifying the cultures of the Third World rather than illuminating them.[15] As anthropologist Fernando Benítez remarks, during the 1930s both state-sponsored *indigenismo* and the fascination of European intellectuals with Amerindian communities caused a "rediscovery" of the native cultures of Mexico, this time, by the rest of their own compatriots (*Lázaro Cárdenas* 133). This re-discovery of indigenous cultures had utopian undertones as it promised the possibility of cultural renewal for a decadent modern society.

Through his fictional character named after this same anthropologist Fernando Benítez (1910–2000), Fuentes examines the impact of Euro-American contact on indigenous peoples five hundred years after the initial encounter, as well as speculating on the future of both Amerindian communities and the social science of anthropology under globalization. Ángel Palomar's Uncle Fernando is homonymous with the author of over two dozen books regarding the history and anthropology of the indigenous tribes of Mexico, including widely known texts such as *Los indios de México* (1967).[16] The work of the real Fernando Benítez combines ethnography, historiography, and travel literature, tracing the history of the remaining indigenous communities in their last areas of refuge. Fuentes's choice of an anthropologist as a character is significant because, as discussed above, in the postrevolutionary era, anthropology and history have been fundamental tools for the integration of indigenous peoples into national identity on an ideological level, while simultaneously these same communities have been excluded from national projects on a practical level. Through his fictional anthropologist's eyes, Fuentes criticizes the effects of the alienation of indigenous groups from the project of modernity by examining the ambiguous relationship between ethnographer and native Other; and ultimately he addresses the question of what the future holds for both Amerindian and anthropologist after the collapse of the Western model of nation.

In *Cristóbal Nonato*, Ángel's anthropologist uncle arrives in a helicopter owned by the National Indigenist Institute to a secluded mesa in the Oaxacan mountains, in an effort to document the Lacandon tribe before they are assimilated. Fuentes underscores the social scientist's panoptical gaze that holds the power to survey the entirety of the country from a privileged perspective:[17] "Vio una angosta nación esquelética y decapitada, el pecho en los desiertos del norte, el corazón infartado en la salida del Golfo en Tampico, el vientre en la ciudad de México, el ano supurante y venéreo en Acapulco, las rodillas recortadas en Guerrero y Oaxaca. . . Esto quedaba" (27). From this aerial perspective, the dystopian image of the nation as a fragmented and decomposing body highlights the alarming effects of globalization as international corporations take over large territories of the country, including the ancestral lands of the indigenous communities. As a result, the anthropologist must acquire permission from the fictitious Chicatam Trustee-ship to interview the last remaining Lacandons "antes de que fuera 'too late'" (235).

Immediately upon introducing his father's uncle, the narrator emphasizes the exogenous nature of Fernando Benítez's ethnic background by referring to him as a blue-eyed criollo historian, calling attention to how the history of subaltern communities has been presented consistently from the problematic perspective of social groups that historically have oppressed them. Upon arriving in the village, the social scientist encounters the lost tribe suffering the effects of poverty, illness, and the lack of adequate nutrition as a result of the marginalization to which colonization and its aftermath have relegated the indigenous population.

Fuentes perceives how communication between criollo anthropologist and indigenous Other is marked by the failure to establish a meaningful dialogue as emblematized in a scene in which the anthropologist murmurs to a Lacandon man who passes by: "Ya no eres dueño de lo que los Dioses te regalaron, dijo en voz baja extendiendo una mano hacia el primer hombre que se le acercó esta mañana en el altiplano asoleado y frío. Pero el hombre se siguió de largo" (230). This telling scene exemplifies the conflictive relationship between informant and ethnographer as the fictive Benítez wishes to communicate with the Oaxacan native but this desired contact is obstructed because the Lacandon man ignores the presence of the anthropologist. Strikingly, Fernando Benítez's reference to the ancient gods is a reminder that his own presence as an outsider is a by-product of what the European search for utopia in the New World has meant for indigenous cultures in the long term:

> El tío Fernando ha pasado la mitad de su vida documentando a los cuatro o cinco millones de indios mexicanos, los que nunca fueron conquistados por los españoles, o jamás se dejaron asimilar al mundo criollo o mestizo, o simplemente sobrevivieron la catástrofe demográfica de la conquista: eran veinticinco millones antes de que Cortés desembarcara en Tabasco; cincuenta años más tarde eran sólo un millón. (229)[18]

Cristóbal's great uncle employs his knowledge of the history of the conquest as a point of departure for re-examining the key moment that transformed the demographic and ecological face of Mesoamerica. Ironically, while the conquest signaled the end of the predominance of ancient pre-Columbian civilizations, it also meant the beginning of modern Mexico, as transculturation in cultural terms and *mestizaje* in biological terms began to reshape the social structure of the Americas.[19]

Fuentes underscores how the segregation of the indigenous population to a second-class citizen status stemming from colonization has created a division between modern civilization and traditional cultures:

> Agitó la cabeza para librarse de la fórmula que le impedía entender el misterio, la ambigüedad de esta tierra adentro de México, semilla de México, pero tan totalmente ajena a su México blanco, de ojos azules y lecturas del Nouvel Observateur y la revista Time y BMWs y pastas de dientes y tostadores eléctricos y cablevisión y chequeos periódicos en las clínicas de Houston y próxima celebración del Quinto Centenario del Descubrimiento de América—hecho totalmente ignorado por los hombres, mujeres y niños que él estaba contemplando: *una población no descubierta porque desconocía su propio descubrimiento, una fecha, un enigma impuesto por otros.* (231; emphasis mine)

This passage from *Cristóbal Nonato* echoes the late anthropologist Guillermo Bonfil Batalla's essay *México profundo* (1987), published in the same year as Fuentes's novel, in which this social scientist contrasts what he calls the "real Mexico" (formed by different indigenous ethnic groups) to the "artificial Mexico" (urban and cosmopolitan).[20] Here the fictional anthropologist observes the distance between the two realities of Mexico, since the westernized elite ignores the implications of globalization for the indigenous Mexican who seems destined to disappear. While the urban leisure class drives foreign cars, watches cable television and celebrates the discovery, the "other" Mexico remains alienated from historical events and from the benefits of modernity. The narrator highlights the problematic notion of globalization, emphasizing how even in the modern nation at the end of the millennium, the "other" Mexico continues silently living and dying in isolation. Through the character of Fernando Benítez, Fuentes details how the notion of modernity based on consumerism clashes with the pressing reality of the disenfranchised communities from the Oaxacan mountains, calling attention to the chasm between the desires of the ruling classes and the reality of marginalized groups.[21]

Fuentes's criticism of the model of nation based on the philosophy of the Enlightenment harks back to his own 1971 essay "De Quetzalcóatl a Pepsicóatl," where this author describes its presumptions for the heterogeneous societies of Latin America:

> La filosofía de la Ilustración, como Jano, tenía dos caras. Mirando el pasado, afirmaba: todo, antes de nosotros, ha sido bárbaro, irracional y supersticioso. Mirando hacia el futuro proclamaba: de aquí en adelante, sólo habrá un progreso ilimitado. Nada en apariencia convenía más a países que querían negar totalmente el pasado indígena y colonial e incorporarse a la marcha optimista del progreso. Sin embargo, la Ilustración fundaba sus ideas en un concepto universal e incambiable de la naturaleza. (*Tiempo mexicano* 32)

Fuentes thus criticizes the negation of the past as barbarous, engrained in the notion of the subject emerging from the Enlightenment and the fallacy regarding unlimited progress, as understood by Latin American ruling classes. In brief, by adopting the Western model of the nation as culturally and linguistically homogeneous, Latin American elites condemn indigenous society to assimilate into the rest of the population and consequently to disappear as distinct cultures. The role of the indigenous peoples in the Mexican Revolution and its aftermath was particularly contradictory: on one hand, they were considered the symbolic origin of the nation-state and possessors of a rich cultural and historical tradition; but on the other hand, they presumably represented the past and not the future of the nation. As Vasconcelos proposes in his essay *La raza cósmica*, the ideal citizen for the revolutionary and postrevolutionary regimes was the mestizo, but as discussed in the introduction to the present study, this image confined indigenous communities to a nationalistic logic of acculturation and ultimately extinction.

In a dreamlike sequence presented in *Cristóbal Nonato* through the fictitious anthropologist's eyes, the narrator presents us the dissolution of the *indigenista* effort when the Lacandon are contrasted to an indigenous community living on an adjacent plateau:

> El pueblo de la otra orilla estaba demasiado lejos; no podía oír lo que decían, aunque sí adivinar sus gestos. Vestidos de blanco, con camisas y calzones almidonados y relucientes, este pueblo era otro, no la tribu abandonada que mi tío quizás acababa de descubrir, por qué no?, con tanto asombro como Cabeza de Vaca a los indios pueblo, sino un grupo de gente con ligas afuera de la aldea. [. . .] Alargaban los brazos como quisieran colmar de un salto la distancia entre aquel pueblo y éste: tendían la mano. (232)

The description of the other group as healthy, clean, and progressive due to contact with the outside world is representative of the state-sponsored endeavor of acculturating the communities and contrasts with the miserable conditions of the Lacandon village. Fernando Benítez becomes aware of the impossibility of dialogue between the indigenous group that he is visiting and the assimilated group on the other side of the ravine as he acknowledges that: "No tenía sentido animarlos a una comunicación imposible. Nada se dirían" (211). The fact that an abyss geographically separates these two communities symbolizes how the events of the last five centuries have culminated in an insurmountable cultural difference between what have become two Mexicos. Even though the revolutionary regimes have intended the inclusion of marginalized ethnic communities, these efforts have failed as the wheels of industrialized modernity and consumerism impose a hegemonic logic that does not allow the self-determination of indigenous societies and their inclusion in the project of the modern nation.

Another key scene in which the division between the two Mexicos is apparent involves Ángel Palomar's other uncle, the conservative Homero Fagoaga. After delivering a lengthy erudite speech to five thousand Mixtec Indians in the state of Guerrero, Fagoaga—who apart from being a politician is also a member of the Royal Academy of the Spanish Language and a staunch defender of the purity of the Castilian tongue—does not comprehend why his audience fails to react to his diatribe. When he asks: "No entendieron mis latines, eso fue?" he receives the reply, "No, señor. No entendieron nada. Ni uno solo de estos aborígenes habla español" (263). This shocking revelation calls attention to the continuing linguistic and cultural segregation of large portions of Mexico's population. Ironically, one of the main points of the learned politician's speech was the idea that the dominant PRI party makes it possible for all citizens to participate equally in the political decisions of the country, a claim which is immediately undermined by the persistence of the linguistic barrier five hundred years after the conquest.

In *Cristóbal Nonato*, the dramatic situation of the indigenous peoples worsens after the limited services provided by the state cease altogether as a result of the novel's fictitious economic crisis of 1990. In Fuentes's dystopian vision the isolated communities abandon their territories in search of a new life, migrating to the already overcrowded Mexico City or crossing the border to the United States in search of the utopian "American Dream." Further problematizing the question of the separate realities of Mexico, at the same time that the protagonist Cristóbal is conceived, a Lacandon couple conceives a baby; needless to say, their offspring will not be eligible to participate in the Christopher Columbus contest. This indigenous couple departs for Chicago in search of a new beginning as the possibilities of surviving in Mexico leave them little alternative but to take their chances by migrating to the north:

> Y la pareja de indios [piensa/dice] nada tenemos, hemos
> regresado a casa, esta tierra siempre fue nuestra, por aquí
> pasamos hacia el Sur, un día hace mucho, primero pisamos
> esta tierra, la recuerdas mujer?, hemos traído a nuestro hijo

a nacer en tierra nuestra, no tierra extraña, no frontera: tierra
nuestra, el Norte, lugar de encuentros. (504)

Here it is clear that the Oaxacan couple does not share the
modern concept of the border separating the United States and
Mexico. For US conservative elites, migration from south of the
border is portrayed as an alien invasion but for these indigenous
characters, it represents the return to a pre-historic place of origin, a return to Aztlán, the Nahua tribe's point of departure.[22]

In this section, Fuentes ridicules the use of modern technology to deter illegal immigration as border guards employ night
goggles, radar, and heat-seeking paraphernalia, but this sophisticated equipment proves unable to detect the border-crossers.
Nevertheless, even though they escape the panoptic eye of
la Migra, when they arrive at their destination the Lacandon
couple discovers that there are no jobs and no promised land
but instead a new form of enslavement as they end up working
in a circus freak show as rare specimens of "primitive" forms
of humanity, just as at the end of the nineteenth century several
key Native American chiefs did, for example, the famous "Sitting Bull" in Buffalo Bill's traveling show. Fuentes satirizes
the conquest of the Wild West pointing to its effect on native
communities across the Americas when he portrays the appall-
ing destiny that awaits the indigenous couple who attempts to
realize the "American Dream."

If the remaining Amerindians face certain extinction in the
rapidly diminishing Republic of Mexico or the dystopian United States of Fuentes's conjectured 1992, the professional anthropologist also represents a dying breed, for soon there will be
no more Others to document. Ángel's uncle Fernando Benítez
demonstrates awareness of the ambiguous function of anthropology since it both serves as a means of preserving a culture
on the verge of disappearance and also ironically contributes
indirectly to that same extinction. Returning to the territories of
the fragmenting nation, "Temió, volando sobre las montañas de
Oaxaca, haber precipitado hoy la desaparición de los últimos
noventa y dos seres de la tribu de la noche eterna" (235). The
anthropologist's consciousness of the peril that the Amerindian
cultures face, and to which he as ethnographer in some sense
contributes, becomes an obsession for the fictionalized Fernando Benítez.

While anthropologists such as the real Fernando Benítez were expected to help incorporate disenfranchised areas into the modern Mexico of the Revolution in order to form a united nation, the eroding effects of globalization end up destroying the last vestiges of native cultures, thus predicting an apocalyptic future for both Amerindian and anthropologist. Looking at the world through his great uncle's eyes, the unborn narrator nostalgically parodies some verses of Ramón López Velarde's famous poem "Suave Patria" (1921):

> Suave patria impecable y diamantina: el bosque de ceibas, la velocidad plateada del río, el cocodrilo y el ocelote, los monos y los tucanes bajo la bóveda vegetal. Y una columna de humo que ascendía desde el corazón de la selva: los bosques talados, las nuevas carreteras, las perforaciones de las Cinco Hermanas, el curso desviado del río, las huellas del pasado borradas para siempre por el lodazal y el petróleo: Yaxchilán, Planchón de las Figuras, la selva lacandona. . . La suave patria invisible. (27–28)

This parody severely critiques the indiscriminate implementation of industrialization and globalization in Mexico as transnational corporations exploit the natural resources whose utilization had promised to bring Latin America out of the Third World. Through this dystopian representation, the narrator denounces the extinction of various animal species, the devastation of the rain forest, and the destruction of the Mayan ruins as rampant capitalism transforms the jungle into mudslides and oil spills.[23] Fuentes's continuing parody of López Velarde's patriotic poem identifies the greed of the Mexican upper classes as the cause of the evils afflicting the nation:

> Patria, tu superficie es el bache, digo
> Tu cielo el esmog estancado
> El niño Dios te escrituró un palacio en Las Lomas y un
>   chalet de ski en Vail
> Y los veneros de petroleo un diablo que vive en el spot
> market de Rotterdam, digo. (247)[24]

By demonstrating the effects of globalization on the indigenous Other and on the environment, Fuentes presses for a project of modernity in which all sectors of society can participate in a more democratic fashion.

Emblematic of his resolution to protect marginalized groups from the abuses of modernized elites, the fictional anthropologist Fernando Benítez meets his own demise while defending poor *campesinos* from the repression ordered by the corrupt politician Federico Robles Chacón to squelch a grassroots rebellion in the state of Guerrero. Benítez's heroic death signals the alliance between the anthropologist and subaltern sectors, while simultaneously shedding doubt on the future of indigenous peoples. His sacrifice underscores the role that the subjectivity of the social scientist plays because while culturally he belongs to a group whose sole presence has promoted the extinction of the indigenous communities, on an ideological level he identifies with the Amerindian. To make matters more problematic, as a professional he struggles to maintain his own scientific objectivity as he is aware that his actions also involuntarily contribute to the annihilation of the same indigenous peoples whom he studies and protects.

Through the character of Cristóbal's great uncle Fernando Benítez, then, Fuentes emphasizes the ambiguous role of anthropology in relation to the native peoples of the Americas. Over the course of five centuries, the imposition of the Western model of modernity has denied a voice to the Amerindians whose identity and political will has been silenced, first by the colonial elites and later by national hegemonic groups. In *Cristóbal Nonato*, Fuentes wonders about the future applications of social sciences—and the role of the state as administrator of services—since the effects of neoliberalism on the state diminish social programs created to solve the problems of marginalization. Ironically, while the encounter with Amerindian societies served as a catalyst for the emergence of modernity, the latest effects of modern economic development and industrialization appear to seal the fate of indigenous peoples. In the following section, we will see how Fuentes revisits two themes associated with utopia—the earthly paradise and the ideal city, represented by Acapulco and Mexico City respectively—as the effects of globalization continue to unearth the contradictions of the project of modernity in Latin America.

Paradise Lost: The Destruction of Utopia in "Acapulcalypse" and "Makesicko City"

Since the 1950s, as a result of the economic boom known as "the Mexican Miracle," the Mexican state has projected both Acapulco and Mexico City as icons of a progressive and cosmopolitan image of the nation: Acapulco has been known idealistically as the "Paradise of the Pacific," while Mexico City has been referred to as the "City of the Palaces." When Acapulco was originally developed, tourism was promoted as a way to diversify the mid-century coastal economy that was mostly based on agriculture and a timid fishing industry. The capital, in turn, has been the site of vital socioeconomic and political activity since pre-Columbian times, when Tenochtitlan administered a huge empire and constituted a commercial hub comparable to Europe's most cosmopolitan urban centers; five hundred years later, the metropolitan zone of Mexico City is central to the project of national modernization as it houses the federal government and most of the cultural, industrial, and economic resources of the republic. Beginning with *La región más transparente* (1958) and *La muerte de Artemio Cruz* (1962), Carlos Fuentes has depicted the Pacific resort and the capital city as areas of multicultural contact and as a projection of the fantasies of status and leisure of the emergent Mexican middle class. Both locations, then, represent the utopian dream of modernity of national elites. Instead of treating them as expressions of a progressive Mexican modernity, however, in *Cristóbal Nonato*, Fuentes portrays both urban centers as sick bodies, parodying the utopian themes of the earthly paradise and the ideal city, while drawing attention to the disastrous ecological effects of industrialization on Acapulco's bay and on Mexico City.[25] In this way, Fuentes's depiction of the port and the metropolis as dystopian products of industrialization contradicts hegemonic notions of progress, emphasizing the subversion of the dream of modernity in the form of a nightmarish future.

In the discourse of Western modernity, the city plays a fundamental role as the symbolic representation of the cohesiveness of the modern national state. The city since classical times has been associated with utopia as it embodies the perfect balance between nature and human genius employed for the common good. Scholar Lewis Mumford has established that "the city itself is the utopia" since it joins the "powers of god" with the design of nature ("Utopia, the City, and the Machine" 3).[26] Since the early modern period, the affluence of urban societies has inspired confidence in the future as people began to abandon the countryside in pursuit of more favorable living conditions. Since Tommaso Campanella's early seventeenth-century masterpiece *La città del sole* (1615) and Sir Francis Bacon's *New Atlantis* (1626), urban life has represented the combination of humanity's wise management of technology and the prudent exploitation of natural resources in order to satisfy the needs of the community. By dismantling the hegemonic notion of progress represented by Mexico City and Acapulco through the depiction of these two cities as sick bodies, Fuentes poignantly questions the Western projects of development which have been imposed by the elites. Throughout *Cristóbal Nonato*, Fuentes reiterates how in Latin America the imposition of foreign projects of modernity is embroiled within the broader structure of the long-standing economic and social relations between Europe and the Americas and between the United States and Latin America.

While Ángel and Ángeles Palomar are at the coast conceiving Cristóbal, Fuentes scrutinizes what the development of Acapulco's beaches has meant in the history of Mexico. As represented in the novel, the fomentation of the tourist industry, rather than turning the port into a cosmopolitan center, has transformed it into a highly polluted settlement. Fuentes describes Acapulco employing images of a sick female body characterizing the decadence that modernization has brought upon the resort:

> [P]layas incendiadas y las torres descascaradas y los peñascos blanqueados como huesos y las laderas miserables donde vivía, dice mi padre, la hiedra humana de Acapulquérrimo, prendida como garrapatas al cuerpo suntuoso, dice, aunque ya blando y agusanado, de *la vieja Acapulca, oh mi núbil niña pescadora con el pelo lacio hasta las caderas* [. . .] *ahora una prometida de la muerte, una cortesana de arenas que se agotan.* (52; emphasis mine)

In this passage, the formerly energetic image of the port city nostalgically contrasts with the current deterioration of the resort that has seen its best days gone by, leaving contamination and decrepitude in place of prosperity and wealth.

The anthropomorphic comparison of Acapulco to the body of an old dying prostitute parodies the European gaze of explorers and conquistadors whose feminization of the American landscape facilitated the enterprise of conquest and colonization. As discussed in the introduction to the present study, Columbus had compared the location of the earthly paradise to a woman's breast. As the admiral had written in his 1498 letter to the monarchs, "But as for this other hemisphere I maintain that it is like a half of a very round pear which had a long stem, as I have said, or like a woman's teat on a round ball. [. . .] I am completely persuaded in my own mind that the Terrestrial Paradise is in the place I have described" (Morison 286–87). While Columbus equates the New World Eden to a seductive young woman's supple breast, Fuentes offers a dramatic contrast through the parodic description of the port as a corrupt and decaying courtesan.

Through the comparison of Acapulco with the body of a decadent prostitute, *Cristóbal Nonato* also significantly begins to elaborate on the theme of Mexico as a dependent economy unable to foster growth and development. Fuentes highlights Mexico's dependence on foreign manufactured goods as Acapulco in his projected 1992 produces limited tangible commodities and instead imports most of its products from overseas in order to satisfy the demands of both national and international economic elites who vacation at the resort:

> [A]sí se escuchaba sin escucharse la entrada y la salida de Acapulco de los camiones foráneos, cargados de los *productos que el estéril balneario necesitaba pero no creaba*: desde el New York Cut steak hasta el papel higiénico, desde las cajas de Taitinger hasta las horquillas para el pelo; papel, pollo y petardos; mostaza, moscatel y manzanas; velocípedos, vaporub y vychysoisse: *todo debía ser traído de lejos* y el rumor de los camiones que lo traía era el más implícito de todos. (31; emphasis mine)

Using Acapulco's dependence on foreign goods as a point of departure, Fuentes highlights how Spain's imperial rule over its colonies failed to produce a modern entrepreneurial spirit capable of developing the industrial and economic base of Spanish America.[27] As a result, Mexico finds itself importing manufactured goods from more industrialized nations in spite of the fact that the country has many natural resources:

> Bubble Gómez, llevando al balneario estéril los víveres indispensables, acarreando de un lugar a otro *la riqueza producida en otra parte, por todos inconsciente de la ironía de la riqueza hispánica, importada, improductiva camino de Santiago, oro de las Indias, tesoros de los Austrias, aparatos electrónicos de Texas,* los tesoros se cuentan como agua entre nuestros dedos, sólo los símbolos permanecen, sólo la continuidad de los símbolos nos pertenece. (32; emphasis mine)

Since modernity is not fully achieved in Latin America, only its icons seem to be accessible for most of the population as the elites accumulate status symbols to which the working classes can only aspire. In Fuentes's account, Mexico passes almost seamlessly from being a political colony of Spain to being an economic colony of the United States, thus manifesting how after nearly two hundred years of political independence Mexico has not been able to create a modern project of nation that incorporates all sectors of society.

While industrial development has benefited some nations, its negative effects are suffered around the world as environmental contamination ignores the borders between countries. Fuentes underscores how nature responds to global industrialization through the climatic phenomenon known as "El Niño" as it approaches the highly polluted beaches of Acapulco:

> Viene corriendo El Niño desde la Isla de Pascua, tibio y malsano, el infante de la muerte por agua, azotado contra las costas del Perú sofocando en su abrazo caliente a las anchoas y las algas, secuestrando la frescura vital de los nitratos y fosfatos ecuatoriales, rompiendo la vasta cadena de la nutrición y la creación de los grandes peces del océano: pesado y sudoroso nada El Niño, arrojando peces muertos contra las paredes del continente, adormeciendo y pudriéndolo todo, el agua hundiendo al agua, el océano asfixiado en su propia marea muerta, el océano frío ahogado por el océano caliente, los vientos enloquecidos y desplazados: El Niño destructor, El Niño criminal arrasa las costas de California, seca las planicies de Australia, inunda de lodo los declives del Ecuador. (23)

As in the passage cited earlier regarding the contaminated sands of Acapulco, here Fuentes again uses the image of a sick body, this time to refer to "El Niño," evidencing how industrialization and the mismanagement of waste affect the balance of nature and life cycles in the ocean. Thus, contrary to what supporters of globalization suggest, in Fuentes's futuristic vision this new phase of capitalism does not result in the improvement of life for the majority of people but rather in the deterioration of the environment and the spread of pollution that transgresses national boundaries, placing in danger the very survival of the planet.

In this dystopian version of Acapulco, the affluent, prosperous, and modern image of the resort sharply contrasts with the poverty and misery of the surrounding hills, as farmers and indigenous peoples who formerly owned the lands have been dispossessed in order to facilitate the construction of hotels financed by foreign capital. In the name of guaranteeing the best lands for developers, the Mexican army has displaced the former residents to the mountains around the bay, away from the view of national and international tourists. Instead of producing benefits for the inhabitants of the port, then, the modernization of Acapulco translates into a littering of its environment and the exploitation of its residents, who have been forced out of their ancestral lands. Fuentes emphasizes how most of the debris of the industrial products imported to Acapulco is deposited into the waters of the bay, causing the coast's deterioration as the garbage of Cap'n Crunch cereal boxes, Heinz Ketchup bottles, Fritos, Pop-Tarts, condoms, and McDonald's hamburgers litters the beaches. Dramatically, the former "Paradise of the Pacific" has become the "Babylon of the Pacific," depicted as a cesspool of corrupt politicians who oppress the port's inhabitants, denying their human rights while lining their own pockets with money from foreign investors rather than investing it in the improvement of the weakened national infrastructure.[28]

The relationship between Acapulco and Mexico City is an important axis in *Cristóbal Nonato*, as Fuentes links the two locations through the representation of the real 1985 earthquake, which originated along the coast of Acapulco; notably, while it did not demolish any of the resort's hotels, the earthquake felled numerous buildings in the capital, causing untold damage and the death of over two thousand people. Fuentes depicts

Cristóbal's father, Ángel Palomar, as strolling along the boulevards of Mexico City after the earthquake with a banner asking for the annihilation of the resort: "Delenda Est Acapulco" (Destroy Acapulco). In the novel's hypothetical 1992, Ángel will embark on a mission dedicated to safeguarding what remains of the disintegrating nation before governmental corruption and globalized consumerism destroy it. Fuentes highlights resistance in the name of popular sectors as Ángel and Ángeles and the Rock Aztec band known as the Four Jodiditos project the image of a world upside down by reversing the course of pollution from the communal lands of Acapulco back to the hotels, causing a brown wave of waste to flush out the Mexican bourgeoisie, tourists, corrupt politicians, and fast food restaurants that defile the once paradisiacal port. Through this revolt, Fuentes accentuates how subaltern groups have recourse to ingenious forms of resistance; for example, the band member known as Hipi Toltec[29] trains coyotes[30] to attack tourists, using the smell of deodorant, shampoo, soap, and spermicidal gel as bait. Even though the Palomars and their gang represent a form of resistance against modernization, their carnivalesque rebellion constitutes a hopeless effort and ends in chaos and disillusion regarding the possibility of reversing the effects of global capitalism. As we later learn, it turns out that our heroes did not in fact cause the destruction of Acapulco, but rather the Mexican government wreaked the death and damage in an effort to eliminate dissenters who were endeavoring to secede from the fragmenting republic.

After examining the impact of industrialization and globalization on the environment in Acapulco, Fuentes takes his unborn protagonist to Mexico City in order to assess the impact of modernization in the major urban setting of the dystopian nation. While the annihilation of Acapulco represents the ultimate nightmarish result of the Mexican elite's dreams of creating a modern paradise, when he follows his characters to the capital, Fuentes redeploys the literary dystopia to critique the government's corruption and poor planning that mar the image of the city as the prototype of the modern utopia.

Since his classic novel *La región más transparente* (1958), Fuentes has focused on the development of Mexico represented primarily by urban life. In *Cristóbal Nonato*'s dystopian version of 1992, the capital houses more than thirty million dwellers who lack the most basic resources such as clean air, potable water, and a safe place to live. The residents of Mexico City have to endure the exhaust of over three million cars circulating through the urban maze of streets. To make matters worse, earthquakes displace large numbers of people who lose their homes and end up living on the street, causing problems with overcrowding and waste disposal, adding to the already critical conditions of the capital. Fuentes stresses the deteriorating effects of industrialization, eroding the utopian image of the city as an orderly representation of the state's power and replacing it with a portrayal of a chaotic, fragmented, highly polluted enclave where the living conditions call into question the benefits of modernity.[31] In his description of Mexico City in the conjectured 1992, Fuentes draws upon the imagery offered by dystopian literature to highlight the negative results of Mexico's ill-planned projects of modernization.

In a systematic fashion, Fuentes dismantles the utopian image of the city as an emblem of a modern centralized state. Utilizing dystopian language, the narrator describes the air of Mexico City as a noxious combination: "Mierda machacada. Gas carbónico. Polvo metálico. Y todo ello a 2300 metros de altura, aplastado bajo una capa de aire helado y rodeado de una cárcel de montañas circulares: la basura prisionera" (91). As a result of overpopulation, the people breathe "El aliento mortal de tres millones de motores vomitando sin límites bocanadas de veneno puro, halitosis negra, camiones y taxis y materialistas y particulares, todos contribuyendo su flátula a la extinción del árbol, el pulmón, la garganta, los ojos" (91).[32] As in the previous pages in which Fuentes describes Acapulco in terms of a sick body, here the narrator depicts Mexico City in acute images of decomposition, pointing to the capital as a source of infection: "[L]a ciudad es un inmenso cráter llagado, la caries del universo, la caspa del mundo, el chancro de las Américas, la hemorroide del Trópico de Cáncer" (326).

While the excesses of modernity have created air pollution, Fuentes also underscores the failure of the state's services at the most basic level such as the capacity to guarantee potable water for daily consumption: "El desplome paulatino de todos los recursos hidráulicos [. . .] ha sido compensado por la llovizna ácida constante provocada por el efecto de invernadero de la industrialización en un alto y ardiente valle encerrado" (327).[33] Because of the unplanned expansion of the city and the industrialization of nearby areas, in Fuentes's dystopia the only precipitation that the Valley of Mexico receives is in the form of acid rain, which suffocates the flora and fauna as it mixes with the smog in a city under continual construction: "La constante de la ciudad es el goteo de los cielos; llueve incesantemente, una lluvia negra, aceitosa, carbonífera, que opaca los más vistosos anuncios luminosos; la sensación de cielo encapotado, oscuro, en cuyas brumas se pierden los esqueletos de los edificios, muchos de ellos sin terminar, hierro oxidado muchos, torres truncas, cués del subdesarrollo, rascatonatiús, otros simples telones como los de la entrada por Puebla, otros más cubos de cartón chorreados de lluvia ácida y muy pocos verdaderas construcciones habitadas" (326). Once again drawing on the metaphor of the sick body, here the truncated buildings appear as skeletons. Significantly, these monuments to an unfinished project of modernity[34] are described as temples of underdevelopment.

As we saw also in the section referring to Acapulco, in his description of Mexico City, Fuentes compares the arrival of the Europeans in 1492 to the apocalyptic 1992 in order to call attention to the ecological disasters that were initially set in motion by the conquest: "[A]bre los ojos el Huérfano Huerta y mira el muro blanco, sin destino, frente a sus ojos abandonados: los lagos muertos, eso ve, los canales convertidos en sepulturas industriales, los ríos tatemados, una coraza ardiente de cemento y chapopote devorando lo que iba a proteger: el corazón de México" (451). These references to roasted rivers and dead lakes contrast sharply with the first description of Tenochtitlan offered by Bernal Díaz del Castillo, a Spanish soldier who accompanied Hernán Cortés in his conquest of Mexico in 1519–21:

> Y otro día por la mañana llegamos a la calzada ancha y vamos de camino de Estapala. Y desde que vimos tantas ciudades y villas pobladas en el agua, y en tierra firme otras grandes poblazones, y aquella calzada tan derecha y por nivel cómo iba a México, nos quedamos admirados, como decíamos que parecía a las cosas de encantamiento que

cuentan en el libro de Amadís, por las grandes torres y *cúes*
y edificios que tenían dentro en el agua, y todos de calicanto,
y aun algunos de nuestros soldados decían que si aquello que
veían si era entre sueños, y no es de maravillar que yo escri-
ba aquí de esta manera, porque hay mucho que ponderar en
ello que no sé como lo cuente; ver cosas nunca oídas, ni aun
soñadas, como veíamos. (159)

Díaz del Castillo's depiction of the Aztec capital resonates with
the image of the utopian city that fueled European exploration
and settlement of the Americas. To the symmetrical design of
Tenochtitlan, Fuentes opposes the image of urban hell in the
shape of the city as a devouring monster, one of the favorite
topics of dystopian literature.

Fuentes underscores how instead of ample modern avenues,
canals, and highways to connect Mexico City to the rest of the
nation, the grotesque "Taco Curtain" impedes the entrance of
disenfranchised individuals from the interior into the already
overpopulated metropolis as he describes:

[E]l súbito hoyo negro que parecía tragarse todo lo que ro-
deaba, en este caso la fila de autos detenidos y la multitud de
personas a pie, algunas descalzas, otras con huaraches, todas
pobres y finas [. . .] agolpados los autos y los peregrinos que
querían entrar a la ciudad de México a través del ojo de la
aguja de una *auténtica Taco Curtain, nada metafórica* [. . .]
que circundaba efectivamente al Distrito Federal, cincuenta
kilómetros a la redonda de la ciudad capital, con ingresos
estratégicos desde Texmelucan, Zumpango, Angangueo, y
Malinalco. (296; emphasis mine)

The governing elites erect the Taco Curtain in order to repel the
migration of people from the rural areas. Because of the displacement of residents from the countryside, several shantytowns
emerge around the capital, making it difficult for the authorities
to provide services for the endless line of incoming migrants.

Ironically, five hundred years after the arrival of the Europeans
in the New World, the former Aztec capital becomes not the
utopia that the conquistadors imagined but rather the dystopia
of an apocalyptic megalopolis that denies citizens the most basic
means of survival, calling into question the advances of modernization. To further his scrutiny of the indiscriminate cloning
of Western modernity by Mexican elites, Fuentes critiques the

failure of the state to facilitate a rational program through which Mexican society could create its own modernity incorporating all spheres of society. As we will see in the following section, Fuentes's questioning of the state's manipulation of mass media, advertising, and nationalistic iconography addresses the theme of democracy and the perfect form of government, key components of the literary utopia since antiquity and one of Mexico's more vexing problems.

Mass Media and Technology in Dystopia

The form of government of the ideal state has been a structural component of utopian imaginings since Plato's *Republic*. As examined above, contact with the New World inspired further meditations on the role of the intellectual in state administration, some of which found voice in literary manifestations such as Thomas More's *Utopia*. During the pre-Enlightenment period of the seventeenth century, Tommaso Campanella's *La città del sole* and Francis Bacon's *New Atlantis* continued this discussion, adding to it concerns regarding the optimum use of science and technology for the satisfaction of human needs.[35] Continuing his systematic dismantling of the topic of the ideal city, Fuentes engages the issue of how to govern when authoritarian regimes in his hypothetical future employ mass media to remain in power, thus coinciding with science fiction novels such as Zamyatin's *We*, Huxley's *Brave New World*, Orwell's *Nineteen Eighty-Four*, and Bradbury's *Fahrenheit 451* in the critical investigation of the manipulation of technology by autarchies. Following this current, Fuentes presents us with a portrayal of a corrupt and hierarchical postrevolutionary Mexican society in which a single dominant party exercises control over the population through the use of technology and mass media. In this novel, the Mexican government and hegemonic groups project a televised fiction of a modern nation in order to maintain control of the starving, unemployed masses that circulate in the disintegrating republic. *Cristóbal Nonato* thus portrays a society along the lines of futuristic dystopian narratives in which the sense of alienation, a rigorous conformity, and a lack of economic opportunities are aggravated by the imposition of consumption as a means to achieve status in society.

Fuentes questions the success of the Mexican Revolution in achieving its promise of social renewal when he represents a monolithic hierarchy headed by Spanish criollos, the "revolutionary family,"[36] and local businessmen with international ties who rule Mexican society in the fictional 1992. The authorities in *Cristóbal Nonato* are divided into two camps: "old boys," such as Minister Ulises López, the aforementioned chief of SEPAFU (Secretariat of Patriotism and Foreign Undertakings); and the new generation of media-savvy governmental representatives like Minister Federico Robles Chacón who is in charge of the SEPAVRE (Secretariat of Patrimony and Vehiculation of Resources). Old criollo sectors, which were supposed to have been neutralized with the Revolution but who ironically continued to wield power through the revolutionary party itself, come to life in the novel in the figure of Ángel's uncle Homero Fagoaga, who among other occupations heads a ministry in defense of the purity of the Spanish language. The lower echelons of society, in turn, are occupied by subaltern races and classes who struggle against the daily bombardment of mass media in the guise of TV contests, advertisements, and official propaganda.[37]

Through his portrayal of ruthless officials, Fuentes records the changing of the guard in the transition between the old boys who achieve their political goals through the use of traditional means such as assassination, fraud, and corruption, and a younger generation that opts to exercise more refined and sophisticated technological control over the masses. Even the old boys utilize in some way the power of media: for example, Ulises López's slogan, plastered all over the country— "Mexicano Industrialízate: Vivirás menos pero vivirás mejor" (181)—encapsulates the drive for industrialization reflecting the Mexican political economy since the end of the 1940s. His nemesis, Federico Robles Chacón, in contrast, proposes that the state exert control over the populace's imaginary through the manipulation of popular cultural iconography, arguing that: "A este país lo único que le interesa es la legitimación simbólica del poder" (38).

In *Transforming Modernity* (1982), cultural critic Néstor García Canclini examines how hegemonic groups appropriate elements of popular culture to maintain the economic status quo. García Canclini's findings regarding contemporary culture parallel the work of historian Serge Gruzinski pertaining to the use of imagery during the colonial period. Gruzinski proposes in *Images at War* (1999) that since the arrival of Christopher Columbus "the image was used as a marker, then became a tool for acculturation and domination" in the newly found territories of the Americas (2). As the historian notes, European colonizers implemented a series of cultural measures aimed at undermining the natives' symbolic system and imposing Western imagery in order to facilitate Amerindian conversion after the conquest. Gruzinski extends his theory regarding the colonial use of imagery to the present use of mass media exemplified by the Mexican consortium Televisa, which through the manipulation of information and in complicity with the long-standing PRI-dominated government has unquestionably become a key figure in Mexican cultural and economic politics since the 1950s. Both García Canclini and Gruzinski help us to understand how hegemonic groups not only control the material conditions of production, but through mass media, religion, and nationalistic propaganda are also involved in the reproduction of the dominant ideology at the symbolic level. Carlos Fuentes in *Cristóbal Nonato* illustrates how the state uses technology to maintain control of its public, promoting modernity as a goal while failing to create the conditions for the development of a democratic society.

In this novel, Fuentes emphasizes how the Mexican government gains legitimacy through the manipulation of nationalistic iconography. Echoing ruling elites from Wells's *The Shape of Things to Come* and Orwell's *Nineteen Eighty-Four*, Minister Robles Chacón demonstrates a profound knowledge of mass communication, Mexican history, myth, and popular culture, especially melodrama. Notably, Robles Chacón creates the figure known as "Mamadoc" by taking a humble secretary and transforming her into an object of national devotion who, as Ricardo Gutiérrez Mouat writes, "is assembled with the raw materials of mass culture and the techniques of cosmetology, [representing] a 'subtle summa' of all the female stereotypes ingrained in Mexican machismo: Coatlicue, La Malinche, the Virgin of Guadalupe, Adelita, [. . .] the movie stars, the devouring women, the vampire [. . .]" (169). In effect, after the meek stenographer is transformed into a nationalistic icon, Robles Chacón presents his patriotic pastiche to the masses, who identify with her image through melodramatic scenes carefully orchestrated by the Machiavellian minister. As Maarten Van Delden sustains, Mamadoc "has been conceived in such a way that the Mexican masses can sublimate in her all their unfulfilled desires" (176). Significantly, one of Mamadoc's principal functions will presumably be to recognize the winner of the Christopher Columbus contest, the male child born precisely at midnight on October 12, 1992, who will serve as Regent of the Nation for life, thus legitimizing state power while doing away with democratic institutions such as elections.

By representing the figure of Mamadoc—Robles Chacón's "Frankedenic" palimpsest of Mexican nationalism—Fuentes problematizes the tradition that renders women as objects created by technology.[38] The character of Mamadoc embodies different forms of hybridity as she combines myth and technology, the public and the private, the past and the future.[39] The radical makeover that she is subjected to constitutes a parody of dystopian novels and films such as Fritz Lang's 1926 classic cinematic piece *Metropolis,* in which uneasiness regarding the future is incarnated in mutilations on a woman's body. Robles Chacón uses a relatively low-tech approach to fashioning Mamadoc by keeping her in isolation for a solid year and forcing her to listen to popular boleros as a form of brainwashing. The people identify with Mamadoc as a maternal figure—represented by Coatlicue and the Virgin of Guadalupe—even though she remains under the thumb of Robles Chacón; this control over her body is dramatized when the minister orders her vagina to be sewn shut in order to guarantee her image as a virgin mother of the nation. As seen here, in the interest of enhancing their sphere of influence, the politicians resort to manipulating icons of popular culture; and as we will discuss below, the state also endeavors to control the flow of information in order to solidify its public image while hiding the crumbling structure of the republic.

Fuentes emphasizes how in his projected future the political and economic elites combine nationalism, mass media, and modern marketing tactics to keep the public happily entertained, primarily through the medium of television. As in *Nineteen Eighty-Four*, *Brave New World*, and *Fahrenheit 451*, the state's use of the media becomes crucial to appease a hungry and malcontent citizenry. In *Cristóbal Nonato*, TV receptors constantly bombard the consumer-spectator with phrases like: "La información es el poder. La no información es más poder" (288). The media also flashes pseudo-news bites with frivolous and meaningless trivia and compels the public to take part in national competitions endorsed by Mamadoc such as the Christopher Columbus contest in which Ángel and Ángeles aim to compete when they conceive the novel's protagonist. The state exerts full control of information: for example, after the annihilation of Acapulco, no news is made public of the catastrophe. This manipulation of the means of communication causes people to feed on rumors, which does not allow for the formation of a well-informed and independent citizenry, but contributes instead to the preservation of public ignorance. As in novels like *Fahrenheit 451* in which the establishment keeps the populace entertained with interactive soap operas, in *Cristóbal Nonato* Fuentes highlights how the state transforms all Mexican reality into a mass media event. As a result, the whole country watches TV contests: "la nación entera inmersa en el concurso, el examen, la efemérides que no les dejaba ni un minuto libre, esperando el golpe de la suerte, la superlotería perpetua de Makesicko Nanny Tú: inútil, exhausta, muerta, la clase media mexicana pudimos decir, al cabo, que nunca se aburrió" (316).[40] Fuentes describes how the authorities are not dedicated to governing because they are focused instead on barraging the masses with commercials that promote consumption, thus giving a technological twist to the Roman idea of "bread and circus" as a deterrent to consciousness-raising. The government's strategy is summarized simply as: "UNION Y OLVIDO y otro de los mensajes sublimados que de tarde en tarde parpadeaban en todos los aparatos de televisión decía redundantemente: CIRCO Y CIRCO" (316).

Fuentes calls attention to how the state employs the power of imagery to represent a mirage of cohesion for the fragmented country. Upon crossing the "Taco Curtain" into the capital, Ángel and Ángeles witness the immense spectacle that the government uses to establish legitimacy in the form of a city composed of cardboard cutouts of famous international monuments—the Statue of Liberty, the Empire State building, the Taj Mahal, the

Great Wall of China, the Holiday Inn at Disneyland—in order to promote the false image of a modern state. For this dystopian administration, governing becomes the performance of a series of empty rituals of power aimed toward promoting a cosmopolitan sense of modernity:[41]

> [E]l señor presidente Jesús María y José Paredes preside un gobierno en el que nada de lo que se dice que se hace, se hizo o se hará: presas, centrales eléctricas, carreteras, cooperativas agrícolas: nada, sólo anunciadas y prometidas, puras fachadas y el Señor Presidente cumple ritualmente una serie de actos sin contenido que son la sustancia misma de los noticieros de televisión: el Señor Presidente reparte ritualmente tierras que no existen; inaugura monumentos efímeros como estos mismos telones pintados; rinde homenajes a héroes inexistentes. (301)

Here Fuentes criticizes how the ruling powers are more concerned with projecting an image of being a modern Western nation rather than taking the steps to actually become one.

Fuentes ridicules state buildings as well, as in his projected future they blend national tradition with a bombastic image of modernity, materialized concretely in the monumental Palace of the Citizenry, which combines Aztec history with dreams of national development:

> Simbólicamente, El Palacio de la Ciudadanía al norte de la ciudad cerró, al ser construido, la Carretera Panamericana a fin de que lo flanqueasen las estatuas de los Indios Verdes. Desde allí se tendió una calzada, rodeada de agua retroalimentada, al vasto islote central donde, deadeveras, un águila posada sobre un nopal devoraba a varias serpientes diarias. (347)

The description of this particular building dramatizes how the government seeks to legitimize itself through what García Canclini would refer to as the "monumentalization of the past."[42] The state combines the Aztec myth of the foundation of Tenochtitlan[43] with the modern infrastructure of the highway, producing a bizarre and grotesque combination of tradition and modernity. The apparent functionality of the building, however, contrasts with the main role of the governmental agencies that occupy the Palace of the Citizenry, which is to register the participants in the aforementioned national contests designed to keep the citizens occupied in mindless entertainment.

In a fashion similar to Orwell's dystopia, Fuentes's *Cristóbal Nonato* elaborates on the state's distorted view of nationalism as it declares wars against real and fantastic enemies that supposedly threaten the physical integrity of the nation. In order to remain in power, the novel's Mexican government provokes a war with the United States, rallying the populace against Mexico's historical adversary, while also conveniently ridding itself of an agrarian revolt.[44] Fuentes emphasizes the performative aspect of this war as another machination of ruling sectors:

> [R]ecuerda que esta guerrita es solo un evento de los medias un espectáculo informativo cubierto por la TV y la prensa para probarle al mundo pero sobre todo a nosotros mismos que somos muy machos y para que el gobierno mexicano le pruebe a su pueblo que hay que unirse para defender al país. (527)

As in *Nineteen Eighty-Four*, these wars achieve the dual purpose of uniting the people against a common enemy while simultaneously alienating them from the ability to gain consciousness of their own oppression and express their frustration.

By highlighting how the state misuses mass media to reaffirm hierarchical oppression, *Cristóbal Nonato* echoes the warnings against the dictatorial use of technology emanating from classic science fiction novels such as Zamyatin's *We*, Huxley's *Brave New World*, and Orwell's *Nineteen Eighty-Four*. Through the representation of a dystopian nation in which the rulers occupy their time in conserving power by any means, Fuentes offers us a pessimistic view of the country's future prospects. As a result of the lack of a guided and organized program of economic growth, marginal sectors of society are faced with the disjunctive options of remaining in the country or emigrating to the also fragmenting United States or to the new utopia represented by Pacífica. In the final section of this chapter, we will see how Fuentes contemplates the future possibilities of Mexico as he weighs different models of development and ultimately advocates for the creation of a truly democratic Mexican modernity.

Globality and Postnationalism:
The Possibilities for Mexico's Future

As discussed above, a fundamental component of Fuentes's examination of modernity in *Cristóbal Nonato* lies in its use of the dystopian literary tradition to deconstruct the image of America as utopia, an image that was fostered during the conquest and colonization of the continent. The novel's final two sections, entitled "No Man's Fatherland" and "The Discovery of America," conclude Fuentes's survey of the ramifications of the events originating in the encounter between Old and New Worlds that shaped our notion of modernity. Fuentes closes his novel with an analysis of different projects of modernity that result from the changes occurring as the forces of the global economy transform the traditional concept of nation and replace it with alternative forms of economic and political organization that we might call "postnational."[45] In the section "No Man's Fatherland," Fuentes dismantles hegemonic conceptions of US modernity, presenting the image of a decadent nation that abuses its power to subject neighboring countries to its will. One of the most salient aspects of this section is Fuentes's discussion of the cultural effects of globalization reflected in the formation of a new entity named Mexamérica that in this fiction represents the transformation of the border region into a country of its own. Finally, in "The Discovery of America," the author presents the unborn narrator's parents with the option of leaving their homeland for a new utopia named Pacífica or remaining in Mexico to participate in the creation of a new project of nation more inclusive of all its citizens. In these final sections, Fuentes's analysis of the implications of utopian thought provides an opportunity for reexamining the possible venues of development for Latin American countries in an age when the institutions of modernity are in crisis.

Drawing on the tradition of the literary dystopia, Fuentes criticizes US neocolonialism as he represents this nation, under the influence of reactionary groups, dominating nearby countries while internally marginalizing ethnic communities. Fuentes emphasizes how a megalomaniacal caste composed of senile right-wing politicians and televangelists—whose maximum incarnation is the Reverend Royall Payne—decides what is important for their own country and the entire continent, imposing their will through military might over other nations as well as relegating people of color to a subservient position within society. As Fuentes dismisses the potentiality of an egalitarian future, the author addresses the US subordination of Latin American countries to a developmental pattern that consigns them to the status of tributaries of the US economy. Along the lines of Huxley's *Brave New World,* in which the dystopian society is divided into Alpha, Beta, Gamma, Delta, and Epsilon castes, Fuentes provides a stratified picture of a future US society in which African Americans and Latinos occupy the lower strata.[46] The image of the United States in *Cristóbal Nonato,* then, is not the ideal society that the Mexican elites dream of becoming; rather, extreme conservatism and corruption have transformed it into a tyrannical dystopia.

The world of *Cristóbal Nonato* depicts the US model of the modern nation as flawed in that democratic institutions succumb to the designs of reactionary forces motivated by xenophobia. Although North American society has sufficient technological know-how to collaborate in the creation of a modern utopia for the Western hemisphere, in Fuentes's futuristic vision, US hegemonic groups have exacerbated the fear of the Other to the extent of limiting the individual rights of ethnic minorities:

> [. . .] [l]a Ley Simpson-Nobody que a cambio de un metafísico control de la frontera norteamericana, sancionó con multas y prisión a los empleadores de indocumentados. Previsiblemente, esta culpa se extendió a todos los empleadores de gente morena, sin averiguar si éstos eran o no nacionales norteamericanos, y desembocó (también previsiblemente) en la necesidad de moverse por las repúblicas del Norte con tarjeta de identidad primero, luego con pasaporte y al cabo dentro de zonas herméticamente aisladas como en Sudáfrica. (500)[47]

These anti-immigration policies engineered to block the entrance of Mexican laborers into the United States have a negative effect on several key sectors of the economy, bringing about the collapse of the labor market and consequently hindering US competition with other global economies. Notably, the expulsion of illegal workers from hospitals, restaurants, transportation, farming, and manufacturing wreaks havoc, occasioning a labor shortage that paralyzes the domestic economy. As a result, the United States becomes dependent on the more advanced utopian Pacífica, ultimately causing Mexico to become, in terms of economic dependence, a colony of a colony.

In the penultimate section of the novel, entitled "No Man's Fatherland," we see that like Fuentes's Mexico, the United States ultimately fragments into a balkanized conglomeration of separate regions reflecting different cultural and economic affinities. These territories include: the Republic of Texas; a region called Dixitlán composed of the Southern states; the economically based Chicago-Philadelphia Steel Axis; the Independent Republic of New England formed by the states of the Northeast; and the new zone called Mexamérica encompassing areas of California, Arizona, New Mexico, and part of Texas as well as the northern Mexican border cities from "Auntyjane" (Tijuana) to "Killmoors" (Matamoros).[48] Significantly for the present study, the remaining parts of California, along with Oregon and Washington and the Mexican coastal states, have joined countries of the Pacific Rim, forming a new utopia named Pacífica. This image of Pacífica evokes Ernest Callenbach's *Ecotopia* (1975), where northern California, Oregon, and Washington have seceded from the Union to create an ecologically sound location in which employees own their own farms and businesses, while limits on the size of the communities defeat overcrowding and pollution. The futuristic utopia has a woman-dominated government and there are no wars. Of the above, Mexamérica and Pacífica represent the most salient options as models of development for Mexico; as we will see, however, each in turn is rejected in favor of finding a specifically Mexican response to the crisis of modernity in Latin America.

As a result of the fragmentation of both Mexico and the United States, then, new socioeconomic areas such as Mexamérica emerge as representative of multicultural relations in a postnational world. In Fuentes's hypothetical 1992, the US-Mexican border no longer exists in its present location; rather, the former border region has become a distinct entity economically and politically independent from both countries:

> Mexamérica independiente de México y de los Estados Unidos, rebanando su faja de maquilas y fayucas y espanglés y

> refugio para los perseguidos políticos y paso franco para los
> indocumentados de la costa del Pacífico a la costa del Golfo,
> cien kilómetros al norte y cien al sur de la antigua frontera,
> de Sandy Ego y Antijane a Coffeeville y Killmoors: inde-
> pendientes sin que mediara proclama alguna el puro hecho
> es que allí ya nadie le hace el menor caso a los gobiernos de
> México o Washington. (26–27)[49]

As an effect of real-life international negotiations between
Canada, Mexico, and the US such as NAFTA, we might expect
a boom in the economic development of the border region; such
is not the case, however, in Fuentes's projected future. Writing
several years before the signing of NAFTA, but speculating
about the potential effects of globalization, Fuentes points to
how Mexamérica's economy is based on maquiladora factories
and informal commerce such as smuggling contraband. As
workers migrate fluidly in and out of Mexamérica, the tenuous
nature of residence in the border region underscores the fragility
of the local economy.

In this fiction, because of the militarization of the border, the
entire region becomes a sort of "alien nation" as immigrants who
wait to cross to the US resign themselves to making their living
in Mexamérica.[50] Beyond the control of both governments, this
territory houses the undesirables from Mexico and the United
States, serving as a sanctuary for political refugees and hopeful
border-crossers. Mexamérica hence becomes an autonomous
political zone "que supuestamente se declaró independiente de
ambos países, aunque en realidad servía a los intereses de ambos, absorbiendo al ochenta por ciento de los indocumentados
que antaño se colaban a Texas, California, hasta el Medio Oeste
y a los Grandes Lagos . . ." (500). Although it is a zone rich with
potential multicultural intersections, Fuentes does not develop
the notion of Mexamérica but rather ends up representing the
region as one through which migrants pass while crossing to
the "other side," which now begins in Baja Oklahoma.[51] As
Mexamérica does not represent a positive model for Mexico's
economic, political, and cultural development, Fuentes's *Cristóbal Nonato* turns to the exploration of other possibilities linked
to globalization and postnational advances.

While the indiscriminate adoption of imported notions of
modernity suggests a bleak perspective for the future, Fuentes

also proposes the possibility of innovative responses reflected in the appropriation of elements of modernity by non-hegemonic entities. In *Cristóbal Nonato*, some popular sectors are able to adapt the rules of the market, transforming them into creative alternatives to the hegemonic project of modernization. For example, Fuentes depicts street vendors in Mexico City participating in informal economies using Spanglish to trade national and foreign products: "Por la avenida Revolución la economía del trueque florece: calzoncillos contra peines, mejorana contra tabaco, manoplas de fierro contra muñecas Barbie, condones con cresta de plumas contra cuadros del Sagrado Corazón de Jesús, dos casettes de Madonna contra un costal de frijoles [. . .] que sólo tienen el valor que se les atribuye hoy" (330). In this spontaneous street economy, the conventional relation between the local and the global is transformed as common folk trade domestic and imported goods following the dictates of supply and demand, without recourse to the official market. As Maarten Van Delden points out in reference to this Fuentes scene: "In this fluid space the people of Mexico City can satisfy their desire for community while at the same time evading the threat of external control" (179). Fuentes's depiction of the barter economy as an alternative economy does also point out that while markets are being controlled by exterior forces, the distribution and satisfaction of social needs still is being satisfied by access.

As the principal agents of this kind of alternative to modernity, Fuentes introduces the truck drivers who transport merchandise between the fragmented points of the nation:[52]

> Fue en agosto cuando las carreteras de la República Mexicana comenzaron a llenarse de esos rumores a la vez esperados e insólitos: los caminos federales, las supercarreteras de cuota, los frigüeys [. . .] habían mantenido una como autonomía respecto a las otras realidades del país; lanzarse a una carretera, la Panamericana a Mexamérica, la Cristóbal Colón a Oaxaca, la Transístmica al CHICATAM Trusteeship, era como dispararse por la patria de nadie y de todos, el territorio libre, las carreteras de los noventas son zonas colchón en las que todo el pesar de la suave patria neomutilada se resuelve en una especie de libertad veloz y pasajera, pero libertad al fin: la carretera es de todos y todo lo reúne. (439)

The identification of freedom with the "frigüeys" (freeways in Spanish transliteration) points toward a new beginning highlighting the importance of the implementation of alternative economic ventures at the local level. Fuentes privileges the highways as fluid spaces, symbolizing the ability of subaltern sectors to formulate their own responses to globalization. Noticeably, whereas the dystopian project of nation separates and disperses its citizens in the urban settings, the road propitiates oppositional agendas that unite the disenfranchised in a shared endeavor. The freeway thus opens up the possibility of creativity and independence from the oppressive nature of the modern state and the economic collapse of the major urban centers.[53]

Fuentes emphasizes how, paradoxically, in the midst of the decline of the nation-state system, subaltern sectors combine their traditions with modern artifacts, as well as the religious with the secular, thus giving birth to a hybrid form of culture:

> Los camioneros empezaron a comunicarse entre sí sus comentarios, a sentirse preferidos, a aliarse entre ellos para que lo anunciado resultara cierto: ellos eran los escogidos de lo que iba a pasar, la virgen les hablaba a ellos, ellos [. . .] eran los Comanches de la Virgen, ellos cabalgaban por los desiertos y las montañas como las brigadas de Guadalupe. No tenían caballos, sino algo mejor: sus camiones, sus Dodge y sus Leyland, sus Mack como corceles rugientes, sus alazanes diesel, los comanches guadalupanos atravesando el país en todas las direcciones, uniendo de nuevo a LA NACIÓN GUADALUPANA. (442)

Fuentes underscores the hybrid nature of the rebellion, which allows the truck drivers to combine technology with traditional forms of affiliation—such as tribalism—renewing their imaginary by combining folk beliefs with modern means of communication such as the CB radio. The fictitious Nation of Guadalupe parodies a national myth of origin since according to Mexican history, the apparition of the Virgin Mary to the indigenous Juan Diego represents the syncretism of Amerindian beliefs and Spanish Catholicism and consequently the birth of Mexico as a cultural entity.[54] Just as the state uses symbolism to manipulate the people, in their revolt the truck drivers also resort to nationalistic imagery. Significantly, the truckers' devotion to the Virgin of Guadalupe also constitutes a response to the state's appropriation of popular iconography. Minister Robles Chacón imposes mandatory secular worship of his creation, Mamadoc, which the truckers counter by juxtaposing images of the Virgin Mary to those of Mamadoc on their dashboards. In an act of resistance, the leader of the truckers' movement announces over the CB that Mamadoc is the "whore of Babylon" as he preaches loyalty to the Virgin of Guadalupe. This insurrection thus represents a return to premodern means of political mobilization and economic systems predating the national state, in a form of what Néstor García Canclini would call "cultural reconversion."[55]

In his hypothetical future, Fuentes describes how following the collapse of the modern national state, communities return to grassroots forms of society. After the initial success of the popular uprising, like the Mexico City street vendors, the truckers begin to exchange their merchandise for other products needed in different areas of the country, circumventing the use of national currency. This substitution of the barter method for the capitalist monetary system favors disadvantaged sectors of society since "[los pobres] sabían mejor que los ricos el valor del trueque, cómo armarlo para y ofrecerse cosas como si fueran regalos suntuosos y hacerlo todo a través de un ejército velocísimo, los camioneros de la república" (446). Fuentes points to how traditionally marginalized groups such as the truck drivers initiate a new sort of market economy, one that does not rely on the state's firm hold over financial institutions but instead on the close knowledge of local and global commerce, underscoring that the economy does not exist on the blackboards of the state offices or in abstract macroeconomic concepts but rather in microeconomic notions of supply and demand. Fuentes's assessment of grassroots movements in the late stages of capitalism parallels what García Canclini examines in *Hybrid Cultures*, as subaltern sectors participate in transnational economies combining their own cultural traditions with international aesthetic and economic agendas. According to García Canclini, economically marginalized groups can refashion their cultural heritage and participate in the global market, negotiating and subverting its rules while bypassing the state's role as regulator of price and circulation. By showing how truck drivers and street vendors intervene and alter the rules of the market on a local level,

Fuentes contests the hegemonic notion of popular sectors as being passive recipients of the fruits of globalization.[56]

In the novel, however, the utopian revolt instigated by the truck drivers is problematized when the original leader, an albino trucker by the name of Bubble Gómez, is arrested and replaced by Ángel Palomar's nemesis, Matamoros Moreno. While initially the rebels limit their resistance to a subversive form of participation in the economy, the sinister Matamoros— who adopts the title Ayatollah—promulgates a violent war with the intent of the extermination of the upper classes, interfering with the possibilities of democratic social reform. The Ayatollah Moreno represents the dark side of popular rebellion as he lacks a program of positive change and growth, instead raping, killing, and destroying everything in his path.

In the face of potential forms of resistance to hegemony, the authorities resort to violence to repress the marching masses led by the truckers who advance upon the capital. In order to halt the popular demonstration, Minister Robles Chacón urges the Ayatollah to appear alongside Mamadoc in an effort to project a mirage of national unity and ratify the state's symbolic control of the people. When the rebellious leader rejects this offer, Minister Robles Chacón mechanically orders armed forces to fire upon the marching crowd.[57] After the repression, Ángel and Ángeles Palomar and their soon-to-be-born progeny escape to Acapulco as Mexico City is destroyed by flames fueled by the tons of garbage that have accumulated in the overcrowded metropolis.

The fact that no grassroots movement is triumphant in the novel coincides with the opinion of Mexican intellectuals of the late 1980s and early 1990s such as Jorge Castañeda who in *La utopía desarmada* (1993) proposes that the left no longer represents an ideology capable of inspiring popular dissent in Latin America.[58] With the failure of the truck drivers' rebellion to create a viable alternative to modernity, Fuentes underscores the dictatorial aspect of modern Mexico as the government regulates the political, civil, and economic life of the nation. Fuentes critiques both the state's inability to engage the public sphere actively in the decision-making process and also the lack of cohesion and vision in the organization of popular groups who have the energy to propose alternatives to the hegemonic project of modernization, but ultimately fail as their leader, the

Ayatollah, manipulates this energy to climb to power, creating a new ultra-violent status quo. Nevertheless, the fact that *Cristóbal Nonato* portrays a popular rebellion—albeit one that is co-opted and eventually repressed by conservative forces—does point to the possibility of resistance and ultimately signals the need for a more democratic society.

Whereas Fuentes represents both the United States and Mexico as sick societies whose projects of modernity have failed to provide the answer for the future, he also offers other possible models of development such as the utopian Pacífica, which represents the East as having fulfilled all the aspirations of the West that did not come to fruition in five hundred years of colonization and independence in the Americas. Pacífica is the ultimate embodiment of utopia as most of the problems created with industrialization—such as the mechanization that leads to ecological damage and the loss of human values and liberties—have been resolved there. As the name Pacífica suggests, the fictitious society manifests a harmonious blend of labor, technology, and governance collaborating in the creation of a Pacific Rim-inspired dream society.

The final section of the novel, "The Discovery of America," follows Ángel and Ángeles Palomar as they make their way back to the polluted beaches of Acapulco escaping the incineration of Mexico City. Upon their arrival at the coast, they are met by two ostensibly Asian characters—who are ultimately revealed to be their friend Orphan Huerta and his brother, Lost Boy—who invite them to leave the Western dystopia that Mexico has become and move instead to the utopian Pacífica:

> [V]amos a Pacífica, el Nuevo Mundo ya no está aquí, siempre está en otra parte, celebren el quinto centenario dejando atrás su viejo mundo de corrupción, injusticia, estupidez, egoísmo, arrogancia, desprecio y hambre [. . .] no le entreguen su niño por nacer al horror insalvable de México sálvenlo, sálvense: vengan a un mundo mejor. (544)

Whereas following the events of 1492 the Americas represented Europe's dreams of paradise, and after independence modernity became a utopian goal for Latin America, now, in the turn-of-the-millennium age of globalization, the Pacific

Rim comes to constitute a potential model for Latin American development.

The new utopia of Pacífica, then, represents the rejection of Western modernity and looks instead toward the East for patterns of progress that promise to remedy the ills of the modern world:

> [V]engan con nosotros al Mundo Nuevo de Pacífica, den la espalda al tiránico Atlántico que los fascinó y dominó durante cinco siglos: cese ya su fascinerosa fascinación fascinada fascista con el mundo Atlántico, denle la espalda a ese pasado miren al futuro [. . .]. Detrás de la máscara de gloria está el rostro de la muerte; renunciemos a la gloria, a la fuerza, al dominio, rescatemos al Occidente de sí mismo enseñándole de nuevo a rehusarle poder al poder, a no admirar a la fuerza. (544)

Thus, the new utopian vision looks toward the Pacific Rim for a better way to understand social relations not based on power and domination but on sharing information and technology.

As do most literary utopias, Pacífica promises the opportunity to realize an equitable community in which individuals are able to enjoy their humanity as well as the advantages of modern technology. One of the aims of the industrial revolution had been the satisfaction of human needs, which technology helped to reach ample sectors of Western society. With time, however, the pursuit of this humanitarian goal was replaced by the large-scale production of unneeded goods for mass consumption. The utopian world of Pacífica discredits some of the most prevalent myths surrounding the widespread use of machinery such as the notion that technology in itself would create happiness by extending life or making it more gratifying. Nevertheless, its inhabitants do not eschew mechanization altogether:

> [T]enemos todo para ser módicamente felices, en nombre de qué vamos a sacrificar los medios técnicos que ahora tenemos para la abundancia, la paz, la creación intelectual, en nombre de qué?, nos preguntamos y no obtuvimos respuestas: a la mano lo teníamos todo, técnica, recursos, inventiva, mano de obra, tenemos con que inventar un mundo nuevo [. . .] más allá de las viejas fronteras separando a naciones, a clases, a familias, a razas, a sexos: por qué no lo empleamos? qué nos lo impide? decidimos que todo esto era posible en una

> nueva comunidad, no una utopía, porque en Pacífica nunca
> perdemos de vista que jamás escapamos al destino, esta fue
> la locura de Occidente, creer que había dominado al destino
> y que el progreso eliminaba a la tragedia. (544–45)

For Fuentes, then, Pacífica represents the perfect realization of
the modern technological society as it offers a balance between
rational production and prudent consumption.

In contrast to the dystopian world of Bradbury's *Fahrenheit
451* in which all novels are burned, the utopian Pacífica em-
braces the role of art as mediator in order to curb the impact of
modern technology on the human condition:

> En Pacífica le dimos la mano a la vez al rápido avance tecno-
> lógico y a la conciencia trágica de la vida, tomando en serio
> lo que dice una novela, un poema, una película, una sinfonía,
> una escultura: decidimos que las obras de la cultura eran tan
> reales en el mundo como una montaña o un transistor, que
> no hay naturaleza viva sin su compensación en el arte, ni
> presente vivo con un pasado muerto, ni futuro aceptable que
> no admita las excepciones al progreso, ni progreso técnico
> que no integre las advertencias del arte. (545)

Fuentes underlines the importance of the arts in a postindustrial
world, as the residents of Pacífica are able to counter the alienation created by modern life by using their aesthetic sensibility
for the betterment of their society, along the lines associated
with the Enlightenment. Although Pacífica offers the solution
for many of the more vexing problems of contemporary society, Fuentes questions whether its advances are applicable to
the context of Mexico, where the fundamental aspirations of
the modern project such as democratization and the opening of
opportunities for all members of society still plague the country. The possibility of Ángel and Ángeles abandoning Mexico
in favor of the new utopia ultimately is rejected as it would
represent a continuation of Latin America's pattern of looking
toward foreign models of development in order to address its
own reality: "[E]l Mediterráneo, el Atlántico, cuna y prisión,
madre y madrastra del mundo durante cinco siglos: ahora ellos
no miran hacia el Golfo, las Antillas, el Atlántico y el Mediterráneo: ahora ellos miran hacia el Pacífico" (543). As we have
seen above, the wholesale adoption of imported paradigms of
socioeconomic development is inadequate because it fails to

take into account the particular socioeconomic, historical, and cultural circumstances of Mexico.

In spite of the promise of guaranteed improvement of the living conditions for their incipient family, the Palomars reject the invitation to migrate to Pacífica, opting instead to remain in Mexico and search for answers for their future. Ángel renounces the Pacific paradise as he emphasizes the necessity of creating a more equitable society using the current resources of Mexico and incorporating the positive contributions that both East and West have to offer:

> Ángeles, Cristóbal, no quiero un mundo de progreso que nos capture entre el Norte y el Este y nos arrebate lo mejor del Occidente, pero tampoco quiero un mundo pacífico que no mereceremos mientras no resolvamos lo que ocurre acá adentro, nos dice mi padre, con todo lo que somos, bueno y malo, malo y bueno, pero irresuelto aún; mujer, hijo, llegaremos a Pacífica un día si antes dejamos de ser Norte o Este para ser nosotros mismos con todo y Occidente. (555)

By refusing to leave for Pacífica, Fuentes's protagonist points to the need for Mexico to search for its own identity and path to development, which has to include all those members of society that the Western project of modernity has marginalized.[59] Ángel and Ángeles's decision to remain in Mexico to aid their country in forging its own response to globalization reaffirms Fuentes's opinion expressed in his 1971 *Tiempo mexicano*: "Imposible Quetzalcóatl, indeseable Pepsicóatl: los mexicanos tenemos la obligación y la posibilidad de inventarnos un modelo propio de vida, una gran síntesis novedosa de los tiempos que nos han marcado, a fin de insertarnos en el tiempo de nuestra memoria, nuestra apiración y justicia verdaderas" (38).[60] Because the return to the pre-Columbian agrarian past is impractical and the option of turning into a dystopia of mindless consumption is objectionable, the project of nation must be malleable enough to include the currents that form modern Mexico in order to forge its future. In the final scene of the novel, Cristóbal is born along with his sister, Baby Ba, broadening the previously exclusive association of national identity with masculinity, and making it clear that both genders will be equally important in the new project of nation that will emerge from the debris of the obsolete model of nation.

As demonstrated in the above, *Cristóbal Nonato* follows a tight program of criticism of serious issues regarding the meaning of Western modernity and its implementation in Mexico on the eve of the signing of NAFTA. Even when this fiction projects a grim picture of the nation's future, however, Fuentes illuminates how popular and marginalized sectors of society can participate in the modern economy by appealing to their own creativity and bypassing the hegemony of the state, which different protagonists manage to accomplish with varying degrees of success. At the end of the novel, it becomes clear that Fuentes forewarns his audience about the potential effects of the fragmentation of the state and the uncritical assimilation of the Amerindians into the modern nation. Notably, Fuentes's novel reflects upon Mexican elites' pursuit of the project of modernity understood solely as consumerism instead of satisfaction of human needs. Fuentes closes his novel by discussing the alternative models of development, thus implying Mexico's need to define its own identity in order to produce its own project of development. Amid all the ecological and demographic changes coming about with the fragmentation of the nation, the final resolution of Cristóbal's parents to remain in Mexico does offer hope for the future. At the moment of his birth, an angel—the Angel of history—touches Cristóbal's mouth, erasing his memory of everything that had happened while he was in his mother's womb. The novel thus concludes with the newborn narrator forgetting all he had learned in the prior nine months of gestation, forming a parallel with the reborn nation that must transcend the history of the previous five centuries in order to forge a new beginning that identifies its own singularity among the concert of nations.

In *This I Believe* (2005) Fuentes has clarified his position regarding globalization: "The sheer speed of technological progress leaves behind [. . .] those countries that are unable to keep up with the pace. Free trade increases the advantages to be gained by massive, competitive corporations [. . .] and crushes small and medium-sized industry" (112). Moreover, Fuentes discusses the role of the state in the global system and underscores how "effective participation in the global arena can only begin with sound governing in the local arena" (115). Far from reducing the role of the state, globalization and neoliberal policies broaden the scope of public jurisdiction and reaffirm the redistributive function of the state via the taxation system (120). Thus Fuentes does not ask for a reversal of globalization but rather for the state to participate with an effective taxing system in order to educate the young to participate in the new millennium.

As will be analyzed in the following chapter, Alejandro Morales's *The Rag Doll Plagues* builds on Fuentes's dystopian thematics by representing a series of epidemics in three time frames: a mysterious plague in colonial Mexico City; AIDS in contemporary Los Angeles; and a chain of plagues instigated by ecological disasters in a borderless mid twenty-first century. Like Fuentes, Morales explores how the colonial marginalization of indigenous communities has its consequences in the contemporary world. Projecting these issues into the future like Fuentes, Morales proposes creative approaches to ethnic and class identity that fall into the category of cultural reconversion.

Chapter Two

Cultural Identity and Dystopia in Alejandro Morales's *The Rag Doll Plagues*

> He wondered again for whom he was writing the
> diary. For the future, for the past—for an age that
> might be imaginary.
>
> George Orwell
> *Nineteen Eighty-Four*

Debates about identity politics have had a significant impact on literary production in Latin America and the United States in recent decades, as is evidenced by the vast number of contemporary narratives on the theme of ethnicity. Inspired by the anticipation of the 1992 commemoration of five centuries of intercultural contact between Old and New Worlds, there has been a proliferation of Mexican novels that reexamine the theme of racial and cultural amalgamation during the period of conquest and colonization of the Americas;[1] these include: Ignacio Solares's *Nen, la inútil* (1992); Olivier Debroise's *Crónica de las destrucciones* (1998); Carmen Boullosa's *Llanto: novelas imposibles* (1992) and *Duerme* (1994); and the novellas in Carlos Fuentes's collection *El naranjo* (1993). For its part, Chicano literary production since the 1970s has included a current that represents cultural *mestizaje* as a response to Anglocentric politics, in works such as Rudolfo Anaya's *Bless Me, Ultima* (1972), Ron Arias's *The Road to Tamazunchale* (1978), and Gloria Anzaldúa's *Borderlands / La frontera* (1987). Alejandro Morales's *The Rag Doll Plagues* (1992) continues in these trends, revalorizing the concept of racial and cultural miscegenation by tracing its evolution in the history of Mexico and within Chicano communities in the United States while adding a dose of science fiction to project the role of multiculturalism into the future.[2] In *The Rag Doll Plagues*,[3] set geographically in both Mexico and California and chronologically in three periods—colonial past, postcolonial present, and post-apocalyptic future—the metaphor of an epidemic[4] serves to call attention to ethnic divisions that have their origin in the colonization of the New World and continue to separate contemporary American and Mexican society. In Morales's novel, for each utopia —the Garden of Eden, the American Dream, and the borderless sanitized future proposed by industrialized capitalism of the late 1990s—the narrator juxtaposes a dystopian alternative that is characterized by recurring plagues caused by ecological abuse.

In this novel, the rhetoric of degeneration, colonial desire, and phobias of contact signal the presence of disciplinary forms of control based on the social construction of race, as Morales creatively combines the theme of miscegenation with medical discourses.[5] In *Illness as Metaphor,* Susan Sontag has pointed to the idea that "Medical imagery has been used widely in satirical attacks on society, and diseases have always been used as metaphors to enliven charges that a society was corrupt or unjust" (*Illness as Metaphor* 42). In *The Rag Doll Plagues,* Morales employs the image of epidemics to analyze societies that experience processes of crisis, transition, and growth. In this context, the metaphor of the plague serves to navigate the limits and borders of colonial, modern, and postcolonial societies, in order to demonstrate how mechanisms of control regulate subaltern communities, who, as in Fuentes's *Cristóbal Nonato*, manage to take significant steps toward social justice through alternative cultural projects.

The Rag Doll Plagues discusses the implications of *mestizaje* in various manners, in terms of racial mixing, intercultural and technological crossings, and relations between genders and social classes. Significantly, although racial miscegenation between different groups is suggested in each of the three sections, it never comes to fruition among the novel's main characters. In Morales's fictionalized past, present, and future, fear of contact predominates, provoking segregation between communities on both sides of the US-Mexican border. Morales highlights the need to create new strategies for intercultural relations beginning with, but not limited to, racial miscegenation and in multidirectional fashion, including people of Hispanic, Anglo, and Asian descent, to reflect the complex cultural composition of contemporary Southern California. Through his genealogy of the dream of *mestizaje*, Morales expands this concept and adds cultural reconversion from the margins as a potential answer for a nightmarish future.

The Rag Doll Plagues is divided into three books, each taking place in a different time frame. The first section, entitled "Mexico City," illustrates how in a fictionalized version of the late colonial period, the capital of New Spain falls victim to a plague that the residents call "La Mona," a mysterious illness that does not discriminate on the basis of race or gender, attacking all ethnicities equally—Spaniards, criollos, mestizos, and native peoples. The first-person narrator is a Spanish doctor named Gregorio de Revueltas, who arrives from Spain with orders from the emperor to combat the disease. To do this, the physician employs both European and indigenous medical resources, but ultimately the plague annihilates a vast sector of the colonial population before running its course. At the end of this segment, the Spanish doctor decides to remain in the New World to raise the daughter of a woman who has died of the plague. In the second part of the novel, entitled "Delhi," Morales again takes up the theme of an epidemic, situating the action this time in a contemporary setting in the Los Angeles area. The protagonists in this section are the narrator, Doctor Gregory Revueltas, a descendant of the colonial physician, and his fiancée, Sandra Spear. These two characters exemplify diverse types of intercultural contact since Sandra is from a wealthy Jewish background while Gregory is a Chicano physician from an upwardly mobile barrio family. In "Delhi" Sandra contracts AIDS through a blood transfusion, and we see how society—including the medical establishment—discriminates against her. Sandra and Gregory travel to Mexico to search for a cure in traditional indigenous medicine; nevertheless, their efforts ultimately fail and Sandra dies. In the final book, "LAMEX," the scene takes place in an apocalyptic future when the plague of "La Mona" reemerges in a deterritorialized Los Angeles–Mexico City corridor,[6] and the only remedy for the afflicted turns out to be a transfusion of the "pure" blood of residents of Mexico City, who have developed resistance from prolonged exposure to environmental pollution. The forced "blood miscegenation" that this cure instigates ultimately results in Mexicans living as virtual slaves, being held captive by "Euroamericans" who harvest their blood. As in the previous section, the narrator of "LAMEX," also named Gregory Revueltas, has interracial relations, in this case with his Asian American assistant Gabi Chung, but does not reproduce with her. Furthermore, Gabi kills herself when she develops complications caused by her rejection of a biomechanical arm that was designed to aid her in performing her medical duties.

While there is *mestizaje* in Morales's novel, the protagonist himself does not produce mixed race offspring within the narration of any section, thus the reader is left to speculate as to the particulars of the Revueltas genealogy. As Manuel Martín-Rodríguez has observed, curiously the main character of each book is represented as a descendant of the previous book's narrator, although the protagonist never produces children with any of his companions and it is unclear where the successive generations of Doctors Revueltas come from (90). Morales suggests *mestizaje* as *one* possible solution for the discrimination against minorities in the United States, but by the end of the third section it becomes clear that miscegenation alone will not be sufficient to address racial issues in a society that continues to be divided along class lines. What we see in *The Rag Doll Plagues* is that even when miscegenation is suggested but not achieved, the dystopian plot helps to conceptualize a different future in which racial, economic, and social barriers can be overcome. In all three time frames, the male protagonist has relationships with female characters who represent different cultural crossings, but each woman dies without reproducing with the doctor, thus showing an ambiguous reading of *mestizaje* as an answer to the ills of a world that remains socially stratified.

The present chapter focuses on the analysis of issues centering around the trope of blood—the link between the representation of the epidemics and the possibilities of miscegenation—in order to demonstrate how *The Rag Doll Plagues* portrays the fear of intercultural contact and points to the shortcomings of concepts such as *mestizaje* to resolve social inequalities, advocating instead for a multicultural agenda able to address the socioeconomic complexities of contemporary society. Significantly, within the novel's three plots, for every representation of the potential miscegenation there is a corresponding questioning of this utopian ideal, symbolizing the resistance to facile solutions implied by the rhetoric of state-sponsored *mestizaje*.

The concept of *mestizaje cultural* was developed as an analogy to the racial miscegenation that was being theorized in late nineteenth- and early twentieth-century Latin America. Concepts such as *mestizaje* have not only been used to define the complex process of cultural transformation that emerged as a result of the colonization of the New World but have also had a great impact on the nineteenth-century Latin American nation-building process, as Doris Sommer suggests in *Foundational Fictions*:

> Miscegenation was the road to racial perdition in Europe, but it was the way for racial redemption in Latin America, a way of annihilating difference and constructing a deeply horizontal, fraternal dream of national identity. It was a way of imagining the nation through a future history [. . .]. (39)

Thus, while in the late nineteenth century, European theories of race were developing increasingly sophisticated pseudo-scientific justifications for maintaining separation between races, at the same time Latin American nation builders in many countries were beginning to posit racial mixing as a positive goal.

Regarding the representation of miscegenation in literature, Sommer suggests that reproductively successful interracial and interclass romances as depicted in nineteenth-century Latin American novels helped to bridge different sectors of the then recently constituted nations. In many nineteenth- and twentieth-century narrations, however, interracial unions fail to produce a harmonious mix and miscegenation falls short, often as a result of the death of the female protagonist. However, through this failed miscegenation, the novels point to the need for changes in social and cultural attitudes. As in these foundational fictions, in *The Rag Doll Plagues*, the doctors' failure to father children of mixed ethnic background within the narration of each section indicates that the conditions of contemporary society are still not conducive to racial harmony.

The theme of miscegenation is related to the discourse on degeneration in nineteenth-century Western thought, since in the rhetoric of progress, the idea of hybridity carries with it the fear of atavism, that is, the fear that contact with "other" races may cause so-called civilized peoples to regress to a more "primitive" state. Since the development of theories of social Darwinism, the notion of degeneration has served in Western culture to erect boundaries between ethnic groups. With colonial and capitalist expansion there emerged a series of racist theories that presented contact between colonizer and colonized as forbidden because of the presumed dangers of cultural regression.[7] Homi Bhabha has argued that the discourse of degeneration—as part of the rhetoric of colonialism—has been used as a mechanism of control whose primordial function is the creation of a marginal space for subalterns who are subjected to a form of vigilance in which social hygiene and phobias of contact are used to regulate the population (70). For Bhabha, the ambiguity of colonial discourse lies not in an open opposition to the presence of the Other, but rather in the projection of a contradictory double operation of "recognition and disavowal" created by the simultaneous identification of the self with the Other and a rejection of this same identification in the name of maintaining the colonizer's cultural hegemony (70–73).

In a similar vein, Robert C. Young in *Colonial Desire* has observed how contact between colonizer and colonized circulates in an ambiguous zone that Young summarizes in reference to nineteenth-century European theories of race:

> Such social theories did not just use notions of hybridity in a merely metaphorical way: [. . .] they were elaborated around the different effects of the conjunction of disparate bodies derived from received knowledge about the literal issue of sexual interaction between the races. In the different theoretical positions woven out of this intercourse, the races and their intermixture circulate around *an ambivalent axis of desire and aversion: a structure of attraction, where people and cultures intermix and merge, transforming themselves as a result, and a structure of repulsion, where the different elements remain distinct and are set against each other dialogically.* (19; emphasis mine)

Colonial desire, then, describes a dynamic of simultaneous attraction and repulsion toward the subjugated Other in which desire felt for the subaltern is repressed by the fear of degeneration, which intensifies the phobia of contagion that coexists alongside the desire for contact with the Other. These types of ambivalent phobias of contact are evident in all three sections of Morales's *The Rag Doll Plagues.*

As discussed in the introduction, in the particular case of Mexico, the term *mestizaje* has been expanded since the second half of the nineteenth century to indicate racial miscegenation as a national and universal goal.[8] José Vasconcelos's *La raza cósmica* (1925) best exemplifies the utilization of this concept to represent a utopian solution for the future of the national project emerging from the Mexican Revolution. However, as Rowe and Schelling observe, "As is usual in theories where race is substituted for culture, there is a hidden hierarchy, and the vision of integration depends on white creole strata for its accomplishments, while the touchstone of the civilized continues to be Europe" (161). Vasconcelos's notion of miscegenation is politically charged since his use of the term *mestizaje* conceals the occidentalization of non-Western communities within nation-building projects through the subtle imposition of European cultural values. Thus, in practice and even in theory, racial miscegenation often coincided with cultural "whitening" or assimilation rather than with cultural mixing.[9] Differently from Vasconcelos, who offers a model of miscegenation leaning toward the dominating groups, Morales offers a resistant version of *mestizaje* as marginalized segments of society struggle against the ruling elites. Thus in *The Rag Doll Plagues* Morales performs a critical analysis of the identity politics that affect relations between different races and classes in the diverse worlds of Mexico and the United States.

The Rag Doll Plagues explores various conceptualizations that describe intercultural contact beyond the utopian *mestizaje* model, including those of transculturation and cultural heterogeneity. In Latin America, since Fernando Ortiz's 1940 introduction of the term *transculturation*, several concepts have been developed to describe the processes of cultural interchange generated by contact between Europeans and Amerindians and also between hegemonic societies and subaltern groups.[10] Antonio Cornejo-Polar, for example, examines cultural blending, which does not always lead to harmonious results as reflected in his term *conflictive heterogeneity*. Mary Louise Pratt's *Imperial Eyes* elaborates on the concept of transculturation by focusing on the unequal relations of power between colonizer and colonized enacted in what she defines as "contact zones." For Pratt transculturation occurs in "[s]ocial spaces where disparate cultures meet, clash and grapple with each other, often in highly asymmetrical relations of domination and subordination—like colonialism, slavery, or their aftermaths as they are lived out across the globe today" (4). Going against the grain of traditional definitions of transculturation as a process yielding harmonious results, Pratt's argument highlights the conflictive nature of intercultural contact in colonial societies, observing how these operations occur as part of larger negotiations of power in the contact zone, "the space in which peoples geographically and historically separated come into contact with each other and establish ongoing relations, usually involving conditions of coercion, radical inequality, and intractable conflict" (6).

Recently, Néstor García Canclini has introduced the concept of "hybrid cultures" to describe a similar dynamic occurring in contemporary global society. Significantly, García Canclini adds interclass exchanges to the dialogue on cultural relations, since as discussed in the previous chapter, through what he calls "cultural reconversion," popular sectors can actively participate in global exchanges circumventing the mediation of the state. While the terms *transculturation, heterogeneity,* and *hybridity* are generally used by scholars, there is also a popular debate surrounding similar issues, using the terms *multiculturalism* and *diversity*. Like *mestizaje*, multiculturalism proposes a harmonious solution to ethnic conflict, although unlike the homogenizing effort behind the original concept of the cosmic race, multiculturalism celebrates diversity as a positive force. All of these concepts to varying extents are drawn upon in Morales's *The Rag Doll Plagues*; while none is rejected outright, the various concepts are examined critically in the novel to illustrate the different possibilities for intercultural dynamics between ethnic groups along the US-Mexican border, with particular attention to the representation of socioeconomic class.

In *The Rag Doll Plagues*, Morales revisits the concept of *mestizaje* that in Mexico from the late nineteenth through the twentieth century had constituted a utopian project involving a series of unresolved contradictions surrounding the question of racial and cultural identity. The idea of racial and cultural mixing, in turn, was intimately enmeshed with the discourse of degeneration, a rhetorical technology that mediated desire for the Other by promoting a fear of cultural regression that would presumably result from interracial contact. Whereas the discourse of degeneration proposed a separation of the races as part of a colonial dynamic of fear of contagion, Morales appropriates this discourse to incorporate it into a project that questions the marginalization of indigenous and Chicano populations during different periods in Mexican and US history. Although *The Rag Doll Plagues* represents various cultures in contact, as Martín-Rodríguez notes, no dialectical synthesis is achieved along the lines of Vasconcelos's notion of miscegenation culminating in a cosmic race. Through the representation of interracial relationships that do not lead to miscegenation, Morales critiques the unproblematic representation of *mestizaje* as the solution for social problems rooted in the boundaries set by phobias of contact.

While *The Rag Doll Plagues* does not resolve the issues emanating from the debates on *mestizaje* and multiculturalism, it does contribute to the discussion of gender, race, and class issues within identity politics. Through the three plots of the novel, Morales encourages his reader to look for other paradigms for exchanges beyond the *mestizaje* model. Morales's fiction does not celebrate miscegenation as an ultimate goal but rather reflects on the ongoing intercultural relations among diverse ethnic groups including Latinos, Anglos, and Asian Americans.[11] Through the image of the epidemics, *The Rag Doll Plagues* underscores the necessity of transcending phobias of contact and inventing new ways to conceptualize relations between races, cultures, and classes beyond the paradigms proposed by hegemonic power structures. In order to analyze this issue from different perspectives, Morales situates his novel in three distinct temporal settings in which miscegenation and its implications—transculturation, hybridity, multiculturalism—challenge the disciplinary methods that colonial, postcolonial, and neocolonial societies have imposed on the questions of race and citizenship. Rather than celebrating transculturation and multiculturalism per se as solutions for society, Morales encourages his reader to rethink the ways we perceive cultural boundaries and social differences, initiating this discussion in reference to the colonial period, extending it to the present, and extrapolating it to a dystopian future.

As the following pages will examine, the first book of the novel, "Mexico City," situated in the late eighteenth century, represents phobias of intercultural contact through the dynamic of colonial desire; the second book, "Delhi," manifests both receptiveness and resistance to interracial and intercultural mixing in California in the final decades of the twentieth century; and finally, the third book, "LAMEX," further demonstrates the possibilities and limitations of transculturation and *mestizaje* in a mid twenty-first-century future that joins the United States and Mexico in a society that is borderless in theory but in practice remains socially segregated. Morales's assessment for the future of the borderlands emphasizes that even when there are multicultural crossings among many ethnic groups, social justice and economic equality do not automatically accompany this transculturation.

Degeneration and Colonial Desire:
Makesicko / "Mexico City"

The first book of *The Rag Doll Plagues*, entitled "Mexico City,"[12] is set in late eighteenth-century New Spain, during the final decades of the colonial period. It centers on the activities of Doctor Gregorio de Revueltas, recently arrived from Spain, who has been entrusted with the responsibility of collaborating with the scarce public services to seek a cure for an enigmatic plague that has come to be known as "La Mona."[13] Gregorio de Revueltas has come to the colony expressly to serve as head of the medical council known as the Royal Protomedicato, an organ dedicated to the preservation of the health of Spain's imperial subjects.[14] In this first book of *The Rag Doll Plagues,* rather than suggesting racial miscegenation as the only means of synthesizing Old and New World ethnic groups, Morales develops the theme of the gradual transculturation of the Spanish doctor as he struggles against this colonial epidemic, as well as against his own phobias of contact and preconceptions regarding the native peoples.

Significantly, Doctor Revueltas arrives in New Spain not motivated by a conviction to save fellow humans from the plague but rather as the result of a royal mandate: "But because the King ordered my presence to help our mutual friend, the Viceroy, *I have come to endure the filth and corruption of this demoralized capital*" (11; emphasis mine). Like Fuentes's narrator in *Cristóbal Nonato*, the Spanish doctor refers to the capital in terms of a sick body, associating the lack of public hygiene with a lack of social order. From his first moments in New Spain, his perspective as outsider and colonizer stands out in his categorization of Mexico City as both physically and morally "degenerate":

> Delicate features distinguished the brown faces of the carved angels sounding trumpets from the opulent baroque doorway of the royal palace in the City of Mexico. [. . .] The cherub's golden wings shimmered in the afternoon sun, which passed over the center of the Main Plaza, and contrasted with the *filthy central fountain where Indians, Mestizos, Negros, Mulattoes and the other immoral racial mixtures of humanity drank and filled clay jugs with foul dark water while they socialized.* (11; emphasis mine)

Here the narrator conflates morality and hygiene in his initial approach to the inhabitants of Mexico City, which is mediated by phobias of contagion as he considers them purely in terms of sick and immoral hybrid bodies.[15] In this passage, the splendor of the official buildings, symbols of colonial power, contrasts with the images of degradation and extreme poverty of the heterogeneous population that gathers in the town square. The dread of racial mixing manifested here indicates the presence of the discourse of degeneration, since the elegance and order of progress that Morales's narrator finds in the monuments adjacent to the plaza is juxtaposed with the chaos and danger that the scientific gaze of the Spanish doctor inscribes upon the bodies of the colonial subjects.

The first contact between the Spanish doctor and the Mexican populace and their environment is referred to in terms of a danger of contamination that threatens the ontological integrity of the colony:

> As we moved deeper into the bowels of the city, I found that the living conditions could only be described as stomach-wrenching. Upon my entering the city for the first time I had observed horrible sanitary conditions in the Central Plaza, but those seemed trite compared to what I was seeing now.

> Only a block from my residence I was shocked by the bodies
> of hundreds of dead dogs in a pile covered with a blanket of
> flies [. . .] above the decaying carcasses. Utterly filthy people
> argued over the freshest ones. (25)

In this passage, the city is described in terms of a decomposing body, opening the door for the doctor as an agent of public health. As is apparent here, the disorder of the colonial world threatens the concept of civilization to which the Spanish doctor adheres. In her analysis of Morales's narrator, María Herrera-Sobek astutely observes that "Don Gregorio's rhetorical mode of speaking identifies him with the colonial project, and the tropes he employs aid in the establishment, continuation, and affirmation of colonial authority" (101). In effect, the rhetoric of empire is patent in the narrator's initial reaction upon arriving in the colony as he describes the residents of Mexico City in terms of otherness. However, during the course of the "Mexico City" section of the novel, we witness a gradual process of cultural identification in the character of Gregorio de Revueltas, whose colonizing mentality is eventually modified by the relationship he develops with the colonized people as he searches for a cure for the epidemic. As the "Mexico City" section progresses, the narrator struggles to maintain a sense of cultural and moral superiority over the native population, both indigenous and mestizos, in spite of a fascination that eventually draws him to the Other.

There is an explicit connection between the practice of medicine and the maintenance of empire in *The Rag Doll Plagues*. In the beginning of the novel, the doctor unequivocally supports the colonial enterprise and uses his medical expertise to promote imperial goals: "The people of the colonies had to be convinced that they were better off living as part of the Empire than separate from it. Therefore I was here to quell the fires of revolutionary fervor by extinguishing the illnesses in the fevered populace" (16). Morales's narrator at first accepts the colonial policy that deems the practices of native healers as witchcraft punishable by the Inquisition, and only later after becoming transculturated will the Spanish doctor look to the *curanderos* for help in fighting the plague.

Since his arrival in the New World, Doctor Gregorio de Revueltas personifies the utopian goal of saving the world through science while at the same time suppressing the medical knowledge of native peoples. Referring to the official role of the Royal Protomedicato, the newly arrived doctor applies the colonizing gaze of science:

> This institute would implement the latest advancements of Europe and apply them here to the native population. The physicians in Mexico would begin to study these new discoveries and make them available to the mass population. In this way, the male and female practitioners of witchcraft, the popular *curanderos*, would be forced out of circulation. These *curanderos* were dangerous and had caused the death of thousands. Worst of all were the Indian *curanderos* who practiced witchcraft *in their native tongue*. They had to be prevented from practicing their evil craft. (15–16; emphasis mine)

As a representative of the European Enlightenment, don Gregorio plans to use medicine to control the influence of the indigenous *curanderos,* whose knowledge is considered a threat to Spanish rule. Medical rhetoric, then, forms a facet of colonial discourse, used not only to defend the idea of the biological superiority of the European colonizers, but also to endorse the implementation of public hygiene with the objective of consolidating imperial power.[16] Significantly, along with the subordination of indigenous knowledge, the narrator describes how the language of the Other becomes the target of elimination through acculturation.

Alongside the discourse of the degeneration and degradation of the colony, the novel also stages a crisis of the compulsory heterosexuality imposed with imperial rule. In his initial inspection of Mexico City, the Spanish doctor observes various scenes in which the destitute sell their bodies in order to survive. The lack of public hygiene and the perceived danger of contagion challenge Western notions of sexual identity as the narrator witnesses acts that the Europeans refer to as sodomy. The colony becomes a theater for transgressing the boundaries of race, age, and class: "I made my way to the fountain where a young man sodomized a boy as others waited their turns. All around the square, men, women and children negotiated a price for their hedonistic carnal acts. After terminating their lustful deeds, a few men, women and children cleansed their genitalia with the murky water" (28).

Colonial society, then, is represented as a zone where order is constantly violated; the transgression of gender roles in particular appears as an affront to the presumably inalterable sexual identity of the conqueror. For example, the account of the New World adventures of the cross-dressing historical character Catalina de Erauso, *Monja Alférez,* or Lieutenant Nun,[17] causes a crisis of the colonial order as it challenges the ability of imperial authority to maintain sexual boundaries.

> She was reputedly the territory's best and most famous muleteer, despite being a woman. [. . .] [T]his woman, known as La Monja Alférez, had rebelled against the authorities of her convent and had run away in male attire. She had made her way from Spain to the New World not only dressed as a man but able to handle a sword as well. (13–14)

As is apparent in examples such as that of the Lieutenant Nun, the exotic New World offers itself as a contact zone in which sexual and gender norms are apt to be transgressed: "Her life came to a climax when she fell in love with the smell, taste, touch and voice of another woman" (14). The narrator of this section—his colonizing mentality still intact—reacts with horror upon learning of the *Monja Alférez* who has not only left her convent dressed as a man but has taken a female lover and killed the lover's husband in a duel, "skewer[ing] the macho from his screaming mouth to his bleeding anus" (14). The doctor reacts violently with a mixture of fear and anger to the story of this woman who has transgressed gender roles both in her dress and in her behavior, and he defends the colonial order with his words: "For the killing of the *hidalgo* I would have made an example of the witch by burning her at the stake" (15). Upon first arriving in Mexico City, Gregorio de Revueltas upholds imperial values, but as we will soon see, his colonizing mentality becomes compromised as the doctor becomes more invested in the colonized people whom he endeavors to cure of the plague.

While controlling the epidemic represents in part a new form of dominance of European civilization over American "barbarism," it also creates the necessary conditions for testing the colonizer's identity in a time of crisis. As is evident in the following, from the beginning the narrator is also drawn toward the New World environment and populace:

> *Poverty and illness attracted me, as if I needed to get closer to that which I rejected.* On the way to Mexico City I had experienced this emotion once before. *The intense colors of the flowers and plants, the beautiful birds and the massive trees and vines of the extraordinary rain forest were the jungle I had read about and imagined.* As my caravan went along, *young natives reached out with open palms and ran alongside the carriage.* (13; emphasis mine)

As discussed in the introduction to the present study, this attraction toward the American landscape as a Garden of Eden is a classic topos in colonizing rhetoric beginning with Columbus's shipboard diary. What is remarkable in this passage is the narrator's attraction also toward sordid elements of colonial life such as poverty and disease. This ambivalent fascination with the Other that we can categorize as colonial desire motivates Gregorio to question his identity as an agent of empire, since his desire for the exotic challenges the assumptions of the conquering mentality, in that it stands as evidence of the need for the presence of the Other in order to define the Western colonizing self.

As part of this dynamic of colonial desire, although Gregorio refers to the native population as wretched and immoral, he nevertheless cannot avoid being attracted to the indigenous women:

> Although some of the clients were foul-smelling, I found no person, man or woman, offensive. People kept their distance. [. . .] With each downward stroke of the stone rolling pin, the older woman's breasts swayed freely into my sight, *absorbing me into a sexual reverie. But, how could any man sin with these soulless creatures of God?* (13; emphasis mine)

This colonial desire creates an ambivalent attitude toward the Other as the colonizer reduces the colonized to mere soulless body, while attempting to repress his own carnality, since acknowledging the existence of that desire would debase the presumably superior moral grounds of imperial power.

The simultaneous attraction and repulsion that the narrator experiences in regard to the indigenous Mexicans is not limited to women but extends to both genders as we see in the narrator's description of the natives who carry his baggage from the coast when he first arrives:

> These Indians were bald and scarred. Their foreheads were
> calloused and deformed from a lifetime of service. *I was
> fascinated by the strength and durability of their emaciated
> bodies.* They kept moving for as long as I advanced. They
> appeared cool and concentrated, as if in a trance. (12; em-
> phasis mine)

This fascination with the inhabitants of New Spain will ultimately facilitate the Spanish doctor's process of transculturation, since desire for the Other's culture sheds a doubt on his
preconceived notions regarding the "barbarism" and degradation of the natives.

The plague itself is the catalyst for this cultural transformation, as it constitutes the original motivation for Gregorio's
arrival in New Spain, and, significantly, it causes him to come
into close contact with Mexican residents of all racial origins.[18]
The plague is in a sense a model for his transculturation, since
it does not discriminate between victims of different races, as
Father Jude, the priest who serves as Gregorio's guide, informs
the doctor:

> A great plague has erupted and poisoned our populace. It has
> ravaged the country and is now moving into the capital. We
> have applied all medical knowledge in vain. The monster
> spreads and horribly kills our people. It first attacked the
> Indians and now it infects the Spaniards. *This disease takes
> everyone, regardless of sex, race, age or rank. It is a just
> disease.* (21; emphasis mine)

The "degradation" that the plague carries with it violates the
boundaries of both race and class, affecting even the colonizers,
and thus placing in danger the "civilizing" enterprise of empire:

> I sat back comfortably in the silk seat of the expensive car-
> riage and wondered how the magnificence of the buildings,
> the wide avenues and the parks had been allowed to fall into
> such disarray and indecency. *Even the well-dressed men and
> women of obvious Spanish upbringing and education walked
> slowly with the pallor of illness upon their countenance.* (15;
> emphasis mine)

If previously the doctor's judgment of the plague victims was
one of disdain and mistrust—based on the racial stigmas associ-

ated with the illness—now the danger of contamination extends to the entire population, forming a notion of a socially hybrid community created by the effects of the epidemic.[19] By the end of the section entitled "Mexico City," the Spanish doctor becomes obsessed with saving the lives of people of all races: "I understood that the saving of *these people* ensured *my physical and mental endurance*, and most important, the survival of *my soul*" (44; emphasis mine). Here we see the extent to which the narrator has become subject to the process of transculturation, since he recognizes the utter necessity of the existence of the colonized Other for the identity of the colonizing self.

Whereas he initially views the plague as a form of divine punishment and as an essential part of the "degenerate" Mexican nature, Doctor Gregorio de Revueltas eventually comes to see the epidemic as a result of insufficient measures to ensure public hygiene, a state of affairs that leads him to question imperial values: "I had noticed that Father Jude always covered his face with a black veil; now I saw it was not because of his mutilation, but for the filthy stench of the city. I finally believed what I was seeing. *This was not a nightmare, but His Majesty's Empire*" (26; emphasis mine). This questioning of the colonial establishment leads Doctor Revueltas to open himself up to new cultural possibilities.

One indication of his cultural transformation consists of the fact that whereas upon first arriving in the New World the Spanish physician resisted the notion that he could learn anything from the native *curanderos*, Doctor Revueltas ultimately begins to employ indigenous remedies in his treatment of "La Mona." While the native plants he uses do not constitute a certain cure for the fatal plague, they do represent the transculturation of the Spanish doctor in his crusade against the epidemic. As a direct consequence of his battle against the disease, Doctor Revueltas experiences a complete turnaround in his attitude toward the native healers; after several months in Mexico, he listens patiently as a critic of the imperial government and the Inquisition stresses the importance of allowing the native healers to practice medicine: "Simply stop ravaging the resources of Mexico. [. . .] The Holy Office must stop persecuting the *curanderos*, for they are a great asset to us. Many are truly learned *texoxotla ticitl*, doctors and surgeons. It is not important that they speak

Latin. They save more lives with their vulgar language than we do with our sanctified words" (40). Thus don Gregorio's effort to combat the scourge at the behest of the king and the viceroy ultimately leads to his questioning of the empire's values and of his own identity as colonizer. While his first feelings toward the native population combine the attraction and repulsion of colonial desire, gradually his transculturation is such that he resolves to forsake returning to his European homeland in order to remain on American soil on the eve of the struggle for independence.

Part of the doctor's challenge is to save children from the plague, and while doing this he adds a new dimension to his personal life. Gregorio meets Marisela, the viceroy's mistress, who has a daughter and is expecting a new baby. Both mother and daughter fall victim to "La Mona" but Gregorio manages to save the baby daughter, whom he later adopts. As a foreshadowing of the cure for the plague that will be developed in the third section of the novel, the arrival of the child Mónica Marisela into the world coincides with the decline of the outbreak: "I remained in Tepotzotlan caring for Mónica Marisela, watching her grow healthy and strong. It seemed as if with her birth, *La Mona*'s attacks on the populace had dwindled to nothing" (61). Like the unborn Christopher's parents in Fuentes's novel, Morales's narrator understands that his destiny is to reside in Mexico City to procure "a better world, a better Mexico for Mónica Marisela" (61). Don Gregorio's transculturation is complete now that he abandons all thoughts of returning to the Old World and begins to think of Mexico as his homeland: "[M]y concerns were no longer of life in the Old World, but of life here in Mexico [. . . .] I waved once and walked away from [. . .] Spain. I returned to my home in Tepotzotlan [. . . .] in my new country" (64–66). As will be discussed below, Tepotzotlan becomes a site of transcultural and transhistorical contact where groups formerly divided by fear come together. Although Gregorio has not been able to save all the victims of the plague, the winds of change of the Enlightenment and the impending independence of the Spanish colonies promise to improve the conditions of the inhabitants of Mexico.

Thus by the end of the first part of Morales's novel, Gregorio has adapted to the native culture to the extent that he determines to remain in Mexico, breaking off his engagement with his Spanish fiancée and adopting a girl whose mother has succumbed to the plague. In this first book of *The Rag Doll Plagues*, we do not see the protagonist himself participating in miscegenation as a synthesis of indigenous and European races; what Morales does highlight is the transculturation of the Spanish doctor as an effect of his struggle against the plague. The possibilities and limitations of *mestizaje* and transculturation for solving the problems of socially divided societies is further explored in the second section of the novel, "Delhi," set in Southern California in the final decades of the twentieth century and with the AIDS epidemic as a central focus.

The American Dream and the Politics of Blood in "Delhi"

Set in late twentieth-century Southern California, "Delhi," the second book of *The Rag Doll Plagues,* continues with the exploration of heterogeneity in the Americas using illness as a metaphor for representing social issues. As in the other two parts of the novel, here an epidemic works as a catalyst to promote intercultural contact among dissimilar sectors of society. While the rhetoric of the American Dream promises equal opportunity and advancement for all, Morales counters this utopia by depicting a contemporary United States that continues to discriminate against those who are ethnically different as well as those marked by the sign of contagion, as hegemonic society treats both Chicanos and AIDS patients as sources of danger. While in "Mexico City" we witnessed the colony of New Spain divided among Spaniards, Creoles, mestizos, and Amerindians affected equally by a fictional plague known as "La Mona," this time Morales demonstrates how in the final decades of the twentieth century a new and real scourge—Acquired Immune Deficiency Syndrome—both breaks down and builds up the divisions between different ethnic and social groups in California. In "Delhi," Morales delivers a fragmented picture of turn-of-the-millennium California on the verge of ecological and social collapse.

In the second book of *The Rag Doll Plagues*, Morales explores the possibility of interracial romance as one means of bringing together different cultures, expanding the traditional focus on Anglos and Latinos to include characters representing other ethnic groups that contribute to the cultural makeup of Southern California. This potential *mestizaje* is represented by the coupling of the Chicano doctor Gregory Revueltas—a descendant of the Spanish doctor Gregorio de Revueltas—who works at a clinic in the Santa Ana *barrio* known as Delhi, and the Jewish actress Sandra Spear, who belongs to one of Orange County's most affluent families. In "Delhi," Morales suggests the possibility of miscegenation in order to bridge the gap between hegemonic and subaltern groups, but as is the case elsewhere in the novel, here the interethnic relationship between the main characters fails to produce offspring because of the female protagonist's untimely death. By pointing to the absence of *mestizaje*, Morales suggests that racial miscegenation—unlike Vasconcelos's utopian dream of a cosmic race—is not the only answer for intercultural relations but part of a larger tapestry of possible ways for different groups to relate to one another and form a just society. Through the representation of the treatment of AIDS victims, Morales calls attention to the deep fracture in the project of modernity represented by an American society that pursues wealth and individual achievement but lacks the compassion to deal with the unknown. Here, as in the rest of *The Rag Doll Plagues*, the simultaneous erection and erosion of utopias function as a narrative counterpoint, demanding solutions for a world in crisis.

In "Delhi," Morales combines the themes of the plague and phobias of contact, creating a dystopian vision of the present to critique the hegemonic culture's attempts to control the heterogeneous population of contemporary border society. This section centers on the description of the illness of the narrator's lover, Sandra Spear—a hemophiliac who contracts AIDS when she receives contaminated blood during a transfusion—to dramatize the effects of the epidemic as well as to represent the process of intercultural contact. Through the representation of this character with AIDS, Morales shows how mainstream society discriminates against groups perceived as suspicious because of their ethnic origin, sexual orientation, or social status, thus establishing parallels between the prejudices experienced by Chicanos and AIDS patients. Through the body of Sandra

Spear, Morales emphasizes the intersections between race, gender, and class in the construction of boundaries between cultures. Even when biological miscegenation does not occur among the main characters of the novel—as will be also the case in the following section, "LAMEX"—in "Delhi," alternative forms of cultural interaction arise among the residents of California and Mexico as the direct result of an epidemic.

In "Delhi," Morales presents us with an industrialized world that isolates the individual, negates tradition, and deprives humanity of the needed connection with its surroundings, as modernity devalues nature in the name of progress: "The behemoth tree was like pure crystal: forever in danger of being broken, cut down by men and women concerned more with industrial profit than the preservation of natural life" (69). Despite his economic success, Gregory struggles to maintain a link with his roots: "Habitually, a multitude of wings or the pandemonium of the city shattered my reverie with nature, but always the cypress endured, peacefully guarding and supporting the sky" (69). Gregory is described as a self-absorbed professional in search of recognition in the mainstream, finding only in nature a place to be himself: "Here, next to this well-planted tree, I felt rooted in this earth. I danced by the little rivulet that meandered down to what once was my family's home, my *barrio*, Simons. I returned often to the people I loved. I came back to fuel my memory" (69). Here the narrator emphasizes the connection between nature, memory, and identity as he stresses the need to develop an ecological and historical consciousness in order to prepare for the future.

The Delhi neighborhood where Gregory's clinic is located is described in utopian terms as a sanctuary where nature and ancient traditions thrive in spite of pollution and the rhythm of modern life: "The *barrios* of Southern California, the real Aztlán, the origins of my Indian past, shared in common the kind of housing built. [They all had] well-tended flower gardens, the beautiful faces marked by the history of young and old Chicanos who worked, studied, loved, hated and helped each other in times of need" (71). As in the classic dystopian novel, here the narrator establishes a contrast between what humanity has lost in its search for perfection and the need to reach a balance with oneself, one's community, and the natural environment. In the middle of a world consumed by profit and status, Gregory will reach to the barrio and to his companion, Sandra, as the means of establishing a connection between himself, nature, and history.

Morales constructs the character of Sandra Spear as a link between Gregory and the environment, employing the problematic association of women with nature. As discussed in the introduction, Western patriarchy perceives women as mediators between nature and culture as well as between modernity and tradition; in *The Rag Doll Plagues*, these operations merge in Sandra Spear's body:

> Her green-blue eyes fixed perfectly into my own almond-shaped brown ones. In an instant she possessed all faces, times and places, none of which were familiar to me, yet I knew them all. I remembered the cypress filled with birds, the great star dancing above, chasing away the clouds of winter. She was the priestess and she drank a cup of blood and raised a sword to the sky and violently thrust it through my soul. Her fingers had grown like roots, penetrated and entwined through my body and soul. (83)

The narrator's male gaze associates Sandra's body with nature in terms of harmonious communion: "I saw the world, the sea, the mountains in her legs, her arms, her face. The cosmos became her body" (70). She is further represented as a conduit to natural life: "I was at her side as she was transfigured into a green-blue cypress and she spoke to me like a tree, a river, a seed. Suddenly she erupted and flew like a hummingbird, like a butterfly" (104). Just as women are depicted as intermediaries between nature and civilization, Sandra will also significantly become an agent of transculturation.

In "Delhi," then, it is a female character who serves as both the embodiment of the epidemic and the primary subject of cultural hybridity. Morales's portrait of Sandra Spear as a mediator between genders, races, and classes shows various facets of intercultural relations occurring on different levels. Since her initial introduction, the narrator makes the reader aware of Sandra's predilection for Latino culture based on its heterogeneous composition: "The apartment was decorated with both modern and ancient objects from North and South America. Sandra had studied in Costa Rica her junior year and traveled from Central America to Tierra del Fuego" (72).[20] Sandra has a particular interest in Mexico, as she has traveled extensively to the ancient ruins of Mesoamerican civilizations as well as to predominantly indigenous towns of Oaxaca. Notably, Sandra is depicted as ethnically marked, since her wavy dark hair distinguishes her from her blond parents. Sandra's body bespeaks the memory of the marginalized Jewish community: "The victims of the holocaust saw through her bones as her body turned into a forest where we both ran on a path in the mountains" (77). As a member of a historically persecuted ethnic group, the Jewish actress is represented as a keen mediator empathizing with the Mexican American population of the Los Angeles area. Sandra's proclivity to transculturation will be especially important when she begins to look for a cure in Mexico after falling victim to AIDS.

Sandra's attraction toward Hispanic cultural production leads her to choose Spanish playwright Federico García Lorca's *Blood Wedding* to be performed at an Orange County theater. In the Delhi barrio where Gregory works, the actress rehearses the play in front of several "homeboys" who receive her with admiration and adopt her as one of their own. On the opening night at the elite Orange County Center hundreds of Delhi residents attend, causing social boundaries to blur as "[. . .] *Barrio* Delhi politely invaded the Orange County Center [. . . .] I estimated there were about three hundred low-riding cars cruising to the house of Orange County culture" (90–91). The local newspaper interprets this low-rider "invasion" as a transgression of privileged space: "The *Orange County Register* severely criticized the disrespectful attire of the people that came from the Delhi barrio. 'How can anyone enjoy a serious play sitting next to someone dressed like a hood?' asked the *Register*'s reviewer" (91–92). Here the hegemonic cultural critics attack not the attitude of the homeboys but their attire as transgressive of cultural codes that dictate the behavior of people of high social standing. By associating them with criminals, the newspaper portrays Chicanos as antisocial and dangerous, thus revealing the mainstream's phobias of contact.

As a reflection on present race relations in Southern California, Morales critiques the dominant society's prejudice against intercultural contact and interracial marriage. Through the relationship between Gregory and Sandra, Morales points to different ramifications of both cultural and biological *mestizaje* in contemporary society. The most openly opposed to their romance is Sandra's father, who is clearly averse to racial mixing: "I just don't know about these mixed race marriages" (74).[21] Even with the continual harassment of her parents, Sandra and Gregory persist in their relationship and even conceive a child, but Sandra miscarries because of her hemophiliac condition: "I looked down. The red rose within her had burst like a river. We saw *our blood* spread over the white tile on the balcony. [. . .] In the white space of the hospital we lost the child and the bleeding ceased" (82; emphasis mine). The implications of the lack of miscegenation between the Chicano doctor and the Jewish actress are significant, for they point to the persistence of cultural barriers that separate ethnically and socially disenfranchised groups. The death of Sandra and Gregory's baby serves as a dramatic turning point, since at the same moment that Sandra's health begins to deteriorate, her desire for intercultural contact becomes more intense as it becomes embroiled in her search for a cure.

Sandra Spear contracts HIV when given a blood transfusion to stem hemorrhages caused by her hemophiliac condition.[22] When she falls ill from AIDS-related complications, doctors and nurses refuse to take care of her, fearing the virus, which was little understood in the 1980s and early 1990s:

> Several doctors and nurses absolutely refused to be in the same room with her. The doctors that treated the pneumonia talked to her by phone or through me. *They considered Sandra a human scourge, a Pandora's box filled with diseases capable of destroying humanity.* Sandra was simply a research case, a human disease puzzle to be solved. The endocrinologist and the hematologist saw her as a job risk. *Their complaint was that they did not get combat pay for endangering their lives with scum like her.* (112; emphasis mine)

Although a member of an affluent class who has access to quality health care, Sandra is rejected by the medical community because of her contagious illness. Thus, Morales demonstrates the prejudice against AIDS patients regardless of their origin, as the expletive terminology used by the medical personnel exemplifies their fear of the unknown.[23]

In this 1992 fiction, Morales projects early twenty-first-century scientists discovering the origins of AIDS as a consequence of the abuse of science and technology: "At the turn of the century the university scientists announced that AIDS was caused by a polluted mutant gene that originally appeared in Pittsburgh, had been taken to Africa where it germinated into a stronger lethal virus, and finally had been returned to the United States" (160). The reference to AIDS as emerging in one of the most industrialized cities of the United States problematizes the traditional conception that epidemics always originate "elsewhere," whereas the first world lies in a pristine state beyond the touch of contagion. This fictional circuit of AIDS from Pittsburgh to Africa and back to North America significantly suggests that otherness is not what we should fear, but rather we should be mindful of the consequences of our own industrial and scientific modernity and technological advances.

During the early years of the epidemic, AIDS patients were presumed to be members of marginal sectors of society such as homosexuals, African Americans, and Hispanics. In *AIDS and Its Metaphors*, Susan Sontag underscores how knowing about the conditions of contamination is important for understanding the dynamics of the panic caused by AIDS. In the specific case of patients who acquire HIV under non-stigmatized conditions, Sontag points to this fact:

> Those like hemophiliacs and blood-transfusion recipients, who cannot by any stretch of the blaming faculty be considered responsible for their illness, may be ruthlessly ostracized by frightened people, and potentially represent a great threat because, unlike the already stigmatized, *they are not as easy to identify*. (26–27; emphasis mine)

The fact that whites and heterosexuals could acquire HIV made it obvious that the association with the stigmatized groups was unjust, contributing to the eventual deracialization and degenderization of the public's perception of the disease.[24] When cases of HIV appeared in recipients of contaminated blood, society was forced to address AIDS victims in a different manner, rejecting the alleged origin of the illness as "God's punishment" or as "the revenge of nature" for alternative lifestyles, as conservative groups had predicated at the beginning of the AIDS crisis (Sontag, *AIDS* 61). Morales's 1992 novel is clearly situated in this early stage of AIDS awareness in that Sandra is described as "scum" in spite of belonging to a privileged class. Her condition as an AIDS patient brings her closer to less privileged sectors of society that are also discriminated against on the basis of race, class, and sexual orientation. Sandra Spear thus embodies otherness by contracting a disease that was initially associated with the stigmas of racial and sexual marginality, and her HIV status notably serves as a catalyst for a variety of cultural exchanges, first with the Chicano youth of the barrio where she is treated, and later in Mexico where she travels in search of a cure.

As in the other two sections of the novel, in "Delhi" the epidemic impels the protagonists to seek intercultural contact. As her condition worsens, Sandra and Gregory embark on a transcultural journey, searching for a cure in alternative forms of medicine in Mexico. South of the border, the travelers find a place where different levels of cultural exchange have created a "contact zone."

> Enchanted by the city, we eagerly allowed our minds to be invaded by a kind of collective hypnosis. A reverie brought about by a continuous differentiation of the old and the new, and the rich and the poor, and the faces of people who represented nomadic *Mesoamerican, European, African and Asian cultures. These were the Mexicans, inheritors of the world's cultural tribes.* (115; emphasis mine)

Whereas Los Angeles is portrayed as socially and spatially divided by class and race, contemporary Mexico City is described as a utopian mix of different cultures, the urban representation of the heterogeneity caused by several layers of transculturation throughout history.

Sandra and Gregory study the curative knowledge of the indigenous communities as their last hope, traveling to the areas surrounding Mexico City and specifically to the monastery-healing center of Tepotzotlan where "thousands of Indians have been cured by the spirits of the buried" (117). There they meet an Anglo woman who practices a transcultural form of medicine in the same building that had housed the hospital administered by the first Doctor Gregorio de Revueltas. At the Tepotzotlan sanctuary Sandra is attended by indigenous *curan-*

deras who show familiarity with the disease: "The *curanderas* [. . .] were not afraid of Sandra's illness. *They gave it a strange name, "La Mona." 'It is an ancient plague. There are records describing it'*" (122; emphasis mine). In contrast to the Western physicians in California, the Mexican *curanderas* attempt to alleviate Sandra's malady without phobias of contact, suggesting that they have power over a scourge that remains a mystery to modern science.

Through this contact Sandra experiences the healing effects of transculturation: "They [the *curanderas*] dressed her in clothes which were many colored and expressed the Indian and modern dress. Her dress was *transcultural, transhistorical.* She was a comet radiating a throng of flaming tails. Surrounded by Indians who touched her in a sacred way, who sang mystic incantations, who moved around her escorting her [. . .]" (125; emphasis mine). This ceremony places Sandra in the role of Coatlicue,[25] the Aztec goddess of fertility and destruction, transforming her into a connection between nature and humanity.[26] Gloria Anzaldúa, in her classic collection of essays *Borderlands / La frontera,* explores the philosophical implications of the Aztec goddess:

> Coatlicue is the mountain, the Earth Mother who conceived all celestial beings out of her cavernous womb. Goddess of birth and death, *Coatlicue gives and takes away life*; she is the incarnation of cosmic processes. [. . .] The rattlesnakes facing each other represent the earth-bound character of human life. *Coatlicue depicts the contradictory.* [. . .] Like Medusa, the Gorgon, she is the symbol of *the fusion of opposites*: the eagle and the serpent, heaven and the underworld, life and death, mobility and immobility, beauty and horror. (68–69; emphasis mine)

The transformation of Sandra into Coatlicue—along with the mysterious origin of her ailment—problematizes the patriarchal medical establishment's appropriation of women's bodies as well as the etiology of the epidemic. Significantly, only subaltern sectors are capable of understanding the true nature of Sandra's illness, thus underscoring the agency of indigenous medicine.

Morales further emphasizes that Gregory's painful experience in searching for a cure for Sandra's illness is also an opportunity to search for an answer for the social problems that vex the Mexican population. The Tepotzotlan seminary is described as a transcultural contact zone where healing knowledge flows regardless of the ethnic origin of the healer or the patient. The sanctuary is also represented as a *transhistorical* hub, since it is a site of time travel among the various doctors Revueltas. Even more importantly, its library contains the colonial Gregorio's manuscripts that his descendants read in the present and future time frames, thus emphasizing the need to historicize the epidemics and their remedies. Nevertheless, this utopia expresses its own ephemeral nature when Sandra leaves Tepotzotlan, and her infirmity takes a turn for the worse. As a result of her illness, the performer engages in intercultural contact that nevertheless does not save her from ultimately falling victim to the symptoms of AIDS.

In spite of the improvement she experiences at the hands of the native healers, back in Los Angeles, Sandra's health declines, and she and Gregory take refuge in another location of transcultural mediation, the Delhi barrio. The close quarters of the urban neighborhood redefine the relationship between tradition and modernity, as Delhi is described as an intersection of nature and culture where characters such as don Clemente, a guardian of tradition, cares for his hummingbird-covered garden accompanied by a pet jaguar. Significantly, one Delhi character, doña Rosina, "the mother of the barrio" who takes care of the homeboys when they get in trouble, represents the creativity of the community. Her house is described as being full of flowers and colors, contrasting with the poverty and crime-infested image of the community depicted in the TV news. We learn that doña Rosina also sews together the jackets of the homeboys, combining new materials with old rags and transforming them into an artistic creation of the Virgin of Guadalupe in what García Canclini would describe as cultural reconversion. This cultural reconversion prefigures the subaltern communities in twenty-first-century California and Mexico that in the "LA-MEX" section will offer an alternative to a segregated world.

Although Sandra's death marks the end of one phase of the transculturation process, the suggestion of potential *mestizaje* in her earlier pregnancy leads the reader to imagine conditions that might result in the reproductive success of intercultural romances such as the one between Gregory and Sandra. As Doris Sommer argues in regard to the function of foundational fictions:

> At the same time as they arouse our sympathies for the love affairs between ideal heroes and heroines, they also locate a social abuse that frustrates the lovers. Therefore they point to an ideal state [. . .] after the obstacle is overcome. Implicitly, and sometimes openly, these novels demand a possible solution to failed romance [. . .]. (173–74)

Along these lines, throughout this section Morales raises our concern for the way that hegemonic society treats both Chicanos and AIDS victims as socially dangerous.

Hence this truncated *mestizaje* highlights the need to create a more egalitarian society in which intercultural understanding, rather than phobias of contact, could become the norm. While Gregory and Sandra's reproductive failure supports Sommer's theory that such novelistic representations suggest that in the future a possible amalgamation could result from the different social groups, Morales also emphasizes the shortcomings of miscegenation as a magical solution for California's multicultural society. *The Rag Doll Plagues* thus avoids celebrating *mestizaje* as a facile answer for a society that still has unresolved racial and class issues. This is exemplified further in the following section taking place in a near future where Latinos and Asian Americans are the majority but still have not reached socioeconomic equality because of the continuing fear of contact.

As we have seen in the first two books of Morales's novel, the crisis of an epidemic spurs communication between social sectors that remain divided on the basis of race and class. In the portions of *The Rag Doll Plagues* that take place in the past and the present, the metaphor of the plague serves to critique mainstream society's discrimination against Amerindians and Chicanos respectively. This aspect will be further developed in the third book, "LAMEX," in which Morales presents us with a futuristic extrapolation of the consequences of these discriminatory practices. In "LAMEX," as in "Delhi," racial *mestizaje* is frustrated by the death of the female protagonist of a race other than the doctor's, but in this as in the other cases, the plague also serves as a catalyst for promoting various forms of trans-cultural contact. The final book presents a dystopian prediction of an apocalyptic future in which the healthcare establishment, rather than bringing citizens of different race and class back-grounds together, actually serves to exacerbate present conditions of oppression.

LAMEX: Dystopia and Hope in a Post-NAFTA World

In "LAMEX," the final book of *The Rag Doll Plagues*, Morales introduces us to a future postnational world in which medical technology, political relations, and consumer economics are regulated by a single overseeing authority. While in the novel's Mexico City past and Los Angeles present it is trans-culturation rather than biological *mestizaje* that predominates, in mid twenty-first-century LAMEX, interracial blood relations represent the cure for a debilitating plague afflicting the population of a new borderless Mexican-Californian megalopolis. In Morales's apocalyptic vision, Mexico City residents have adapted to conditions of human and ecological exploitation such that they have developed biological defenses against the plagues that a hypertechnologized future creates in its wake. It is therefore in part on a biological level that marginal sectors offer alternatives to salvage their own culture, since the sup-posedly "pure" blood of Mexico City residents becomes a rare and valuable commodity for the "Euroamericans" who suffer from the new plague and can only be saved through a blood transfusion. Thus, as in the previous two sections, in "LAMEX" Morales highlights the theme of intercultural contact employing the metaphor of an epidemic to represent the future society in terms of a sick body, literally in need of new blood.

In the third part of *The Rag Doll Plagues*, then, Morales continues his clinical examination of the borderlands from the perspective of a fragmented dystopian world in which global-ization ostensibly has erased—but in reality has heightened—national differences and racial and class inequities. As was the case of the "Mexico City" past and the "Delhi" present, the futuristic world of "LAMEX" is narrated through the scientific gaze of Doctor Gregory Revueltas, a descendant of the initial protagonist. An expert in "medical-biological-environmental genetics," Gregory—like his colonial ancestor who was the director of the Royal Protomedicato—plays a cardinal role in public hygiene as Medical Director of the Los Angeles–Mexico City Health Corridor, a geographic zone that extends from Los Angeles, passes along the coastal region incorporating San Diego, and continues south to encompass Mexico City. As did his homonymic forefathers, Doctor Gregory Revueltas of "LA-MEX" works to stem the tide of incessant epidemics that afflict the population of the Los Angeles–Mexico City Corridor as a result of ecological and human deterioration.

Although the world of the future provides citizens with tremendous technological innovations in transportation and medicine, Morales's LAMEX deprives the individual of autonomy and a sense of purpose, thus coinciding with science fiction dystopias such as *We*, *Brave New World*, and *Nineteen Eighty-Four*. Doctor Revueltas is successful in his career but he lives in isolation in his medical-technological world, where he is incapable of effecting change in the community or even enjoying personal freedom. For example, there is no distinction between professional and private life, as the narrator asserts regarding his relationship with his assistant and lover, Gabi Chung: "My personal guide and assistant in work and in life (there was no difference) was Gabi Chung" (135).

Through the character of Gabi Chung—an Asian American doctor—Morales expands beyond the traditional pattern of *mestizaje* between Europeans and Amerindians. Dr. Chung also embodies a radical expression of otherness reflected in the conjunction of technology and medicine, since she has agreed to have one arm amputated in order to install a biomechanical limb that allows her to perform her medical duties more efficiently: "The Triple Alliance Directorate maintained that apparatuses like Gabi's computer arm would bridge the infinite and minute space between us and perfection" (182). Significantly, Gabi's presence is always associated with the smell of burning flesh.[27] When pressured by the ruling powers to replace his arm as Gabi has done, Gregory's spectral advisors Grandfather Gregory and Papá Damián counsel him "not to deconstruct my humanity" (143). As in classic science fiction novels, here the utopian dream of reaching perfection through technological advancement leads to excessive mechanization and consequent dehumanization.

In this futuristic vision, Canada, the United States, and Mexico have formed a block that Morales refers to as the Triple Alliance, a clear reference to the North American Free Trade Agreement which was signed the same year as the publication of Morales's novel.[28] Echoing the autocratic regimes of Zamyatin's One State and Huxley's World State, as well as Orwell's Big Brother, Morales's Triple Alliance is governed by a central unit called the Directorate that controls the flow of people, commerce, and information in the areas dominated by the Triple Alliance. This new multinational configuration—which is run as a corporation—promises that the inhabitants of this borderless region will have basic rights, including access to jobs, benefits, and services, without regard to national or ethnic origin. Although these measures solve contemporary problems such as illegal immigration and unemployment, new issues emerge in the Triple Alliance as phobias of contact continue to maintain racial, economic, and cultural segregation in the LAMEX corridor. Notably, the armed forces are primarily composed of Mexican soldiers who are responsible for suppressing riots and quarantining victims of the numerous outbreaks of plagues caused by ecological disasters. The Triple Alliance also displays neocolonial tendencies in that it economically and ecologically exploits populations outside the region, for example "the Philippine Islands, one of those countries whose territories we rented for military use and synchronously converted into a waste dump" (143). Thus in "LAMEX," the politics of control observed in "Mexico City" and "Delhi" continue to be enacted by a new set of governmental authorities that combine science, technology, and medicine in the exercise of power.

In the generations following the NAFTA treaty, the former border region has been developed as an industrial hub as a result of the *maquiladora* factories that in this fiction have come to be dominated by the Pacific Rim Multinational Manufacturing Center. In line with science fiction novels such as Huxley's *Brave New World*, in which humans are categorized in vocational classes from Alpha to Epsilon, despite economic progress, Morales's new global reality is far from being utopian, as people are separated into clearly defined socioeconomic castes.

The tri-national conglomerate known as the Triple Alliance claims to have provided uniformity in the standard of living for all citizens of the region, but in actuality in LAMEX we witness a society sharply divided along class and consumption lines into communities designated as Higher Life, Middle Life, and Lower Life Existence.

The "Higher Life Existence" zones are inhabited primarily by "Euroamericans" and constitute independent suburbs where only the upper classes may enter. Although the very wealthy live on private islands, the affluent also have compounds in Baja California, since, ironically, as Mexicans have migrated north, "Euroamericans" have taken over regions of Mexico.[29] The "Middle Life Existence" areas, in turn, are populated by apathetic conformists dedicated to a machine-like consumption of the products that an overdeveloped society makes accessible to its citizens. Between Mexico City and Los Angeles there are also numerous pockets of misery known as "Lower Life Containment" concentrations inhabited by individuals who have been displaced from projects of massive production and consumption but who have labored to forge their own alternative multicultural communities. With time the Lower Life Existence settlements—which originated as penal colonies—have become autonomous units operating beyond the control of the state. Tellingly, the only centralized governmental organ that remains active in these settlements is the Directorate of the LAMEX Health Corridor—an agency that parallels the colonial institution known in history and in Morales's fiction as the Royal Protomedicato—of which the third Doctor Revueltas is appointed director. Although hyperconsumption dehumanizes the higher echelons of LAMEX's society, as we will see, the underprivileged sectors carve out a determinant role in guaranteeing the survival of their own culture.

Morales's fiction describes Mexico City as the most polluted urban area in the Triple Alliance, with a population of over one hundred million inhabitants. In contrast to the colonial "La Mona" plague whose origin is unknown, the epidemics of the twenty-first century explicitly represent nature's response to humanity's disrespect of the environment:

> Totally unpredictable, these spontaneous plagues could appear anywhere. *Produced by humanity's harvest of waste,*

they traveled through the air, land and sea and penetrated populated areas, sometimes killing thousands. Scientist [*sic*] throughout the world had identified thousands of these living cancers of the earth. [. . .]. *From our pollution we had created energy masses that destroyed or deformed everything in their path.* (138; emphasis mine)

As in Fuentes's *Cristóbal Nonato,* where the "El Niño" phenomenon transgresses national borders functioning as a metaphor for globalization, here ecological emergencies are declared when contaminated waste comes ashore infecting the earth:

Born in the depths of the Pacific Ocean about one hundred miles offshore, three huge masses of filth had developed organically and begun to move of their own accord. The Triple Alliance ships circled the energy masses, keeping them stationary. If these masses of living waste were to throw themselves onto the coastal shores, there would be unavoidable catastrophe. (139)

In Morales's apocalyptic future, land and ocean respond with devastating rancor to humankind's pollution. Significantly, mother earth transforms into an angel of death who from her womb metes out fatal destruction: "The initial infecting gases had evaporated or returned to the earth and probably to the sea, where from its *mother's wet warmth* it *nourished and gathered more vigor, to strike again*" (185; emphasis mine). Here we see the depiction of nature as an avenging figure that responds to human neglect with cataclysmic effects to which modern technology has no answer.

Like *Cristóbal Nonato, The Rag Doll Plagues* describes the conditions of ecological deterioration of Mexico City as a direct effect of uncontrolled growth:

For a time, it was the fastest developing city in the world. It overdeveloped into chaos and the lowest quality of urban life in the Triple Alliance. As the population grew, the ecological balance of the city was destroyed, its public services overwhelmed and natural resources decimated. Above all, water had been the greatest problem facing humanity [. . .]. (163)

Like Fuentes, Morales perceives the ultimate origins of this urban nightmare as rooted in the conquest and colonization of Tenochtitlan. As seen in the "Mexico City" section, the problems of overpopulation and inadequate services of the Mexican capital stem from poorly planned expansion and overexploitation of resources beginning under colonial rule.

While it brings the promised economic growth, globalization also translates as more pollution for an area already overwhelmed by human waste:

> Mexico City was the most contaminated city of the Triple Alliance. [. . .] Daily, a brownish haze covered the Valley of Mexico. This thick smog consisted of thousands of tons of metals, chemicals, bacteria and dirt so thick that it darkened the sky like mahogany. Nevertheless, the Mexicans had lived in this irreversibly polluted toxic air for more than a century. These conditions were responsible for the steady rise of human biological mutations. (163)

Mexico City is represented here as a post-apocalyptic megalopolis that has exceeded its resources. Morales portrays Mexico City as a vortex of regeneration and recomposition, and emblematic of the incessant condition of modern change.

In the midst of this ecological nightmare, the narrator finds in the people of Mexico City a miraculous will to survive and transcend the devastation of their surroundings. Daily exposure to chemical waste has had a cumulative effect on the bio-chemical constitution of Mexico-City-born individuals, forcing the creation of blood mutations, as Doctor Revueltas discovers:

> Something wonderful, biologically wonderful, had occurred to some of the people of Mexico City. Some time in the recent past, a great chemical transformation had taken place. [. . .] These people [. . .] had been transformed genetically to produce a blood that was able to sustain life in the most polluted conditions on earth. (165)

Curiously, the extreme ecological damage resulting from heavy industrialized exploitation creates the possibility not only for resistance against disease but also for providing a cure. This medical discovery will be highly prized when a new eruption of the "La Mona" pestilence attacks the Higher, Middle, and Lower Life Existence concentrations around Los Angeles where people fall victim regardless of their ethnic or class origin.

Coinciding with Orwell's assertion in *Nineteen Eighty-Four* regarding how autocratic states can control the future by manipulating the past, in the apocalyptic world of LAMEX, nature, history, and literature have become the exclusive patrimony of the ruling elite. Describing the home of the Director of the Triple Alliance, Morales's narrator writes:

> Gabi and I walked through an expertly manicured herb garden which I imagined contained every herb in existence. The fortress was built into the side of a mountain and the only access was by helicopter. Beyond the *gardens and patios* there was open space, hundreds of feet direct to jagged hills below. As I followed Gabi through several corridors and rooms, I noted walls with *thousands of books, the old books as in my grandfather's library.* [. . .] *The house was a huge depository of knowledge stored in the old manner, in ancient and beautiful books.* (189; emphasis mine)

In what he refers to as the "fortress of knowledge," Gregory finds his grandfather's novels describing the medical crises of the past which serve to highlight how because humanity does not value history and literature, it is destined to repeat its mistakes.

Although, as in Bradbury's *Fahrenheit 451*, in Morales's apocalyptic future paper books have become obsolete, the doctor searches for the remaining vestiges in his ancestor's archives and in the process runs across a novel written by his grandfather entitled *The Rag Doll Plagues* which points to the idea that the answers for the problems of the future lie in the past. Reading this book makes him realize that literature represents an important means of interpreting history: "As I read *The Rag Doll Plagues*, I grasped my inability to discern fact from fiction. Grandfather Gregory's novel became a history. I began to read exclusively for the pleasure of information [. . .]" (159). Gregory salvages history through both the humanities and the sciences: "The text in Grandfather Gregory's library taught that, in the time of the Aztecs and in his time, scientist [*sic*] were heroes. Now, no scientific heroes were allowed to exist. We were all caught in the asymptote of knowledge, never quite touching the perfection humanity pursued" (181–82). Thus, although LAMEX has utopian ideals, in reality it appears as an anti-intellectual dystopia.

A notable case of humanity's failure to learn from the past occurs when a plague assaults a Baja California Higher Life Existence compound and the Directorate of the Triple Alliance opts to obliterate all trace of the affected community: "The military had just demolished one of the ecumodern habitats. In a few days, the area would be scraped clean. *We humans had a bad habit of erasing the calamities caused by our mistakes; never did we learn from them*" (152; emphasis mine). As in Fuentes's *Cristóbal Nonato* where the government suppresses news of the "Acapulcalypse," here the Directorate controls not only the flow of information, but also the reality of the situation as the buildings are bulldozed and the salvageable materials recycled while the bodies of the victims are cremated and the survivors designated as "primitives" since they have lost the ability to communicate as a result of the disaster. This erasure of history underscores the loss of value of human life, which in this dystopia is subject to the absolute control of the omnipotent Directorate.

The three plots of *The Rag Doll Plagues* are intimately linked through the science fiction motif of time travel, as the doctors from the past, present, and future have fleeting contact with one another, transgressing the barriers of time to discover the cure for the plagues. Reinforcing the need for historical grounding, Gregory's guide is his grandfather Gregory who travels with his own grandfather Papá Damián to the colonial past to search for indigenous remedies for the plagues of the future. The young doctor looks to his ancestors for wisdom regarding the prudent use of scientific knowledge: "I searched desperately for a clue as to what I should do with the knowledge that I safeguarded. What I had discovered terrified me. *In the written text, there exists an answer*" (170; emphasis mine). Notably, these forefathers direct Gregory toward the science fiction classic *Frankenstein, or, the Modern Prometheus*, by Mary Shelley, pointing to the lessons that literature and history have to offer about the value and limits of science. Underscoring the importance of using his medical knowledge consciously, a shaman warns Gregory, "Whatever the secret you possess, guard it well, for it can lead to great harm as well as good" (175).

Both the time travel and archival research of the successive protagonists suggest the need to understand history in order to avoid committing the same mistakes that previous generations have made: "Grandfather Gregory and Papá Damián continuously pursued a better past. They understood that we created the past and not the future in the present. Now, I too, strove for a better past" (141–42). Thanks to the experience of his elders, Gregory is able to acknowledge his own limitations as a scientist: "This plague was beyond my experience. But I had read similar descriptions of it in Grandfather Gregory's books. [. . .] [Grandfather Gregory and Papá Damián] wrote what they had observed" (186). Hence, Morales's characters highlight how the combination of history and personal memory are fundamental to the forging of a new identity able to deal with the changes that the future brings with it. As a result of the dialogue among the three doctors Revueltas, a form of historical synthesis is achieved, ultimately pointing in the direction of a cure for the epidemics.

When the plague reemerges in the future, Gregory accidentally stumbles upon a cure consisting of a transfusion of the mutated blood of long-term residents of Mexico City. In order for the cure to be effective, the transfusion must go from male to female or from female to male, thus underscoring the notion of the remedy as a kind of miscegenation. Although Gregory's experiment is successful, the Triple Alliance at first refuses to facilitate the distribution of the prodigious blood, leading "Euroamerican" citizens to opt for the grotesque solution of "adopting" or purchasing on the black market Mexico City Mexicans, or MCMs as they come to be known, to live with them virtually as pets in order to ensure a supply of curative blood. A crucial element of this section of Morales's novel, then, revolves around the idea that the blood of Mexico City residents becomes a precious and vital commodity necessary to sustain the "Euroamericans," who condemn them to a life of "privileged enslavement":

> The Euroanglo population became the most aggressive in hiring and maintaining a Mexico City Mexican, an MCM, in residence. [. . .] Many MCMs moved right in with the family and signed an agreement to offer their blood for sale. In months the MCM blood business soared to become a multimillion-dollar industry. Mexican blood was offered at reasonable prices to those that could not afford *their own Mexican.* (194; emphasis mine)

As a direct impact of the plague, MCMs cause a northern migration wave that ironically is welcomed since it represents the only cure for the illness: "The population of people from Mexico City tripled in a matter of weeks. They came with their identification documents, birth certificates and letters of residence, certifying that they were born and had lived in Mexico City [. . .] all their life. These people from ancient Tenochtitlan were in demand" (194). The need for transfusions leads the Euroamericans to resort to extreme measures such as the creation of "blood farms" in which "Mexicans were contracted and flown in from Mexico City to live in luxury and produce blood" (194). Even with these drastic steps, the blood available is inadequate to fill the demand. As a result, "The newspapers carried articles about families fighting over one Mexican, or a family of Mexicans that refused to be separated. *Euroanglos always wanted to be photographed with their Mexican at their side. People took their Mexicans everywhere [. . . .] Millions of MCMs signed contracts for blood enslavement*" (195; emphasis mine).

As we saw in "Mexico City" where the plague had served to trigger the Spanish doctor's colonial desire and ultimate transculturation, ironically, within the globalized region of LAMEX—one that is theoretically egalitarian but in practice is racially and socially segregated—the plague instigates the creation of a new form of forced *mestizaje* that consists of mixing the blood of affluent "Euroamericans" and poverty-stricken "Mexico City Mexicans." Although in theory this intermixing of blood would imply a sort of metaphorical biological miscegenation, what Morales highlights is not the harmonious blending of the cosmic race but rather a new form of subordination, since "Euroamerican" households keep captive Mexicans to guarantee their blood supply. This circumstance highlights the conditions of unequal exchange that occur in the "contact zone," since in this dystopian vision Mexicans are forced to sell their most precious raw material—their very blood—in order to survive. Even when we have blood mixing, then, Morales points to how miscegenation does not resolve all racial and class issues.

This exploitation of the MCMs leads Gregory to meditate upon the history of marginalization:

> In the past, it was Mexican Indian blood that was sacrificed to the sun forces; it was Mexican blood that was spilled during the conquest; it was Mexican blood that ran during the

> genocidal campaign of the Spanish Colonial period [. . .] it
> was Mexican blood that provided cheap labor to California
> during the first half of the nineteenth century and that now
> provided the massive labor force in the *maquiladora* factory
> belt. (195)

In this light, it is ironic that it is the historically marginalized
Mexican strata of LAMEX that provides the cure for the illness
afflicting the people of California: "It was Mexican blood that
guaranteed a cure [. . .]. In a matter of time Mexican blood
would run in all the population of the LAMEX corridor. Mexican blood would gain control of the land it lost almost two hundred and fifty years ago" (195). This reference to recuperating
the region through blood mixing parallels Fuentes's assessment
in *The Crystal Frontier* of a "chromosomic reconquest" of the
Southwestern United States.

As has been evident throughout *The Rag Doll Plagues,* the
politics of identity have a direct impact on the private choices
that individuals make to participate in the various forms of
blood mixing. A constant characteristic in the novel—as we
have seen in the case of the intercultural relations of the various
generations of doctors in the three plots—has been the protagonist's lack of direct participation in racial *mestizaje* within the
narration of each section. In "LAMEX" also Gregory does not
procreate, since his Asian American lover, Gabi Chung, elec-
trocutes herself when she finds out that her body has rejected
the cybernetic arm that was supposed to bring her professional
success. As in the previous sections, here the main female
character dies much as the heroines of nineteenth-century Latin
American foundational fictions routinely did. Morales seems
to imply that even the world of the twenty-first century is not
ready for the cosmic race, as his apocalyptic California is represented as a hedonistic consumer society that achieves surprising
technological advances and conquers illnesses such as cancer
and AIDS but lacks a sense of purpose and community. Rather
than a solution, Gabi Chung's biomechanical hybridity creates
additional problems and serves as a further demonstration of
the dystopian society's lack of humanity. Through the truncated
relationship between Gregory and Gabi Chung, Morales once
again underscores the difficulties facing a society that has not
yet transcended ethnic divisions.

Morales suggests that we have various alternatives for future intercultural exchanges including, but not limited to, racial miscegenation. While in "LAMEX" on the negative side we see the forced blood mixing created as a response to the plague, we also have a positive solution in the form of the resurgence of intercultural relations. Notably, the world of LAMEX does feature a trend toward interracial marriage between members of subaltern communities:

> Monterey Park/East Los Angeles was a center for Mexican/ Asian culture. Chinese, Japanese, Koreans and Southeast Asians had migrated in great numbers at the turn of the century. [. . . .] In order to survive and coexist, the Mexicans and Asians united economically, politically, culturally and racially. *The common cross-cultural, racial marriages were between Asians and Mexicans.* (148; emphasis mine)

One of these couples, formed by Ted Chen, who is a third generation Chinese American, and Amalia, a native "Mexican Californian," represents the hope for a better future. As in the novel's "Mexico City," in which the Spanish doctor Gregorio decides to stay in the New World in order to procure a better life for his adopted daughter, in the final book of the novel the last Doctor Gregory Revueltas decides to keep watch over Ted and Amalia's newborn baby, who represents "the hope for the new millennium" (200).

In addition to portraying racial and cultural mixing, Morales describes how disenfranchised groups in both Mexico and California propose creative solutions for the survival of heterogeneous cultures. These alternatives come from subaltern communities such as El Mar de Villas in California and El Pepenador in Mexico City. Like "Delhi" in contemporary California, both communities are described as contact zones in which innovative forms of solidarity emerge from marginal cultures that create a utopian world inside the barrios of the major urban centers of the LAMEX corridor.

As in the previous sections in which surviving practitioners of native medicine are called upon to help heal victims of the plagues, in "LAMEX," Morales introduces the character of don Antonio Pérez, resident of the Lower Life Existence settlement El Mar de Villas as "a master *curandero*, [who] had tried to cure his friend by using modern and ancient treatments available to him, but all efforts failed against the infection caused by the pernicious gas cloud [. . .]" (173). Once again Morales represents the blending of modernity and tradition as one of the possible answers for the future but resists presenting facile solutions, thus insisting on the need to think beyond the cultural options endorsed by the hegemony. In El Mar de Villas, don Antonio is treated ceremoniously as a "man-god" just as in Aztec society men of science were regarded as representatives of the supernatural.

In this Californian Lower Life Existence community, Mexican and Asian Americans appropriate elements of hegemonic society to perform what Néstor García Canclini would call a "cultural reconversion" in order to survive, inventing new ways of inscribing cultural projects from the margins.[30] In his first visit to El Mar de Villas Gregory describes the place as a site of encounter and promise: "The practicality of objects was simple. What struck me were the brilliant windows made from the glass of broken bottles" (173).[31] This community represents a response to the ecological desolation caused by the prevalence of consumerism, since its inhabitants recycle materials deemed disposable by the consumer society. The narrator describes the threshold between the modern world and this Lower Life Existence settlement in terms of post-industrial hope: "The entrance to El Mar de Villas was a wide street that at one time functioned as a freeway. But after the ecological disasters and demographic change in the Los Angeles area, nobody wanted to go where the freeway led. It was a road abandoned to gradual decay" (173). As in *Cristóbal Nonato*, here we see how the symbols of modernity such as the freeways are appropriated by marginalized groups and given a new function, as the former road becomes the entryway to a new kind of community, leading to a more inclusive future.

This cultural reconversion occurs not only in California but also in one of the most polluted areas of Mexico City. This community is El Pepenador, a scavenger colony that houses families who recycle the garbage produced by the capital: "Twice a week large trucks drove tons of waste out to the garbage colonies, where millions of people scavenged and lived off the salvageable waste" (164). This community in the midst of the most dramatic conditions of poverty is able to convert discarded material into ecologically sound solutions for the future as Gregory describes: "That night I found myself wrapped in a wonderfully baroque cover made from a multitude of colorful waste materials" (168). In this way we see that in LAMEX, alongside racial miscegenation, disenfranchised groups perform operations of cultural reconversion that create a positive impact for the future.

In the world of LAMEX new cultural and political forms continually transform society. As a result of the chaos and abuse of power that surround measures for controlling the blood supply, several social structures wane, including the LAMEX Corridor Health Directorate. Unable to tolerate the corruption, Gregory abandons his position as director and joins the inhabitants of the marginal zone El Mar de Villas in taking steps toward social justice. In the utopian vision that emerges from the LAMEX dystopia, it is apparent that in order to salvage their culture, subaltern groups must take a determinant role in making decisions that affect the future of their civilization. Significantly, as El Mar de Villas develops into the most powerful sector of the LAMEX corridor, the Mexican members of the Triple Alliance insist on better representation in the leadership of the Directorate. Residents of the subaltern communities such as the son of the *curandero* Antonio Pérez come to occupy top positions in the reorganized Triple Alliance, along with Gregory Revueltas, who is granted the Directorate's library as a reward for his service to science and humanity. Thus it is only when multicultural groups—such as the one described in El Mar de Villas with Chicanos, Asians, and less affluent Anglos—deploy a democratizing agenda that the centralized government loses control and the conditions of oppression in society change.

While miscegenation on the racial level and transculturation on the cultural level have been traditional ways to conceptualize identity in Latin America's heterogeneous societies, Morales shows that *mestizaje* alone is not the answer for a harmonious future. Nevertheless, transculturation along with the transformation of modernity by marginal groups through cultural reconversion represents hope for the future of the Americas and in particular for the borderlands. Departing from the notion of *mestizaje* as a nation-building project which in postrevolutionary

Mexico represented the utopia of an egalitarian society, Morales insists on the need for subaltern groups to partake in the government of their community and to form alliances to fight for environmental protection and social justice across ethnic and class boundaries. *The Rag Doll Plagues* thus refuses to posit the cosmic race as the answer for societies that continue to be divided along racial and class lines. Instead, Morales proposes that racial miscegenation can be one part of broader projects of cultural and political transformation while underscoring that any effort to transcend the social barriers created with colonialism and continuing into the postcolonial age must necessarily include the recuperation of historical knowledge and a critical consciousness of how science and technology can be employed wisely for the benefit of humanity.

Like *The Rag Doll Plagues*, Carmen Boullosa's *Cielos de la tierra,* examined in the following chapter, constitutes a critical view of utopian dreams in three different dystopian societies throughout the history of Mexico. In addition, Boullosa's novel questions the project of modernity by incorporating an overview of the history of racial relations in an attempt to explain how Mexican society arrived at conditions bordering on apocalyptic. Unlike *Cristóbal Nonato* and *The Rag Doll Plagues,* in which female characters have no historical memory, in the novels by Boullosa and Aridjis, subjects of the remaining chapters, female and indigenous characters will take a more active role in efforts to evade the ecoapocalypse through the preservation of nature, literature, and history.

Chapter Three

The Dream of Mestizo Mexico

Memory and History in
Carmen Boullosa's *Cielos de la tierra*

> History is bunk.
> Aldous Huxley
> *Brave New World*

Like Chicano writer Alejandro Morales's *The Rag Doll Plagues*,
Mexican author Carmen Boullosa's *Cielos de la tierra* (1997)
examines the transformation of utopian dreams into apocalyptic
nightmares in the colonial past, postrevolutionary present, and
postnational future, pointing to the disjunction between nature
and humanity.[1] Dramatizing the paradox posed by the pursuit
of industrialized development without regard for the cost to the
environment and to humanity's sense of community, *Cielos
de la tierra* calls the reader's attention to notions of power and
knowledge deeply ingrained in the discourse of modernity.[2] In
addition, Boullosa develops the issue of the colonial construction of cultural difference—thematized in earlier works such as
Son vacas, somos puercos (1988), *Llanto: novelas imposibles*
(1992), and *Duerme* (1994)—emphasizing how the marginalization from history of indigenous knowledge in contemporary
Mexican society is the product of several centuries of sedimen-
tation. In this novel, Boullosa proposes the need to rethink the
development of Mexico at the turn of the millennium when the
project of nation initiated by the Mexican Revolution suffers
its most dramatic historical crisis. Incorporating elements of
science fiction, *Cielos de la tierra* questions Latin America's
new utopian goal of globalization through the representation
of a dystopian future in which the by-products of industrialization—air pollution, destruction of the natural habitat, and
dehumanization of society—have led to the annihilation of
humanity. Through the juxtaposition of three different societies

where the utopian dream of progress has gone awry, Boullosa points to our need to learn from the teachings of history and literature in order to avoid the ecoapocalypse.

In contrast to *The Rag Doll Plagues*, in which each plot occupied a separate section of the novel, *Cielos de la tierra* is composed of thirty-one fragments, alternating among three time periods: the colonial past in the initial decades following the conquest of Tenochtitlan; contemporary Mexico City; and a postapocalyptic future society named L'Atlàntide. In these fragments, Boullosa represents three different communities where the desire for a perfect society is expressed but never realized as each utopian dream becomes a dystopian nightmare. The first community is the religious utopia represented by the College of Santa Cruz de Tlatelolco in colonial New Spain, which strives to combine European learning with the knowledge of the indigenous communities after the fall of the Aztec empire. The second time frame represents contemporary Mexican society where we witness the projected utopia of integration through the model of racial and cultural *mestizaje*. And lastly, we have the super-technological future community of L'Atlàntide in which people live in the skies, since the earth has become uninhabitable as a result of pollution and nuclear fallout.

In these different plots, Boullosa introduces protagonists who represent marginalized perspectives within their respective cultures. In colonial New Spain, we are introduced to the indigenous friar Hernando de Rivas who is one of the first native Mesoamerican children to be admitted to the College of Santa Cruz de Tlatelolco where he learns to write in Latin. In the contemporary time frame, Estela Díaz, an anthropologist living in twentieth-century Mexico City, rescues Hernando's manuscript from oblivion after it has been hidden for five centuries. And finally, in the postapocalyptic L'Atlàntide, we find Lear, an archaeologist who searches for the human past while her society moves toward cultural and historical amnesia. Lear recomposes Hernando and Estela's narratives, resulting in the final manuscript interweaving all three perspectives. The separate plots and temporal frames forming Boullosa's novel are thus unified through the literary device of the newly found manuscript, which narrates the birth of Mexican modernity and forecasts the destruction of humanity.

In *Cielos de la tierra*, Boullosa highlights the problem of transmitting knowledge as the characters recover information from previous generations and convey it into the future. First of all, with the story of Hernando de Rivas in colonial New Spain, the problem lies in the difficulty of translating the surviving knowledge of indigenous societies to hegemonic forms of communication, in this case Latin. Then in postrevolutionary Mexico City, Estela takes on the task of translating Hernando's manuscript from Latin to Spanish. And last, in a dystopian future, Lear attempts to preserve the previous manuscripts while adding her own story. Through these interwoven narratives, Boullosa points to the problems raised by the act of translation when the respective protagonists disseminate knowledge from Nahuatl to Latin, from Latin to Spanish, and from Spanish to the disappearing language spoken in Lear's community. This operation is problematic since the last transcribers, Estela and Lear, modify the original text written by the indigenous scribe Hernando by including their own personal stories, thus emphasizing the multiplicity of voices involved in the act of narrating.

Throughout *Cielos de la tierra*, Boullosa highlights the importance of memory as well as the challenge of transmitting knowledge. At the beginning of the novel, for instance, there is a disclaimer signed by one "Carmen Boullosa" expressing concerns about the climate of violence and destruction experienced in Mexico City during the 1990s, which has compelled her to write *Cielos de la tierra*. Following this, we have a note from a second narrative voice, Juan Nepomuceno Rodríguez Álvarez, stating that these three stories were given to him to construct a novel. His intervention appears just before an impending nuclear holocaust threatens to destroy humanity and all creation: "La guerra intercontinental se ha desatado. Si no llegan las potencias a un arreglo expedito, si no se solucionan las pugnas internas de los territorios en que hubo naciones, pocos meses quedarán al hombre y tal vez a la naturaleza" (14).

In true science fiction fashion, *Cielos de la tierra* opens in the distant future with Lear, an expert in archaeology from the Center for Advanced Studies who recovers historical documents and transcribes them into archives called *kestos*.[3] Boullosa's L'Atlàntide is a society characterized by its technological successes after conquering cancer, AIDS, and even death, making its forty-two surviving inhabitants—who live in a crystal bubble floating above the earth—virtually immortal.[4] Boullosa observes how even after achieving this high level of technological sophistication, the community faces its most formidable challenge yet in the effort to survive in a barren world while attempting to reconstruct nature. In an interesting twist, most of the efforts of the inhabitants of L'Atlàntide focus on the systematic erasure of all records of what they call the "man of History," since according to their beliefs, humankind's emphasis on history led to the destruction of the earth's ecosystem. As a result, the Atlántidos labor incessantly on what they call the Language Reform movement, consisting of different tasks, ranging from the rewriting of history to simply banning all forms of linguistic communication. Paradoxically, however, this Language Reform causes the end of their society, for confusion and chaos ensue as the Atlántidos become unable to communicate with each other, thus repeating the tragic fate of humans in the biblical tale of the Tower of Babel. Therefore, at the end of Lear's story, such measures doom the Atlántidos in a descending spiral that situates them in a state of barbarism and anarchy, finally destroying their possibilities of cultural survival. The story of Lear teaches us that the pursuit of utopia, while accomplished on the technological level, can ultimately lead to the loss of humanity's perspective, since knowledge of the past is necessary to forge a viable future. As the Atlántidos begin to show signs of regression to a less than human state, Lear takes refuge in translating Hernando's colonial manuscript, becoming the last survivor of the erstwhile paradise, while in the end a ball of dust approaches signaling the final destruction of L'Atlàntide.

The first fragments of the novel follow an inverse order, coming from the future to narrate the history of Mexico City in the 1990s and from there to the capital of New Spain in the early colonial period. After introducing Lear, Boullosa presents us with the first segment referring to anthropologist Estela Díaz, who, while working at the Library of the National Institute of Anthropology and History (INAH) in contemporary Mexico City, discovers Hernando de Rivas's sixteenth-century manuscript. Estela translates the document from Latin to Spanish, adding her own memories of growing up in mid twentieth-century Mexico. Estela's narrative traces the history of racial hatred in postrevolutionary Mexico, including her personal conflicts with prior generations represented by her grandmother's bigotry against native peoples and disdain toward everything that has not passed through the sieve of refinement.

Following the initial fragments portraying Lear and Estela, we meet the producer of the original manuscript, the indigenous Hernando de Rivas, a former student of the Colegio Real de Santa Cruz de Santiago Tlatelolco, and one of the first native scholars who helped to salvage the knowledge of the Nahuas in the years following the conquest of Tenochtitlan. Through the institutionalization of systems of transmission of knowledge, the conquering elites used schools like the College of Santa Cruz de Tlatelolco as a tool of acculturation of the Mesoamericans. As will be discussed below, such schools became zones of intercultural contact where indigenous children learned the language and culture of the conquerors while European intellectuals—assisted by native scribes—recorded the traditions of the vanquished communities in order to extend their sphere of domination. Ironically, thanks to these institutions, knowledge of indigenous customs was partially preserved for posterity, in great part by the silent and often ignored participation of Nahua scribes, of which Hernando is a fictionalized example. In his manuscript, Hernando chronicles how the European colonizers prevented the Amerindians from participating in the political and economic structure of the colony by creating a hierarchical division between the "República de españoles" and the "República de indios." From this character's perspective, we learn of Nahua customs at the time of the conquest as well as of the demographic and ecological conditions of the Valley of Mexico, which drastically changed in the decades following the fall of the Aztec rulers at the hands of Spanish conquistador Hernán Cortés in 1521.

Through the narratives of Hernando, Estela, and Lear, Boullosa demands equal respect for the teachings of history, the environment, and the rights of the indigenous peoples, linking these concerns with the critical edge of dystopian fiction. In colonial New Spain, Hernando's testimonial narrates the collapse of the imperial college, highlighting how since the defeat of the pre-Columbian communities, there has been a systematic exclusion of indigenous cultures in Mexican society that has prevailed until today. Estela's tale, in turn, focuses on the fiction of contemporary Mexico as a presumably egalitarian mestizo society, which in reality has not surmounted the discrimination against native peoples stemming from the conquest. Finally, Lear's story critiques the impact of globalization, consumerism, and the dependence on technology, since in her future, humans are destroyed by their inability to communicate with one another. What all three narrative threads have in common is a utopian dream—the New World as earthly paradise; the Revolution's dream of a mestizo Mexico; L'Atlàntide's perfect society in the sky—but these utopian dreams go sour, as a result of each culture's failure to respect all human beings, safeguard the natural environment, and attend to the lessons of history.

Although the three plots intertwine throughout *Cielos de la tierra*, this chapter will examine each time frame separately in chronological order rather than in the order in which the narrative fragments first appear in the novel. The first section will discuss how Boullosa dramatizes the construction of modernity in Mexico through what Walter Mignolo would refer to as "la colonización de la memoria," that is, the systematic erasure of indigenous systems of knowledge in order to promote colonization and assimilation. The second section will focus on Estela Díaz's comments on the failure of the Mexican Revolution to achieve its goal of creating a harmonious mestizo Mexico. The third and final section, centered on Lear's world, will discuss the future implications of the present model of Western modernity, which in L'Atlàntide ultimately leads to the extinction of life on Earth. Through the representation of utopian societies that have collapsed, Boullosa questions the adoption of a neoliberal model of development for Mexican society.

Hernando's Time: The Franciscan Utopia and the Colonization of Memory

Since the publication of *Llanto: novelas imposibles* (1992), the history of the vanquished native communities and their transformation as part of the Mexican national patrimony has been a unifying theme in Carmen Boullosa's narrative.[5] Five years later, in *Cielos de la tierra*, she revisits this issue in the fictionalized story of the historical nobleman Hernando de Rivas,[6] one of the first indigenous scribes to collaborate in the preservation of Nahua customs and traditions within the confines of the Franciscan academic structures. In his old age, Boullosa's Hernando remembers the changes that affected the Valley of Mexico during the first fifty years after the fall of the Aztec capital of Tenochtitlan. Through the historical perspective of this fictionalized native chronicler, Boullosa reminds us of the difficult negotiations made by the indigenous intellectual elites to save and transmit their knowledge in the face of colonization and cultural assimilation.

After the fall of Tenochtitlan in 1521, the European conquerors implanted a system of administration incorporating religious institutions such as the Franciscan missions, which in turn became central components of colonial society, since they provided the key service of indoctrinating the newly converted Mesoamerican leaders and educating their offspring. The Franciscans founded missions in several parts of Mexico, becoming a mediating juncture between the colonial authorities and the indigenous communities. As Georges Baudot points out, the original charge of the Franciscan schools was to watch over the spiritual and cultural conversion of the dominated communities, as well as to instruct the children of the recently converted nobility—thereby taking the place of the indigenous *calmecac*—but these religious institutions were also crucial for the preservation of native knowledge.[7] One of the main proponents of these schools was the Bishop Fray Juan de Zumárraga, who in 1536 established the Colegio Real de la Santa Cruz de Santiago de Tlatelolco.[8] The Franciscan attitude toward the Amerindians is ambiguous at best, since although the order constructed churches, schools, and monasteries with the intention of creating a utopian society based on the neo-Platonic principles of the Christian Republic, the Franciscans were also in charge of the "extirpation of idolatries." The missionaries undermined the intellectual, religious, and social infrastructure of the indigenous communities by imposing an overzealous observance of religious dogma that facilitated the assimilation of the surviving tribes to Western culture. The express function of the College of Tlatelolco was to form a generation of native clergy capable of attending to the spiritual needs of the New

World. The establishment of the Franciscan schools also demonstrated the political alliance that legitimized the presence of Hernán Cortés in Mexico, since the vanquished Mesoamerican elites had sworn to send their young to be instructed in the governance of their territories as a demonstration of allegiance to the Crown and personal loyalty to the conquistador.

Since the early 1990s, scholars dedicated to the study of colonial Latin America such as Walter Mignolo and Serge Gruzinski have addressed the problems of preservation of pre-Columbian history, coining useful terminology such as the "colonization of memory" and "the war of images." In Mignolo's words: "La 'colonización de la memoria' consiste, precisamente, en o bien ignorar la producción cultural e intelectual de las comunidades colonizadas, o bien reconocerlas y aún valorarlas convirtiéndolas, al mismo tiempo, en objeto descrito y analizado por medio de los tipos discursivos empleados en la comunidad colonizadora" ("La colonización de la memoria" 198).[9] For Mignolo, the most formidable apparatus of conversion of the native communities entailed the appropriation or destruction of their modes of recording their collective memory. After the conquest, colonial authorities incarcerated the *amatlacuilos* who were in charge of the preservation of oral tradition and burned their *amates* or paintings, for fear of inciting a return to the former idolatrous practices.[10] The surviving *amates* were the object of dual operations of erasure or appropriation within a hegemonic framework of transmission. The few surviving codices were translated into Latin and Spanish and were interpreted within a Eurocentric logic. This practice extended well into the twentieth century until scholars such as Ángel María Garibay, Miguel León-Portilla, and Alfredo López Austin undertook the challenge of re-examining these texts within their original cultural context and reconstructing the indigenous intellectual framework.

In several monographs, Serge Gruzinski has extensively studied the impact of the conquest on the native communities, focusing on how these groups have adapted the European systems of representation to their needs. According to Gruzinski, the Amerindians—in the early years of the conquest—combined elements of both indigenous and European systems of representation: the European based on phonetic writing and the Amerindian based on the iconographic representation of sound and image. Gruzinski posits a transcultural view of these responses to colonization in which sixteenth-century native scribes borrowed images from Christianity and added their own interpretations of the sacred. Boullosa extrapolates the consequences of these mechanisms of cultural survival and dramatizes them to illuminate the process of preservation of memory. While the systematic destruction of indigenous cultures underwrote the European settlement of the New World, Boullosa highlights how there was also a counter-discourse from marginal sectors, who from the beginning were "talking back" to colonization.[11]

In the fragments of his manuscript transcribed by Estela and Lear, Hernando examines the function of the so-called "Indian colleges" as they inculcate the young generation of a now dispossessed nobility who send their children to these schools to save them from the disguised form of slavery known as the *encomienda*.[12] Hernando's version of history begins soon after the conquest of Tenochtitlan during a period of radical transformation, when the social structures of the Anahuac Valley are rapidly being replaced by the new colonial codes of behavior and association. His first memories are of the aftermath of the defeat of the Aztecs and the ensuing dispossession, of which he and his mother are victims since their status in the burgeoning society is uncertain. Hernando is not from Tezcoco but from Tlatelolco, but his mother has hidden his noble heritage so that he can be saved from the *encomienda* or even death as inheritor of the crown of Tlatelolco.[13] Hernando narrates the colonial administration's mistreatment of the Aztec nobility. For instance, as a young child, he witnesses the assassination of a Tezcocan noble, internalizing the violence of colonization. In spite of their noble origin, Hernando's mother does not feel safe and takes refuge in the home of her relatives, the inheritors of the Tezcoco crown, in order to escape the violence of the Spaniards.

Hernando and his mother find support in the house of Tezcoco with the noble family Ometochtzin. Later on, Hernando will be used to protect an heir to the crown of Tezcoco, by taking his place in the College of Santa Cruz de Tlatelolco.[14] Hernando's entrance into the imperial college exemplifies the series of operations that the Mesoamerican nobility contrived to resist the destruction of the pre-Hispanic political system, including sending substitutes to take the place of heirs to the crown of their communities in order to resist assimilation or assassination. As a result of this strategy, of hiding his noble origin, Hernando declares:

> Mi fiesta de mi nacimiento no fue para mí. Mi padre no fue mío. [. . .] Mi Tezcoco no era mío, porque yo era tlatelolca. Tlatelolco, mi tierra, no me perteneció. Pasé a formar parte de los alumnos del Colegio con un nombre que no era el mío; otro que no era yo había sido elegido para ocupar el lugar, y yo ocupaba el lugar de uno que nada tenía que ver conmigo. Mi mamá fue quitada de toda mi compañía sin saber que la que ellos creían mi madre no era la mía. (268)

Boullosa finds in early colonial Mexico a propitious locale from which to subvert notions of origin and identity. As in her other historical novels *Llanto* and *Duerme*, the author is interested in presenting a contested view of the foundation of Mexico in which the colonization of memory is resisted as subaltern sectors appropriate hegemonic preconceptions in order to guarantee their own cultural survival. In this case, the indigenous nobility manipulates the Spaniards' notion that "all Indians are the same" by having Hernando take the place of the heir to the house of Tezcoco in order to protect Carlos Ometochtzin from acculturation and potential harm at the hands of the colonizers.

In the beginning, Hernando describes his experience at the College of Santa Cruz de Tlatelolco as both emotionally painful because of the separation from his mother and also as a physical limitation of his sensory capability, associated with the loss of culture, which he perceives as a metaphorical amputation of his hands. The young student recognizes the importance of his hands as a means of communication with the world: "Porque las manos son aquello con que el cuerpo le habla al cuerpo, con que se deja tocar y toca. Sin manos, el cuerpo se queda sin tocar al mundo" (143). By educating him in their culture, the monks offer him a new set of hands: "Alimentado con los cuidados de los frailes, en mis muñones brotaron otras manos, unas manos nuevas, éstas con que escribo" (143). In compensation for the limitations of his body, the scribe, who in his old age is confined to a wheelchair, expresses how he has gained a different power in writing. Hernando thus summarizes the experience of colonization as an ambiguous exchange, which on the one hand, identifies the loss of the body as a site of experience, but on the other, in his particular case, has provided the opportunity to transcend distances and imagine different realities.

After his experience at the college, an elderly Hernando reconstructs the customary laws that governed the pre-Columbian communities of the Valley of Mexico[15] and contrasts these with the chaotic image of Mexico City under colonial rule. For example, he refers to the Nahua world before the arrival of the Spaniards as a humanly designed Garden of Eden due in great part to Tezcoco's rulers who planned the irrigation of large portions of the land. Hernando admires the knowledge of waterways demonstrated by the kings, a father and son both named Netzahualcóyotl, describing his own childhood in which he could still drink from the wells established by these monarchs. After the arrival of the conquistadors, however, this ecological balance is violently overturned, as water overflows from the irrigation system, which has not been maintained under colonial rule. Instead of the regulated water flow, the adjacent territories have become deserts, foreshadowing the apocalyptic future described in the novel's third and final story.

Like the historical chronicler Bernal Díaz del Castillo, writing several decades after the events narrated, Hernando not only reconstructs his life within the religious confines of the College of Santa Cruz de Tlatelolco but also digresses in his commentary by relaying broader events that have transformed Mesoamerica. Hernando emphasizes the power of writing as a means of resistance to the colonization of memory, fashioning himself as a humble but truthful witness: "A riesgo de escribir disparates, pues soy persona sin lumbre de fe, contaré aquí la historia que creo preciso anotar para que no la desvanezca el olvido o el caos" (69). From the beginning of his manuscript, Hernando is aware that the customs of the Mesoamericans are under siege as a result of the colonial destruction of systems of knowledge, and he thus positions himself against this erasure of native memory. The scribe—as a representative of the *pipiltzin* caste—intends to save his community's history through writing, following the scholastic principles learned at the Franciscan college. As was customary under the Renaissance rules of rhetoric, the fictionalized chronicler resorts to the trope of false modesty in order to legitimize his authority before the Holy

Roman Emperor, who was the ideal reader of all official writing during this time. The purpose of his text, like those of colonial indigenous and mestizo scribes such as Diego Muñoz Camargo, Inca Garcilaso de la Vega, Felipe Guaman Poma de Ayala, and Fernando de Alva Ixtlilxóchitl, was to present his own version of history and discredit colonial misconceptions regarding the native communities of the New World.[16]

Boullosa situates her fictionalized scribe in the position of mediator, since he is both a member of the indigenous ruling class and an aspiring novice of the Franciscan order.[17] Hernando interprets the historiography of his people as a form of resistance aiming to dispel the myths spread by the early explorers of the New World:

> Fray Andrés de Olmos convenció al visorrey Mendoza de que en su propio palacio había hallado los huesos del pie de un gigante, los osezuelos de los dedos del pie, y del falso hallazgo fingieron deducir que en estas tierras otros días habitaron gigantes.[18] [. . .] Aquí no hablaré de gigantes ni de ninguna otra clase de fantásticos engaños [. . . .] *Diré lo que mis ojos vieron y mis oídos consideraron cierto. Pondré en palabras aquello de que fui testigo o que me fue dicho por quien presenciara los hechos.* No habrá más engendros que los reales [. . .]. (69; emphasis mine)

Through his eyewitness account, the Tlatelolcan scribe begins to dismantle the colonizer's version of America as a land of fantastic creatures, opting for a modern attitude toward learning based on empirical knowledge. To prove his point, Hernando uses the scientific method of observation and experimentation rather than relying on scholastic tradition.

When not basing his information on his own personal experience, Hernando draws on the vast resources of orality to problematize the monologic version of "official history" by pointing to how events are reconstructed by individual accounts that represent different perspectives. The narrator resists presenting events that he cannot verify through eyewitnesses, thus limiting his ability to recount the history of pre-Hispanic Mesoamerican civilization. Along with their language, he adopts the ethnographic gaze of the Franciscan order and internalizes their evangelizing ideology: "Escribo porque quiero dejar anotadas las insensateces de quienes no conocieron la luz de Dios" (106). The scribe appropriates hegemonic tools, opting to write in Latin as a form of preserving the memories of his community, "porque es la lengua en que sé hacerlo con menor torpeza y porque sé es lengua que, como ha resistido el paso del tiempo, vivirá en el futuro" (70).[19] Hernando's writing shows an individual caught between two worlds, negotiating his own authorial gaze between the ancient traditions of the Nahuas and the scholastic principles learned in the Franciscan college. Nevertheless, contrary to historical scribes such as Felipe Guaman Poma de Ayala, Fernando de Alva Ixtlilxóchitl, and Diego Muñoz Camargo, who sought to disseminate their writings during their own lifetimes, Hernando prefers to save his manuscript for a more open-minded generation in the future who may be capable of valuing his experience. Thus, he hides his memoirs inside a chair at the monastery where they are found centuries later by a former schoolmate of anthropologist Estela Díaz.

Through the eyes of this sixteenth-century friar, Boullosa reconstructs the climate of violence and uncertainty in the years following the conquest. With Hernando as a witness, we are told how the Inquisition ordains a trial against Carlos Ometochtzin, heir to the crown of Tezcoco and in real life a former student of the College of Santa Cruz de Tlatelolco. Through the trial, Hernando unmasks the veil of colonial subjugation when the Spaniards—including Zumárraga—attack the Tezcocan prince under false pretenses, accusing him of committing acts of idolatry.[20] Hernando narrates how the enemies of don Carlos plant evidence against the nobleman, emphasizing how hegemonic sectors use indigenous knowledge as a weapon of colonization, in a transparent effort to eliminate the native nobility:

> [A]lguien acusó al sabio y buen don Carlos de cavar los restos de prácticas funestas al pie de unas cruces en el pueblo de Chiautla, allá en Tezcoco. Las autoridades hicieron cavar a los pies de las cruces, y encontraron cosas de sacrificios, ciertos papeles con sangre, pedernales a manera de cuchillos de sacrificar arrancando los corazones, [. . .] así como figuras de ídolos esculpidas en las peñas. (280)

Through his narration of don Carlos of Tezcoco's trial, Hernando underscores how the Inquisition was used as an instrument of disenfranchising the already beleaguered native nobility. Ironically, the false accusations of idolatry directed against the indigenous nobleman are based on the cultural practices that the Franciscan ethnographers were interested in documenting. Hernando emphasizes how the accusations of idolatry actually may have been cases of the colonial authorities framing Amerindians for political reasons: "Si estaban ahí bajo las cruces o ahí las pusieron cuando escarbaron al pie de ellas, esto nunca lo sabremos, pero su hallazgo, ya fuera falso o verdadero, hizo que empezara el juicio contra don Carlos Ometochtzin, el Chichimecatécotl" (280–81).[21]

As the noble Tezcocan is attacked for his alleged heterodox beliefs, the narrator observes that his enemies have constructed false allegations with the help of jealous adversaries. One such adversary who has served as a witness for the prosecution declares that don Carlos made the following heretical statements regarding Christian doctrine:[22]

> ¿[Q]ué son las cosas de Dios? No son nada: por ventura hallamos lo que tenemos, *lo escripto de nuestros antepasados*; pues hágote saber que mi padre e mi agüelo fueron grandes profetas, e *dixieron muchas cosas pasadas y por venir, y ninguna dixieron cosa ninguna de esto*, y si algo fuera cierto esto que vos e otros decís de esta dotrina, ellos lo dixieran, como dixieron otras cosas muchas, y esto de la doctrina xpiana no es nada, ni en lo que los frailes dicen no hay cosa perfecta: más hay que eso, que eso que el visorrey y el obispo y los frailes dicen, todo importa poco *y no es nada, sino que vos e otros lo encarecéis y autorizáis y multiplicáis a muchas palabras,* [. . .] y *no cures de andar en eso ni andar haciendo creer a los indios lo que los frailes dicen, que ellos hacen su oficio, pero no porque sea verdad lo que dicen.* (284; emphasis mine)

In the above passage, it is of note that the Tezcocan nobleman calls attention to native forms of knowledge as a gauge with which to measure the truth value of the Christian doctrine that the Franciscans are instilling in the Amerindians. His statements are clearly an example of resistance to the colonization of memory, as they aim to indict a colonial mentality that marginalizes indigenous culture.

Through her representation of the inquisitorial prosecution of don Carlos de Tezcoco, Boullosa stresses the importance of the Mesoamericans' resistance despite their subjection to a sustained harassment that undermined their culture and religion almost to the point of extinction. As Gruzinski points out, the execution of this historical leader had dire consequences for the remaining artifacts documenting native cultures: "The death at the pyre of this important figure of the aristocracy of the valley of Mexico seems to have had a profound effect. Many of the panic-stricken Indians decided at that point to destroy their 'paintings,' or to give up these compromising objects" (*Conquest of Mexico* 19). Hence by prosecuting prominent indigenous figures, the colonizers undermined the native nobility, delivering a severe blow to the Mesoamerican systems of self-representation and self-government.

After don Carlos's execution, Hernando indicates that there is an increase in attacks against the College of Santa Cruz de Tlatelolco and its students, diminishing the Franciscan dream of acculturating the indigenous groups through education into the norms of Western society. Nevertheless, when some of the students successfully rose among the religious ranks of the Franciscan order, the narrator stresses how indigenous knowledge was held to be inferior to its European counterpart. Although the protagonist contributes to several scholarly works either as a translator or as firsthand writer, he bitterly points to how the colonial academic establishment does not acknowledge native intellectual expertise: "[L]ibro que era allá, mientras que aquí se reducía a rayones trazados por un indio" (222).

As Hernando writes, many members of the religious hierarchy disapprove of the very idea of educating the Mesoamericans: "[L]a doctrina es buena que la sepan [los indios], pero el leer y escribir muy dañoso como el diablo" (279). Intolerance continues to inhibit the formation of a native clergy, as later on, the indigenous friars have to face the bigotry of their own Franciscan brothers, who deny them their right to learn the fine points of Catholic doctrine: "¡Teología! [. . .] Dejemos eso fuera de toda discusión, que no hay indio bueno siquiera para deprender bien la gramática, que el latín *exige de la mente un refinamiento y un tino que no tienen de dónde extraer los naturales*" (300). The Spaniards oppose the admission of the indigenous students into the clergy of the monastery, revealing that they do not really intend to have the Amerindians mixing in matters of religion.[23] Through the opposition of the Franciscans to indigenous monks, Boullosa demonstrates how the systematic colonization of memory and imposition of cultural homogeneity has affected the construction of Mexico since colonial times.

Furthermore, the opponents of indigenous education accuse the native friars of mimicking Latin rhetoric as if they were parrots without really understanding it.[24] The most conservative forces even oppose their instruction in Latin:

> [A]ndaban diciendo que estaba muy mal que latín nos enseñasen, que a los indios esto les podía muy mal, que hereticaríamos, que hacíamos mal uso de todo. Que los indios no éramos sino niños, y que como a tales debieran tratarnos, manteniéndonos fuera del latín conocimiento. (304)

Disenchanted after witnessing don Carlos's unjust trial and punishment at the hands of the Inquisition, and experiencing firsthand the general mistrust of the Franciscans, Hernando realizes that the native nobility has little future in the new world order of the colony apart from blind obedience to authority.

The fragments of Hernando's manuscript transcribed by Estela and Lear emphasize how the Spaniards began to systematically attribute an entire repertoire of emblems of otherness associated with America to the indigenous friars and students of the college. The Amerindians are considered as aberrant and accused of idolatry and sodomy in order to prevent further native admissions to the school and to the order:

> [E]ntre los cristianos seglares andaba presto el mismo dicho, que en todas las bocas rondaba un NO hacia los frailecillos indios, y que el peor motivo de escándalo era que a dos de nosotros, no contentos con darnos armas para hereticar, nos hubieran dado hábitos de religiosos, que qué creían que podríamos enfundados en ellos hacer, *sino iniciar a hispanos y a indios a nefandos pecados*? (304; emphasis mine)

Clearly, the Amerindians are perceived here within the scope of the rhetoric of degeneration in which the Spaniards project their own fantasies of same-sex sexual encounters under the guise of imposing heterosexual conformity.[25] Even though the Franciscans have asserted that the indigenous peoples are equal in matters of religion, deep down they mistrust Amerindians, projecting on them one of the quintessential marks of otherness: sodomy.

Hernando uses his knowledge of both Old and New Worlds to respond to accusations of alleged indigenous sodomy. When a peer looks over his shoulder as he writes,[26] the scribe shifts from recording his memoirs to writing about pre-Columbian practices:

> [Para ahuyentar al monje que mira por arriba de mi hombro mientras escribo] haría yo uso de costumbres infames, que si se atribuyen a mis ancestros es porque sin duda las tuvieron, que no parece haber rincón del mundo no plagado de esos males, si las ha habido en todas latitudes desde tiempos remotísimos. ¿O, por decir un ejemplo, nos miente Juvenal? [. . .] No niego que es mala costumbre [. . .]. Pero aún siendo así, yo no gastaría mi pluma quejándome tanto de este vicio, que *peor es la envidia, peor la arrogancia, peor matar prójimos, peor abusar de ellos* [. . .]. (187)

Notably, Boullosa's character does not deny the existence of same-sex practices in Mesoamerica but rather observes that such practices have also existed in Western culture since classical times, citing a prominent Roman philosopher to lend authority to his writing. He further comments that these "perverted habits" are not as immoral and damaging as the treachery and violence committed by the colonizers among themselves and against the indigenous communities.

Hernando's dream of forming part of an intellectual elite comes to an end when the higher echelons of criollo society voice their opposition to Amerindian admissions to the Royal University. The Spaniards consider the indigenous peoples as benighted and barbarous, incapable of rational thought. However, as Hernando demonstrates, the native students are erudite, mentally agile, and well disciplined, as he conjectures that they were excluded from admission to the university because of their intellectual superiority. In the face of accusations of preparing a native clergy to break away from Rome, Bishop Juan de Zumárraga withdraws his assistance to the College of Tlatelolco in 1555. Although this institution continued to operate until the seventeenth century, access to the school was only granted to Spaniards and criollos, thus limiting the ability of the indigenous nobility to participate in the academic endeavors of the colony (Baudot 106).

At the end of Hernando's life a renewed consciousness of displacement emerges as the colonial system relegates the indigenous population to an inferior social position. Having seen his dreams of rising within the hierarchy of the monastery or returning to the status of his ancestors shattered, Hernando's final condition represents the uprooted situation of the native elite whose role in colonial society is severely limited:

> No soy de aquel tiempo [. . .] donde los quequezalcoa, tle-
> namacac y tlamacazqui, los tres grados de sacerdotes [. . .]
> regían con sabiduría el orden de estas tierras, ni soy tampoco
> de allá, de las nieblas y nubes del cielo de donde creyeron los
> míos ver descender a los franciscos doce primeros, ni de las
> crueles tierras europeas. (364)

Referring to the past as a lost order as a result of the colonization of memory, Hernando sees that colonial society offers little future to indigenous peoples. This religious figure writes from a nostalgic perspective, since the land and time where he was born have gradually been transformed by colonization, epidemics, and transculturation. He bitterly identifies the loss of the paradise represented by the Anahuac Valley with the loss of his desire to aspire to the heavens through Catholic doctrine. His remarks remind us of the status of colonial hybridity or the in-between state called nepantilism experienced by some sectors of the dominated communities after the destruction of their world and the emergence of colonial society.[27]

With the end of the sixteenth century also comes the end of the character Hernando de Rivas, who dies of old age before completing his memoirs, as an anonymous note informs us:

> Aquí terminan los escritos de Hernando de Rivas, quien fue
> de los primeros hijos del Colegio Real de Santa Cruz, natural
> de Tetzcuco, muy gran latino, y que con mucha facilidad
> traducía cualquier cosa de latín y de romance en la lengua
> mexicana, atendiendo más al sentido que a la letra, el cual
> escribió y tradujo de cosas diversas más de treinta manos
> de papel para fray Juan Bautista. Murió el año de noventa y
> siete a once de septiembre. (366)

While in the beginning, the scribe refers to the imperial college in utopian terms, at the end he bitterly expresses his conclusion that "los indios han sido condenados ya a la ignorancia y a un eterno sometimiento" (177). Hence the former heavens on earth, the utopian dreams of the Franciscan missionaries, ultimately become the colonial nightmare upon which contemporary Mexico is cemented.

The portions of the novel dedicated to Hernando de Rivas help us to understand the roots of the unequal treatment of native peoples in Mexico, as the rhetoric of empire presented them as children and consequently as incapable of self-rule. As the next section will develop, the implications of the colonization of memory will have a crucial role in the second plot, taking place in Mexico City in the late 1990s. Through the narrative of anthropologist Estela Díaz, Boullosa links the colonization of memory with the failure of the dream of postrevolutionary governments to forge an egalitarian society, since in contemporary Mexico despite the dreams of *mestizaje*, segregation of the indigenous communities continues.

Estela's Time: The Utopia of Mestizo Mexico

Boullosa locates the action of the second narrative strand of *Cielos de la tierra* in a chaotic and decadent contemporary Mexico City reminiscent of the socially and racially stratified societies depicted in Fuentes's *Cristóbal Nonato* and Morales's *The Rag Doll Plagues*. Through the perspective of fictitious anthropologist Estela Díaz, who works at the library of Mexico's National Anthropology Museum, the author makes us aware of the exclusion of indigenous cultures from full participation in national governance, underscoring the failure of postrevolutionary regimes to fully integrate all Mexicans despite the official policies of *mestizaje*.[28] Through Estela's own memories and those of her grandmother, Boullosa takes up the issue of racial segregation initially identified by Hernando and links it to Mexico's treatment of the indigenous communities from the decades following the Mexican Revolution through the mid century and into the 1990s. Estela describes the failure of postrevolutionary Mexico to realize the modern utopia of *mestizaje* imagined by ideologues such as José Vasconcelos, as well as the failure to undo colonial structures to produce a radical transformation of society.

Drawing on the narrative technique of the found manuscript, Boullosa shows how Hernando's memoirs fall into Estela's hands when a former classmate of hers finds the manuscript hidden in an antique chair. After describing the living conditions in contemporary Mexico City, Estela begins to translate the manuscript from Latin to Spanish, adding her own memories of growing up on the haciendas in mid twentieth-century southern Mexico where life for native laborers has changed little since the time of the colonial *encomienda*. Her reflections on indigenous cultures begin early on because of her complexion, for she has dark skin, differentiating her from her white criollo relatives. Her relationship with her grandmother, with whom she spends a great deal of time while her parents are absent conducting missionary work, is conflictive: on the one hand, her grandmother is a strong female role model who is iron-willed, independent, and hardworking, while on the other hand, she is extremely prejudiced against the indigenous workers who provide the raw materials for the family fragrance factory in Tabasco. By presenting this woman's bigotry, Boullosa demonstrates how the institutions of racism are passed from generation to generation, maintaining the colonial system of segregation.

Seen in the light of the blatant racism of her own family, Estela's translation of Hernando's manuscript can be interpreted as an act of personal rebellion against the fantasies of superiority of her grandmother's social class:

> Porque soy mexicana y vivo como vivimos los mexicanos, respetuosa de un *juego de castas azaroso e inflexible*, a pesar de nuestra mencionadísima Revolución y de Benito Juárez y de la demagogia alabando nuestros ancestros indios. Y porque, creo, *nuestra historia habría sido distinta si el Colegio de la Santa Cruz de Santiago Tlatelolco no hubiera corrido la triste suerte que tuvo*. (64–65; emphasis mine)[29]

Estela chooses to translate the colonial manuscript for several reasons: the racism of her own family; the duplicitous language of the Revolution; her sense of guilt about her missionary parents' contribution to the acculturation of native communities; and lastly, because her recognition that the conditions of indigenous peoples in contemporary Mexico might have been different if projects such as the Imperial College had met with more support in the colony. Furthermore, her reasons for taking on the translation of the colonial document hinge on the potential ability of oppressed sectors of society to form alliances of solidarity with one another; in this case, Estela's marginalization as a woman makes her more sympathetic to the plight of indigenous laborers.

As in indigenist novels by other Mexican women writers, such as Rosario Castellanos's *Balún Canán* (1957) and *Oficio de tinieblas* (1962), and Silvia Molina's *Ascensión Tun* (1971), Boullosa's protagonist is a woman raised in a regional society where the colonial hierarchy remains intact even after the winds of change represented by the Revolution have swept past without deep social reforms. Estela's narration begins with memories of her childhood in Tabasco in the mid twentieth century, while conversations with her older relatives allow her to map out the racial and cultural ideologies of the first half of the century. Estela's family serves as a microcosm of the nation in terms of racial issues. For example, her grandmother represents the fear of contagion as she attempts to "whiten" her family by enforcing the racial boundaries between criollos and indigenous peoples. Although Estela's father is light-skinned, her mother has dark skin and dark hair that Estela inherits. Notably, the narrator remembers her grandmother's efforts to monitor her pigmentation through admonishments that Estela should stay out of the sun and take care to avoid being "like an Indian."

As a representative of the large landowning class, Estela's grandmother expresses her mistrust of native workers: "*Los indios vivían cerca de la finca. Los varones pastoreaban el ganado de los blancos y las mujeres cosechaban el café de las tierras de los blancos, pero no vivían en la finca. El abundante servicio doméstico era únicamente de mestizos*" (42; emphasis mine). As in Morales's *The Rag Doll Plagues*, here we clearly see the presence of phobias of degeneration that lead the criollos to resort to inbreeding to keep social structures unchanged and the rights over the land unquestioned. Estela's grandmother believes that all her family members should marry whites in order to "mejorar la raza"; as the result of these beliefs, Estela's relatives end up with endogamous relations in order to maintain the racial hierarchy. In spite of these efforts to preserve the status quo, the postrevolutionary government forced Estela's grandmother to parcel out her hacienda and pay fair wages to the native laborers. Nevertheless, as Estela observes, agrarian reform was never fully implemented by any of the postrevolutionary administrations.

Estela demonstrates how after the Revolution the colonial structures of dominance continued to be deeply ingrained within Mexican society:

> Eso del racismo es algo muy feo, pero [para mi abuela] los chinos eran sucios y rateros, los negros haraganes malolientes y los indios no eran gente de razón, así de claro. En cuanto al racismo . . . ése era un pecado horrendo de los alemanes. Digamos que si los indios no trabajaban en la casa de la finca, era porque olían muy feo y eran sucios, y mentían, pero no porque fueran indios. (43)

The narrator reflects upon her grandmother's ambiguous attitude because on the one hand, she is racist—although she does not admit it—and on the other hand, she herself married a dark-skinned mestizo whose complexion is inherited by Estela. While her grandmother fails to recognize the discriminatory nature of her words and actions, Estela sheds light on the contradictions of Mexicans in ethnic matters, implicitly calling for a shift in cultural norms. The grandmother's discriminatory beliefs cause Estela to consider herself as a second-class citizen within her own family and by extension within Mexican society, as she internalizes this notion of the inadequacy of dark-skinned individuals. In this way, Estela establishes a subtle correlation between the lack of a complete and accurate record of native Mesoamerican history—as a result of the colonization of memory—and its effect on the national psyche, which continues to ignore the validity of indigenous cultures. That is, we see the effects of what Hernando witnessed in colonial times through Estela's descriptions of a fragmented contemporary Mexican society.

Gradually, Estela's narration calls attention to the contradictions in the utopian myth of *mestizaje* and in particular to the paradox of attempting to create a revolutionary culture without fundamentally modifying the colonial structure upon which the system of landowning was built. Notwithstanding the efforts to salvage native cultures undertaken by postrevolutionary regimes, Estela calls attention to the hypocrisy of contemporary Mexican society and its mirage of racial harmony: "Es cierto que vivo en la ciudad de México, que *comparto la fantasía de un posrevolucionario país mestizo,* pero es también la verdad que tengo muy cerca a mi abuela, y que ella habitó un pasado diferente, un pasado que es colectivo y que, además, tiene bastante de presente" (48; emphasis mine). Estela's comments unmask the fiction of Mexico as a genetically unified and culturally mixed country, in spite of the ideals of the Mexican Revolution.

Estela criticizes previous generations for setting the tone for racial discrimination and social injustice but also emphasizes her own generation's inability to radically alter the cultural values of Mexico. While her peers grew up searching for sexual liberation and proclaiming that "Black Is Beautiful" and "Brown Is Down," their lack of conformity with the system did not entail a sound and lasting political commitment. Estela's most salient criticism is directed toward the literary utopias with which her generation nourished their youth, such as Nobel Prize-winning author Gabriel García Márquez's 1967 masterpiece *One Hundred Years of Solitude*, which ultimately supported the ideals of patriarchal *criollismo*:

> [L]o que me llama la atención es que en el *Edén garciamarquiano los indios no son "actores"* de este re-nacimiento de *la realidad.* El tataranieto del criollo se casa con la tataranieta del aragonés para fundar la estirpe de los Buendía. *Los indios no participan en la recreación del mundo, de un mundo que les pertenece,* y los nuevos Adán y Eva pertenecen ilícitamente al mundo, no consiguen su legitimidad a pesar de tanta anécdota, de tanto suceder, de tanto salir del cuerno mágico del que fluyen sin parar historias. (203; emphasis mine)

Poignantly, Estela observes how even the most progressive forces of the 1960s and 1970s blindly ignore the presence of the indigenous peoples, thereby excluding them from participating actively in the construction of the utopian societies envisioned by the authors of the Latin American literary Boom. By founding a patriarchy on marriage between European immigrants and criollos, García Márquez's imagined community reinforces the racial boundaries that Estela's grandmother so adamantly promotes within her own family. Of crucial importance is the fact that even forward-thinking intellectuals, politicians, and social actors are unable to conceive of an alternative world in which the Amerindians are protagonists of their own history.

As a major criticism of the failure of Latin America's project of modernity, Estela emphasizes the lack of options for the future if even literary utopias are unable to project a heterogeneous future:

> *Cien años* escribe una utopía hacia el pasado porque Latinoamérica soñaba "modernizarse" por medio de la revolución socialista, siguiendo el modelo cubano. El sueño cubano que antecedió al fracaso cubano están ahí presentes [*sic*]. [. . .] Macondo es un sueño de José Arcadio Buendía. Él va hacia la fundación de la utopía, "hacia la tierra que nadie les había prometido." Mi generación asistía al nacimiento de un Nuevo Adán y de una Nueva Eva, y de un Nuevo Paraíso. (202–03)

Notwithstanding their vehement reaction against the government's violent repression of student dissidents on October 2, 1968, the members of Estela's generation who lived through the Tlatelolco massacre were unable to bring about democratic reforms and social justice.

The narrator points to how even the utopia of the Cuban Revolution, which represented a panacea for that generation, transformed into a nightmare years later. The disenchantment with socialism and the lack of a model of modernity capable of addressing the marginalization of large segments of the population have had a negative effect on Estela's generation, who never brought to fruition their dreams. Estela further laments how her peers sold out to mainstream Mexican culture's commodification of ethnic communities as folkloric instead of demanding their inclusion in the economic and cultural system of the nation. The anthropologist calls attention to how the embrace of indigenous cultures on the part of the "Jipitecas" (Mexican hippies) was reduced to wearing huaraches, Mazagua blouses, and Tehuana skirts rather than fighting for social justice to radically transform the socioeconomic structure of the past. Thus, Estela stresses how the lack of genuine reformist aspirations in her generation has consequently contributed to the stagnation of society.

Coinciding with Fuentes's *Cristóbal Nonato*, Estela denounces how indigenous groups face extinction in isolation, while also underscoring the ecological damage resulting from industrialization as the rain forest begins to disappear:

> Condenados a la miseria, [los indígenas] vagan en lo que resta del bosque tropical, donde hace cientos de años fueron a refugiarse, como cuentan las crónicas de la Conquista, para rehuir el maltrato a que los sometían los invasores. Los años han demostrado que ni así consiguieron rehuirlo. (47)

These ethnic groups remain subjected to the systematic violence initiated with the colonial *encomienda* system, prolonged by Porfirian *latifundios*, and worsened when postrevolutionary governments failed to effectively implement agrarian reform. Furthermore, even in cases where land redistribution did take place, the Mexican government's neoliberal policies in recent decades have negatively affected small-scale farmers, as now they must compete against more developed economies in the global marketplace. Thus, as discussed above, it is not a mere coincidence that the Zapatista Rebellion in Chiapas began in 1994 on the very same day that NAFTA went into effect.

Estela regrets that the dream of a true Mexican modernity is not realized but rather has become a dystopian nightmare as the social, economic, and ecological structure of the country begins to crumble as a result of the indiscriminate pursuit of global capitalism by unscrupulous government officials: "De la Colonia venimos, en la Colonia estamos. Nuestras riquezas salen a Suiza, a Luxemburgo, a las Islas Fidji y Caimán, a Cuba (eso se dice, que hasta Cuba, ya no hay sueños, ya no hay)" (147). In a fashion similar to *Cristóbal Nonato*, Boullosa notes how Mexican politicians swindled the country out of its wealth, funneling currency and assets to foreign locations where the law cannot reach them.

As a result of this imposition of a Western model of development relying heavily on industrialization as the most viable way to modernize the country, the Mexico City depicted by Estela is plagued by pollution, overcrowding, and a widespread sense of hopelessness reflecting the economic crisis of the 1990s:

> La pobreza creciente, [. . .] la sobrepoblación, la carencia
> total de oportunidades para las nuevas generaciones, la
> suspensión de crecimiento económico y el decrecimiento
> productivo, etcétera, etcétera . . . Ninguno de los males men-
> cionados parecen [*sic*] expresar del todo el horror que puede
> sentir la gente de mi generación: *de pronto somos como los*
> *forasteros de nuestra propia patria.* No ha habido un golpe
> de estado, sino un golpe radical, y nos han echado fuera de
> nuestro propio país, sin siquiera darnos otro a cambio. *Somos*
> *extraños en lo nuestro.* (148; emphasis mine)

Estela reflects on how her situation under the present trend of
globalization is similar to that of Hernando, as she experiences
dispossession and disenfranchisement, thus establishing a parallel between the displacement of indigenous groups in colonial
New Spain and that of late twentieth-century Mexicans under
neoliberal governments.

Summarily, Estela indicates how postrevolutionary Mexico
has not achieved a radical transformation of its colonial roots:
"Conservamos así la estructura colonial y colonialista, nos
alejamos de nuestro propio poder a base de tanto cuento y tanta
historia, y nos orillamos al silencio, y al peor silencio, peor aún
del que hieden sin parar los cadáveres: el silencio que se escu-
cha cuando ha muerto el Sueño" (204). According to Estela, because twentieth-century Mexicans did not resolve the problems
of racial discrimination that tied them to the sixteenth century,
these conditions are destined to repeat themselves. Bitterly, she
refers to the death of the utopian dreams of an equitable society
while meditating upon a modern nation that mirrors the colonial
world where Hernando lived.

This impossibility of realizing heaven on earth becomes a
centerpiece in Estela's rendering of the failure of her generation
to imagine an inclusive and democratic future:

> No soñé, ni yo, ni mi generación, con un sueño que borrara la
> estructura suicida de nuestro pasado colonial. Yo reparo mi
> pena de la mejor manera: me aplico a traducir del latín al es-
> pañol el texto de un indio que mejor quedara de ser traducido
> al náhuatl, si éste se enseñara en las escuelas. No recibimos
> esa lección porque nosotros nos contentamos con vestirnos y
> con poner ante nuestros ojos sus artesanías, incluso diré que
> huarache al piso nos volvimos más ciegos, más sordos, más
> culpables. Merezco el silencio. (204)

Estela opts to take refuge in translating Hernando's manuscript from Latin to Spanish, addressing the need to recover the indigenous languages and cultures concealed from the mainstream by the colonization of memory.[30]

Throughout all three plots of *Cielos de la tierra*, Boullosa demonstrates how the problems of the present are deeply rooted in the past. In Estela's time, we see how the lack of respect for indigenous peoples goes hand in hand with a disregard for the natural world: "A los ojos de mi abuela, la naturaleza era inclemente, peligrosa y detestable. Nada como un patio con piso de cemento y bien limpio" (47). The aversion that Estela's grandmother has to nature anticipates an apocalyptic future in which humanity loses the ability to understand its place in the larger picture.[31] Ironically, this predilection for "civilization" will lead to the destruction of the planet: "Nunca pensó [mi abuela] que el hombre pudiera ser capaz de vencer la selva destruyéndola, y que al acabar con los bosques tropicales pusiera en riesgo el resto de la vida en el planeta" (47–48). Estela's words foreshadow the portrayal of the ecoapocalypse narrated in the fragments of the novel devoted to the character known as Lear.

Through the eyes of this anthropologist in contemporary Mexico City, Boullosa traces the effects of the colonization of memory initiated with the conquest of the New World and follows its repercussions to Mexico's present in which the exploitation of natural resources and the by-products of industrialization lead to ecological disaster. In the following section we will discuss how in the distant future, the dream of modernity and the use of technology have caused the complete destruction of humanity's habitat. Through the story of Lear, the problems of history and humankind's relation to the environment will reach a critical juncture such that the people of L'Atlàntide will suffer the total collapse of the ecosystem as well as the elimination of the human past as a source of knowledge.

Lear's Time: The Horrors of Reason and the Loss of Community in L'Atlàntide

The last narrative thread of *Cielos de la tierra* in chronological terms, the story of Lear, takes place in a postapocalyptic society called L'Atlàntide,[32] in which the suppression of history and

161

the abuse of the environment reach a critical climax. Through Lear's narration, Boullosa highlights the effects of the dependence on technology and the consequences of ignoring the teachings of history. As in the other two plots, in which the protagonists are dedicated to the preservation of knowledge from previous generations, Lear is an archaeologist who works for the Center for Advanced Studies, collecting the scarce remains of the written past in archives called *kestos* that are housed in an institute called the Museum of Man.[33] While conducting research, Lear finds Estela's document hidden in an old table from the Colegio de México, which she later translates into the language of L'Atlàntide, saving it from oblivion.

The world of the future is a mixed bag of surprises and disillusions as Lear recounts that because of their technological advances, the Atlántidos are practically immortal, having defeated old age as well as conquering all fatal illnesses. Furthermore, these superhuman beings have converted air into solid materials used to construct their dwellings.[34] They have erased national and cultural differences while creating each member of society as equal with the same talent and opportunities. However, contravening these portentous achievements, the Atlántidos have self-imposed a sort of historical amnesia that identifies language and history as the direct causes for the destruction of earth, as wars of ethnic cleansing have annihilated most of the population, destroying vegetation, polluting air and waters, and eliminating the possibilities of living on earth's surface for centuries to come.[35] These beliefs cause the community to lose its critical sensibility regarding literature and history both as means of humanizing society and as cautionary tales warning people to avoid repeating the mistakes of previous generations. While the other sections focus on the destruction of the pre-Columbian societies and the construction of modernity, Lear's story dramatizes the consequences of searching for perfection without valorizing the lessons of literature and history.

Lear depicts L'Atlàntide as a crystal sphere floating above the barren space of Earth constituting the last materialization of the mythical earthly paradise:

> Es nuestra casa el Paraíso Terrenal (como el del primer hombre y su primera mujer en la leyenda que retoma la Biblia), un paraíso sin vegetación, suspendido en el medio del cielo.

Vivimos en esta enorme esfera achatada y transparente, sin
paredes ni pisos visibles [. . .]. Y no tenemos cosas, no usa-
mos, no hacemos cosas. Solamente nos acompaña el agua.
(18)

Although these ethereal beings refer to their world as the realization of heaven on earth, this reference is rather paradoxical,
since the destruction of life on the planet's surface has forced
the Atlántidos to migrate to the clouds in order to avoid living
on the polluted ground: "Vivimos suspendidos en la atmósfera
de la Tierra, alejados de la superficie, evitando las radiaciones,
las ruinas, la destrucción, las tolvaneras y nubes tóxicas de las
tormentas" (16). This description of utopia does not coincide
with the harmonious and placid portrayal of the ideal worlds
imagined since classical times by philosophers and artists alike,
but rather the description of L'Atlàntide stands out for its som-
ber and depressing nature.

Besides discovering medical applications for their technological might, the Atlántidos find in science a substitute for
basic human activities. The narrator highlights how technology
replaces humanity at the most basic level, since human beings
are artificially engineered and reared inside a machine called
"the Cradle," which replicates the functions of the maternal
womb: "[La Cuna] [e]ra un lugar para sentir [. . .] tibia y móvil
[. . .] y nos abrazaba, nos envolvía, nos deglutía casi en su
masa de falsa carne, meciéndonos, arrullándonos incansable.
[. . .] Era un grandísimo cuerpo de madre, un cuerpo que nos
envolvía a cada uno de nosotros" (164). As in classic science
fiction novels, this futuristic society artificially controls human
reproduction.[36]

While the Cradle suffices as a substitute for the maternal
womb on the biological level, on the intellectual level, the Atlántidos are socialized and indoctrinated by another machine
known as the Image Receptor through which inhabitants of the
future society are programmed to receive a standardized notion
of identity, personal history, and their individual role in the
community. Thanks to this machine—similar to the media conglomerate depicted in Fuentes's *Cristóbal Nonato* and Aridjis's
"Circe of Communication"—the Atlántidos remedy some of
the most serious problems that hinder contemporary society,
since the Image Receptor erases racial and ethnic differences:

"Aquí no cuenta la 'raza,' porque todos somos de una distinta, y porque, auxiliados por el Receptor de Imágenes, los hombres que hicieron a los sobrevivientes crearon en cada uno de nosotros un protagonista igualmente meritorio de belleza y respeto" (108). Thus, the Atlántidos have forcibly eliminated the discrimination that we saw in the Mexican past and present. Nevertheless, this homogenization of humanity creates additional problems, since the community is not able to appreciate cultural difference, opting instead for uniformity and conformity, resulting in the alienation of the individual.

Through the representation of machines such as the Cradle and the Image Receptor, Boullosa underscores how in this postindustrial world, where the relation of humankind with its biological and cultural surroundings has been modified, humans nevertheless depend on machines in order to survive. Problematically, through these devices, the Atlántidos rewrite their history, avoiding any mention of earth, humanity, and the historical circumstances that have led to the massive destruction of the planet:

> Durante La Conformación, nos transmitieron en el Receptor un sinnúmero de imágenes de nosotros mismos, como éramos ya y cómo se podía conjeturar seríamos de adultos. Estas imágenes fueron fijas y móviles, planas y de tres dimensiones. En ellas se nos vio junto a los más dispares paisajes, visitando lugares de la Tierra con la apariencia que tuvieron antes de ser destrozados por el hombre de la Historia. (108)

The series of pictures projected by the Image Receptor evades the painful memories of the earth's destruction,[37] but in doing so renders the community unable to learn from the mistakes of their predecessors.

Through the systematic erasure of the past, the Atlántidos have been conditioned to forge a new genealogy, distancing themselves from what they call the "man of History":

> En las imágenes no había huella de la Humanidad ni de su voracidad y su deseo de destrucción, ni de la tontería que terminó por conducir a su aniquilación y al desastre que azotó la Tierra. En ellas no se sabía que el hombre había maltratado a la Naturaleza, ni que un día había ardido la atmósfera.

> Las imágenes fueron creadas por los hombres que hicieron
> posibles a los sobrevivientes, y no *tenían nada que ver con
> la realidad.* Yo me vi [. . .] y vi a la Tierra sin huella de la
> destrucción cuando ella no era ya sino un páramo devastado,
> poblado solamente por los desechos y el viento iracundo y
> sucio. (110; emphasis mine)

This revisionist past implanted in the newborns by their creators
does away with all notions of historical knowledge, as it reflects
the reasons for the nuclear holocaust that destroyed Earth.
Furthermore, Lear identifies the artificiality of these images in
that, like Fuentes's mass media and Aridjis's Circe as well as
turn-of-the-century "reality shows," they do not reflect the way
people really live, but rather, project distorted fantasies of an
idealized society, while the world around them crumbles from
the neglect of the natural environment.

The Atlántidos censure humankind's obsession with consumer goods, identifying it as the primary cause for the ecoapocalypse. In grotesque fashion, the sole monument to the
"man of History" is a pile of debris:

> La relación del hombre con la materia trabajada por él, alte-
> rada por él, devino sólo en una sucesión de equívocos. [. . .]
> [P]ongo mis ojos en la montaña artificial que hicimos los
> atlántidos (macabro monumento al amor que los hombres
> tuvieron por las cosas), cuando acabábamos de fundar nuestra
> colonia. Esa montaña artificial está hecha de fragmentos de
> cosas de plástico, pañales desechables, bolsas, empaques, apa-
> ratos eléctricos o electrónicos, muebles, ropas, etcétera. (24)

As in Fuentes's *Cristóbal Nonato,* where Acapulco is overwhelmed by cereal boxes and hamburger wrappers while the
inhabitants of utopian Pacífica have transcended hyperconsumption, the minimalist Atlántidos have come to deplore the
senseless overproduction of goods. The fact that the Atlántidos
have reduced humanity's heritage to nothing more than a mountain of garbage underscores contemporary concerns with the
neoliberal model of development that Latin American countries
have pursued at the cost of the environment and indigenous
societies.

Lear points to how the Atlántidos hopelessly work to recover
nature from the ruins of humankind:

> [M]is ojos no pueden admirar la rama de un árbol, una flor, siquiera una hoja, porque en los lugares donde los escombros me esconden tesoros no queda nada de eso. Existen los jardines que los sobrevivientes hemos cultivado con las semillas o la memoria de los despojos que cosechamos de la destrucción. (24)

Thus, where in the previous section we saw how Estela's grandmother cherished the superposition of "civilization" over nature, here we see the effects of these values in the long run, as the world of the future has been destroyed in part by the abuse of technology.

One of the most notorious aspects of this apocalyptic culture is the lack of reference to the origin of L'Atlàntide, in a compulsive effort to distance this society from the deeds of the "man of History":

> Decir L'Atlàntide es una invocación al tiempo de la Historia. Es cierto que ya nadie menciona de dónde proviene nuestro nombre. Nadie se acuerda del continente sumergido en el mar, ni de su huerto de naranjas de oro [. . .]. Nadie habla tampoco de quiénes soñaron con La Atlántida, de quién la describió, de quién aseguró haberla visto. *Quieren enterrar la memoria de los que nos precedieron, explicando que todos sus actos y conocimientos orillaron a la destrucción, y que los sobrevivientes debemos rehuirla.* (19; emphasis mine)

The inhabitants of L'Atlàntide thus live literally in the air, above the desolate planet that stands as a constant reminder of the mistakes of their predecessors. They even avoid historicizing their own myths of origin, which would connect them to the "man of History."

As in the other plots, in the story of L'Atlàntide Boullosa underscores the strong connection of the narrator with the recollection, transcription, and communication of written history. In this order of things, Lear is the only member of her community concerned with recovering, classifying, and documenting all surviving information about the past, whether it be literature or history. Lear's interest in memory, language, identity, and individuality distinguishes her from the rest of the members of her community who—like the inhabitants of the dystopian society described in Zamyatin's *We*—use numbers to identify themselves. As an act of rebellion, she chooses her own name and names some of her fellow citizens. This act of rebellion against the dehumanizing culture of L'Atlàntide expresses her keen sense of the role of history and memory. Significantly, Lear's profession as an archaeologist emphasizes a personal quest in which she attempts to salvage the past for future generations: "[P]orque con mis estudios vuelvo a nuestros padres, los reconstruyo. Con mi trabajo, urgo [*sic*] en nuestros orígenes, en el tiempo de la Historia" (15).

While the Atlántidos attempt to revive nature in their own version of the Garden of Eden, Lear is committed to establishing a dialogue with history to reconstruct human civilization and recover the past:

> Dicen que es sólo necedad innecesaria batir mis pies entre ruinas cuando hemos conseguido alzar de la yerma tierra paraísos "donde parece no haber llegado la mano del hombre," recintos artificiales que imitan lo que un día fue Naturaleza. ¿Han creado un jardín donde pasean evas y adanes inmaculados, sin haber aún pecado, porque no han reconstruido a su serpiente? (24–25)

Facing the scorn of her fellow citizens, Lear denounces the futility of re-creating the earthly paradise without understanding the historical circumstances that led to the annihilation of humanity and its habitat. The archaeologist hones in on the need to incorporate history to save the community from repeating the same mistakes that led to nature's destruction, while her peers occupy themselves in going forward with their notion of utopian perfection, excluding any knowledge of history and ultimately eliminating language altogether.

Within her culture, Lear stands out, since she tries to see in the actions of the past a lesson for the future, while her fellow Atlántidos are only interested in the present without grounding it in historical understanding: "Mientras me inclino hacia el pasado, los demás habitantes de L'Atlàntide se empinan hacia un presente perpetuo y se utilizan para reconstruir lo que los hombres de la Historia se empeñaron en destruir, la sublime Naturaleza. Yo sí recuerdo al hombre de la Historia, y dialogo con él. A él es a quien le explico [sobre L'Atlàntide]" (16). For the Atlántidos, man's creations seem unworthy and dangerous, since they incubated the chain reaction that ultimately destroyed life on Earth. While Lear's colleagues embark on the design of a means for rescuing nature, this enterprise is rather contradictory, for the Atlántidos save the smell of the orange and the color of the banana but do not pay attention to their own society and to their loss of the ability to communicate with each other.

In her fragments, Lear narrates how her community embarks on a gradual disintegration of its means of communication. She observes that the Atlántidos' efforts to erase the past lead into chaos, as the denial of history implies the elimination of the notion of culture and identity:

> De ser verdad, como se piensa ahora en L'Atlàntide, que sólo debemos atender al presente y al futuro, que es una necesidad imperiosa olvidar el pasado porque fue únicamente lección de errores, porque en él se edificó la destrucción de la Naturaleza, si fuera cierto, como se dice, que sólo hay que poner el entendimiento en el presente y en el futuro, si fuera esto verdad y se practicara rigurosamente, como lo piden, al borrar el pasado, Tiempo, o lo que conocemos como tal, se disolvería. Flotaríamos en una masa amorfa donde Tiempo no tendría cabida. (18)

As in Bradbury's *Fahrenheit 451* where books are burned systematically, the Atlántidos ban history, considering it dangerous, thus preempting the possibility of learning from the mistakes of previous generations.[38] Lear's warning about the future of life without the notion of time foreshadows the debacle of the Atlántidos who, like Icarus from the Greek legend, fall victim to their own utopian aspirations to soar above the earth. In an attempt to control imagination, the Image Receptor edits out the master narratives of Western civilization: "Pero ni domamos el fuego, ni vencimos un dragón, ni cortamos la cabeza de la Gorgona, ni arrojamos la piedra a Goliat, ni Pegaso nos subió en su lomo" (109). While the inhabitants of the future world rewrite the past with the intent of avoiding the horrendous mistakes that caused the end of life on Earth, this erasure of memory also obliterates the critical capacity of the Atlántidos, ironically condemning them to repeat the mistakes that annihilated humankind.

In spite of being successful in technological matters, the Atlántidos face severe problems, as the future of their civilization is uncertain because of the lack of space and resources in the crystal-like sphere. One afternoon while coming back from her daily walk, Lear finds a fellow Atlántido hiding a small child in a cave that was fashioned by the nuclear blasts that destroyed Earth. In its interior, Lear discovers that the Atlántidos practice infanticide in order to preserve the scarce resources for their survival. She graphically describes how dead babies are piled one on top of another to save space, foreshadowing the end of humanity. After this disturbing discovery, Lear recognizes that her species has few alternatives for survival, since there are no more children to educate and the adults of L'Atlàntide are not interested in preserving their culture: "Pero aunque el tiempo transcurra, no habrá hijos, ni quién intente explicarse lo que fuimos, porque nosotros siempre seremos, y no tendremos descendencia, no gestaremos descendientes, nadie nos suplirá sobre la faz de la Tierra" (184). Lear comes to the realization that her community will have to live in a perpetual present where the human stages of birth, growth, maturation, and death have ceased to exist as a result of the scientific advances that perpetuate their lives. In this way, Lear underscores the loss of the meaning of life, ironically caused by the advance of technology.

The ultimate downfall of the Atlántidos comes from an unregulated desire to realize the utopia of perfection. In order to complete the erasure of their past, the Atlántidos endeavor to eliminate language altogether, as explained by a fellow citizen who tries to dissuade Lear from speaking: "Entiende que sólo sin lenguaje, sin gramática, podremos fundar un hombre nuevo, uno que no hable del dañino bicho que con ese mismo nombre destruyó la Tierra" (117). In order to achieve this purpose they self-impose what they call Language Reform, which consists of different measures ranging from the elimination of writing to the final eradication of all communication, through such radical procedures as the performance of voluntary lobotomies.[39] At first, they replace verbal exchange with a series of codes discernible only to the forty-two members of the society, but as time goes by, each member ends up creating his or her own code, leading to a complete lack of communication and ultimately chaos.

This Language Reform movement resembles the gradual process of linguistic substitution represented in George Orwell's

Nineteen Eighty-Four in which new dictionaries of "Newspeak" are continually produced in order to revise history and modify public opinion. In *Cielos de la tierra*, the reorganization of communication causes the demise of imagination, which leads to the Atlántidos' incapacity to imagine the future, since there is nothing to guide them in their decision-making. Atavistically, the ultimate inheritors of humanity, who had managed to defeat problems of racial discrimination, illness, and even death, have regressed, thereby leading them to meet their own end.

Boullosa presents us with the irony that the most technologically advanced society sees the annihilation of its own culture because of its desire to reach perfection. The utopian society tries to reinvent its own cultural tradition by abolishing the past, leading to undesired results, as the community from this point on begins to descend into anarchy and barbarism.[40] Lear's pessimism regarding the future is clearly stated as she loses all hope of saving her community: "Creo que hemos perdido por completo. Su reforma del lenguaje, la insistencia en el olvido, nos ha borrado. No somos nada ya. He perdido toda esperanza de que volvamos al tiempo del Tiempo" (322). As a result of the Language Reform and the elimination of writing, the cultural identity of the Atlántidos begins to disappear.

Like Hernando's fragments, in which the colonization of memory amounts to the erasure of the indigenous cultures, Lear's story emphasizes how this self-imposed eradication of history and language brings about the final destruction of the remains of human society. In a series of interconnected events, the narrator describes the effects of the loss of communication on the Atlántidos who enter a descending spiral, only to find themselves reduced to prior stages of human development. Lear depicts how the Atlántidos perform acts associated with the alterity attributed to native cultures under colonization, as she describes them engaging in bestiality, sodomy, and finally cannibalism. Ultimately, the Atlántidos are reduced to less than animals when they turn to anthropophagy: "Comen chicos, qué horror, son unos cerdos. Mis divinos atlántidos, que algún día alcanzaron un estado de perfección que rebasaba cualquier sueño humano, al borrar de sus personas la palabra han devenido en cerdos, comedores de carne de bebecitos muertos" (277). Thus, the former proud "owners of the air" descend into the most barbarous condition as they transform themselves into cannibals, obliterating traces of their own humanity.[41] While the discourse of modernity imposed an optimistic notion of endless progress, based on the confidence of human development aided by machines and an assembly line mentality, the last community regresses to a pre-human state.

Importantly, as Lear recognizes the degeneration of her fellow Atlántidos, she also realizes that she is the last specimen of humanity:

> Soy el último ser humano que resta sobre la Tierra. Los atlántidos no son ya hijos del hombre y de la mujer. Ahora son lo que desearon, los hijos de sí mismos. Los seres sin dioses, sin padres, sin lenguaje, sin tierra, sin Natura, sin tiempo, sin dolor, sin sentido. (306)

From this point forward, Lear decides not to continue to struggle against the debacle of her society and, like Hernando and Estela, she opts to write the memories of her community as a way to escape the present by entering into the province of history: "No puedo permanecer ya con mi comunidad. Voy a intentar brincarme al territorio que puedo compartir con Estela y con Hernando, volverme de palabras" (368).

As a last resort, Lear has chosen to seek in the written word the only possibility for transcendence:

> Los tres perteneceremos a tres distintos tiempos, nuestras memorias serán de tres distintas épocas, pero [. . .] ganaremos un espacio común en el que nos miraremos a los ojos y formaremos una nueva comunidad. La nuestra se llamará *Los cielos de la Tierra*. L'Atlàntide pertenecerá al pasado, como la vieja Tenochtitlan, como el México de Hernando y el país de Estela. (369)

Curiously, Lear conceives of an imaginary community in which the past, the present, and the future establish a dialogue and invent an alternative destiny for humanity. Ironically, while Lear decides to write her own history, it is not clear who is going to benefit from reading of the Atlántidos' demented efforts to reach perfection without weighing the lessons of past generations.

Sadly, Lear shows that when the Atlántidos had overcome the problems that had vexed terrestrial culture, ironically their own desire to perfect their community through the erasure of the past ends up destroying their society:

> Ah mis bellos. Todo lo hemos perdido. En la última comunidad de hombres y mujeres, todos fueron iguales, nadie hizo menos al otro por razón de raza, sexo o apariencia. Nadie fue rico ni pobre, poderoso o esclavo. Se vivió en armonía, se venció la enfermedad, la vejez y la muerte. En esa comunidad idílica que pudo ser eterna, *el horror al pasado impuso la destrucción de la especie.* (362; emphasis mine)

Boullosa's critique of the erasure of history is crucial, since all three of the narrative threads point to how the annihilation of systems of knowledge and memory have devastating effects on the future of humanity.

By tracing the potential end results of the advancement of capitalism through industrialization, *Cielos de la tierra* questions the legitimacy of Mexico's entrance into the global market system, showing the possible costs on both human and cultural levels. Through the depiction of three utopias that have failed to understand the value of language, history, and culture, in *Cielos de la tierra* Boullosa questions the present model of development for Mexico during the late 1990s when the negotiations for a reaffirmation of the NAFTA treaty were taking place. The superhuman Atlántidos choose voluntarily to delete humankind's history from their own, creating a paradoxical situation, since their unwillingness to attend to the lessons of history leads to the destruction of their presumably perfect society. Hence, in a similar operation to what we saw as the colonization of memory, in which the indigenous past is eclipsed by the hegemonic imposition of modernity, the Atlántidos attempt to eliminate history altogether with devastating consequences. While the rhetoric of modernization has been linked to the notion of limitless progress, the disturbing end of Boullosa's novel suggests that if achieved, globalization may be more disastrous than the original situation of underdevelopment that it was supposed to remedy. While the pessimistic end of Boullosa's dystopia signals the end of humankind, it does not mean the end of all creation, since new organisms crawl on the sandy beaches of Earth symbolizing that humanity was just another species in the long history of the planet, and sadly, the only one capable of destroying it.

In the final chapter, the ecoapocalypse of Homero Aridjis's novels *Leyenda de los soles* and *¿En quién piensas cuando haces el amor?* offers a dystopian view of Mexico's future utilizing the science fiction mode to attract attention to the deleterious effects of industrialization on the environment in Mexico and around the globe. In contrast to Boullosa's *Cielos de la tierra*, Aridjis's novels have more hopeful endings, implicitly proposing the reform of the project of modernity in Mexico by calling for a direct involvement of the citizenry of all races and both genders in the creation of a more democratic and ecologically conscious future.

Chapter Four

Surviving the Ecoapocalypse in Homero Aridjis's *La leyenda de los soles* and *¿En quién piensas cuando haces el amor?*

> If they give you ruled paper,
> write the other way.
>
> Juan Ramón Jiménez,
> epigraph to Ray Bradbury's *Fahrenheit 451*

While in the previous chapters, we read how Morales's *The Rag Doll Plagues* and Carmen Boullosa's *Cielos de la tierra* trace a pattern of racial exclusion and ecological devastation of nature in three different time periods, in Homero Aridjis's novels, we see the environmental and human cost of industrialization in Mexico City in a single time frame, a hypothetical 2027. While Latin American officials and intellectuals were debating the implications of the then upcoming Quincentenary of the Discovery of America, in the late 1980s and into the 1990s, the Mexican author published several literary works dealing with the ramifications of colonial contact for the project of nation in Mexico.[1] Aridjis began with the historical novels *1492: vida y tiempos de Juan Cabezón de Castilla* (*1492: The Life and Times of Juan Cabezón of Castile*, 1985) and *Memorias del Nuevo Mundo* (Memories of the New World, 1988), in which the past is rewritten through the lens of the present. He further explores transhistorical themes in *La leyenda de los soles* (Legend of the Suns, 1993) and *¿En quién piensas cuando haces el amor?* (Who Do You Think of When Making Love?, 1996),[2] this time utilizing the powerful imagery provided by the science fiction genre to present a playful combination of popular culture and ecological criticism in order to project a disfigured image of Mexico one generation into the future. These latter two novels underscore the capacity of dystopian writing to criticize the present environmental deterioration and social stratification of

Mexican society, while suggesting alternative possibilities for the future. Building on Carlos Fuentes's depiction of the capital in *Cristóbal Nonato*, both of Aridjis's futuristic novels center on Mexico City in the early twenty-first century when the deplorable living conditions have been further exacerbated by the effects of ill-planned development, massive migration from the countryside, and an autocratic government, turning the Mexican capital into an apocalyptic nightmare. Most originally, in these two novels, the author uses the Aztec myth of the Fifth Sun as a metaphor for the devastating effects of industrialization, poorly planned growth, and political corruption, symbolizing the crisis of Mexican modernity.

Both *La leyenda de los soles* and *¿En quién piensas cuando haces el amor?* find in the Mesoamerican myth of the Fifth Sun their inspiration for describing the effects of rapid modernization on contemporary Mexico, thus linking the past with the future in creative fashion. The title of the former novel links it to the historical *Leyenda de los soles* (also known as the Chimalpopoca Codex), a colonial document written by an anonymous scribe working in the College of Santa Cruz de Tlatelolco, under the direction of fray Bernardino de Sahagún.[3] According to the surviving accounts, at the time when the Spanish conquistadors arrived in the Valley of Mexico, the Aztecs believed they were living in the fifth era of creation (the Fifth Sun) and that four previous suns had been destroyed. They believed that Omehtecuhtli, the original creative duality, unfolded in forces representative of the four elements, earth, air, fire, and water, and that each in turn had created its own respective sun. The First Sun's inhabitants were giants, and their era ended when ocelots devoured those who lived under its sign. The Second Sun was destroyed by wind, and its people were turned into monkeys. The Third Sun ended engulfed in fiery rain and volcanic eruptions, and its inhabitants turned into butterflies, dogs, and turkeys. The Fourth Sun was destroyed by floods, and those who lived during this time became fish. Lastly, the Fifth Sun differentiates itself from the other four in that it represents cosmic balance because no single element predominates. According to the Aztec cosmovision, for every sun destroyed, a new one, better equipped and stronger, emerged until the era of the Fifth Sun.

Nevertheless, the Aztecs held that the Fifth Sun was marked for destruction as well, this time by earthquakes and famine, and just as in the case of the previous four, after its destruction, a new, stronger sun would emerge. According to Enrique Dussel, the Aztecs believed that the arrival of the Spaniards and the conquest of Mesoamerica constituted the realization of the predicted end of the Fifth Sun: "The Aztecs [. . .] had anticipated their own tragic dénouement when the very arrival of the strangers under Cortés's authority evoked terror and weeping. Almost from the start, they interpreted these events as foreboding the end of the world and the fifth sun" (109). For the Amerindian communities, colonization also marked the beginning of a period of enslavement that continues until today. Nevertheless, the Aztec interpretation of the end of the Fifth Sun also encompasses the hopeful belief in a Sixth Sun that would deliver the indigenous population from the slavery and oppression that ensued upon the conquest of their territories (Dussel 109).

The oral tradition of the Fifth Sun had an important role in the Aztec calendar, since in order to avoid the end of the world, every fifty-two years throughout the Valley of Mexico all fires were extinguished and the people made a pilgrimage to Teotihuacan to take part in a ceremony to renew the fire.[4] It was believed that if the fire were not re-ignited, the *tzitzimime* (night demons) would come from above and devour men and women, marking the return of Tezcatlipoca, god of the First Sun.[5] Since the time of Tlacaelel, one of the most important statesmen of the Aztec empire, blood sacrifices in honor of the sun—especially the offering of the human heart—formed an important ceremony to ritualize and legitimize authority. As scholar Miguel León-Portilla observes: "El sacrificio y la guerra florida, que es el medio principal de obtener víctimas para mantener la vida del Sol, fueron sus ocupaciones centrales, el eje de su vida personal, social, militar, y nacional" (*La filosofía náhuatl* 126). Significantly, Aridjis's two apocalyptic novels, *La leyenda de los soles* and its sequel *¿En quién piensas cuando haces el amor?*, establish a correlation between the Mesoamerican myth of origin and the present conditions of material and moral decay that afflict contemporary Mexican society. Aridjis employs this legend to question the Western myth of unlimited progress through global industrialization, presenting a vision of how, paradoxically, the reliance on technology along with political corruption brings about the end of Western modernity in Mexico in the first decades of the new millennium. In this inquiry into the future, Aridjis incorporates the Aztec version of the apocalypse as a warning, parodying the Mexican nation's traditionally solemn appropriation of the indigenous past, which has served as one of the main strategies of legitimization since the early stages of the modernizing project, amply used by the regimes following the Mexican Revolution.

In order to offer an articulate criticism of the potential effects of industrial growth and to speculate on Latin America's current pattern of development, Aridjis presents us with two novels that employ an ecocritical view of Mexican society. *La leyenda de los soles* is composed of forty short chapters in which two different but interconnected plots are developed by an omniscient third-person narrator: the revival and return to power of the Aztec gods of war and pestilence; and the hunt for El Tláloc, "the messenger of the dawn," a mysterious kidnapper.[6] *La leyenda de los soles* begins with the resurrection of the ancient sorcerer and god of betrayal, Tezcatlipoca,[7] and ends with his death at the hands of the police as they discover that he is the mysterious perpetrator of the rape and murder of young girls. The action of this novel and that of its sequel occur simultaneously, beginning a few days before the earthquake that announces the demise of the Fifth Sun. The sequel, *¿En quién piensas cuando haces el amor?*, is composed of thirty-nine chapters centered on the life of the first-person narrator Yo Sánchez. As in *La leyenda de los soles*, this novel narrates the story of the protagonist against the backdrop of the natural and man-made destruction of the planet in the year 2027.

The action of *La leyenda de los soles* begins with the resurrection of Mexico City's Chief of Police General Carlos Tezcatlipoca after his death in a car accident. Following this character's revival, the novel introduces Juan de Góngora, a painter who depicts life in the early twenty-first century, and his friend Bernarda Ramírez, a photographer whose daughter, Ana Violeta, has been kidnapped by the mysterious Tláloc. Intertwined with their search, Aridjis introduces the Aztec *tlacuilo*,[8] Cristóbal Cuauhtli, who in science fiction fashion has traveled through time to entrust Juan with the recovery of the last page of a sixteenth-century manuscript entitled *Codex of the Suns*, which was stolen by General Tezcatlipoca.[9] Cristóbal warns Juan that if Tezcatlipoca retains the manuscript, the future of Mexico will involve the return of senseless violence and human sacrifice. But if Juan is successful in recovering the missing page, then the Sixth Sun will be the Sun of Nature, overseen by the Blue Goddess, implying a return to a harmonious relationship between humans and the environment as well as the possibility of avoiding a complete Mexican apocalypse. In *La leyenda de los soles*, the quest for the manuscript and the search for Ana Violeta serve as the pretext for Aridjis's examination of Mexico's projected post-NAFTA future, a future in which political corruption and the destruction of nature have called into question the goals of global industrialization.

Critiquing the Western notion of progress, Aridjis portrays Mexico City in dramatic terms as a sick society in the midst of an ecological apocalypse where global warming, acid rain, and severe drought hinder the growth of any natural life in the megalopolis, while the population explosion and the automatization of modernity promote alienation, anxiety, and insecurity. In search of the kidnapped Ana Violeta, our characters travel across diverse areas of Mexico City, visiting fictitious cities such as the nearby Moctezuma City and encountering along the way a cross section of Mexican society living in hopeless conditions. One day, Cristóbal and Juan penetrate General Tezcatlipoca's estate in an attempt to steal back the missing page of the *Codex of the Suns*, but they are discovered by the guards, who kill the Aztec sage. These ventures serve as the main plots, but the narrative is ultimately subordinated to the discussion of the ecological damage of Mexico and the moral degradation of its people in the year 2027, that is, one generation after the signing of NAFTA.

As in Fuentes's *Cristóbal Nonato,* Aridjis's novels identify the actions of corrupt public functionaries as one of the most imposing hurdles impeding the realization of Mexican modernity. In addition, in *La leyenda de los soles* and *¿En quién piensas?,* we see the irreverent conflation of characters based on Aztec mythology with political figures from the recent past such as José López Portillo and Carlos Salinas de Gortari, presidents of Mexico during 1976–82 and 1988–94, respectively, periods of economic and political crisis. In Aridjis's satirical novels, these historical figures are personified by the fictional President José Huitzilopochtli Urbina, who leads the corrupt PUR (Only Party of the Revolution)—also referred to as the Only Party of Corruption—a parody of the historical PRI, and General Carlos Tezcatlipoca, who is Mexico City's cruel and corrupt chief of police.[10]

As the reincarnation of the Aztec god of violence and pestilence, General Tezcatlipoca keeps a tight control over the city with the help of the "*nacotecas*," a merciless horde of sectarians who assault and murder civilians, imposing a reign of terror.[11] Characterized by an equally abusive nature, President Huitzilopochtli Urbina, the reincarnation of the Aztecs' principal deity, constitutes an antipode of democratic principles of government.[12] These two formidable figures rule the country through fear and force, particularly directed against the young women of Mexico City. In order to dramatize the extreme violence against nature's creatures, Aridjis portrays General Tezcatlipoca killing endangered species as well as his own sister, Natalia, who lives in one of the last natural refuges in the Desierto de los Leones. As in Aztec history, in which the two gods battle for political supremacy, in Aridjis's version of the future, General Tezcatlipoca eliminates President Huitzilopochtli, only to be killed himself soon afterwards. With the death of both corrupt politicians, there is a revival of Aztec gods of life and death such as Coatlicue and Toci,[13] the goddesses of earth renewal, and Xipe Tótec, the god of spring and agriculture, as well as the abominable night demons, or *tzitzimime*, who announce the destruction of the Fifth Sun.

Aridjis calls attention to the dictatorial quality of Mexican political life, restaging the 1968 Tlatelolco massacre, in which, as discussed above, hundreds of protesters were killed by government forces. In *La leyenda de los soles*, when anonymous masses celebrate the end of the Fifth Sun and the rebirth of pre-Hispanic Mexico while marching over the fallen ruins of the capital, General Tezcatlipoca orders the *nacotecas* to fire against the crowd. In the middle of the massacre, as was predicted in the novel's fictitious *Codex of the Suns*, a massive earthquake—resembling the one that occurred in reality in September 1985—strikes Mexico City, aggravating the already apocalyptic circumstances. During the upheaval, General

Tezcatlipoca is killed while resisting arrest, after being found to be Tláloc, the author of the kidnappings and murders who had terrorized young women in Mexico and Moctezuma City. At the end of *La leyenda de los soles*, Juan and Bernarda are able to escape death at the hands of the *nacotecas* and flee the destroyed capital toward the neighboring state of Michoacán. A new era is born under the auspices of the Blue Goddess, deity of the environment, thus auguring an optimistic future for Mexico with the possibilities of a renewal of both human and natural order.

In *¿En quién piensas cuando haces el amor?*, Aridjis continues his exposition of the maladies of Mexican society—ecological decay, social fragmentation, and political corruption—in the same year of 2027. In addition, through the narrator Yo Sánchez, an Amazon-like figure who is distinguished from the rest of the population because of her extraordinary height, Aridjis builds on the theme of the subordination of women in Mexican society. Along with Yo, Aridjis introduces a series of other female characters who resist the ecological and moral apocalypse, including a middle-aged actress named Arira, a performer in Moctezuma City's National Theater Company; Arira's sister María; and a former schoolteacher named Facunda. As the novel begins, María's twin, Rosalba, has just died, and Yo, Arira, María, and Facunda cross the city on foot from the cemetery to Arira's house in Moctezuma City.[14] These four characters wander around the capital describing the human and material decadence of the metropolis. While violence against women formed one of the central themes of *La leyenda de los soles*, in this novel, the author expands his analysis of Mexico's systematic gender oppression while at the same time expressing more hope for the future by representing his female protagonists as more empowered than the women in his previous novel. Although in *Leyenda* we also see women represented as environmentally conscious, in *¿En quién piensas?*, Aridjis emphasizes how this sector of society holds answers for a more inclusive and egalitarian project of modernity, thus taking the question of the relationship between women and the environment to the level of a coherent ecofeminist political project.

As in *La leyenda de los soles*, the action of *¿En quién piensas cuando haces el amor?* occurs in the days preceding the earthquakes announcing the end of the Fifth Sun, and references are made to some of the same characters and events as in the previous novel, such as the felonies perpetrated by politicians Carlos Tezcatlipoca and José Huitzilopochtli. In this sequel, Aridjis further develops the theme of political corruption in the figure of Moctezuma City's Mayor Agustín Ek, who like President Huitzilopochtli and General Tezcatlipoca abuses his influence to line his pockets. Mayor Ek acts in the name of economic progress without consideration for the ecological impact of his numerous business endeavors; among other things, he owns pharmacies and crematoria that not only take advantage of human tragedy in the megalopolis but also contribute significantly to the already excessive air pollution. Through characters such as these, Aridjis depicts unscrupulous public officials who are less interested in improving their society than in maintaining control of the population by any means, from the use of mass media and the imposition of a culture of terror to widespread violent repression.

In *¿En quién piensas cuando haces el amor?*, the characters' odyssey through the decadent capital becomes the background for the description of the deplorable conditions of the urban environment in the early twenty-first century. Along with the criticism of the city as an ecological and human nightmare, the narrator details the strategies for survival devised by the female protagonists amidst the chaos of an unpredictable future. As Yo Sánchez perambulates through the capital with her friends, she gradually relates her life story in this first-person narrative. After losing her father, Yo narrates, in flashbacks, how she finds a position as a lighting technician at Moctezuma City's National Theater Company, after escaping the harassment of her stepmother and stepbrother. While working at the theater, she establishes a solid friendship with the famous actress Arira, her sister María, and her coworker Facunda. After moving into Arira's house with the three women, Yo searches for a companion and meets Baltazar, a tall and enigmatic character who only appears after an earthquake or an accident has struck the city. In spite of the uncertain future, Yo and Baltazar fall in love and dance to the tune of the bolero "¿En quién piensas cuando haces el amor?" which becomes their song. Therefore, like Fuentes in *Cristóbal Nonato*, Aridjis stakes the future of society on a regeneration of both the human and cultural landscape of Mexico in 2027.

Amidst the moral disintegration of social and familial structures, Yo finds companionship with her friends on their trek through the nightmarish metropolitan area. With graphic descriptions, Yo narrates the lives of our characters as they traverse areas of Moctezuma City where young boys and girls are sexually exploited, demonstrating a world that holds little respect for human dignity, and neither safeguards its youth nor provides them with an education to prepare them for facing the challenges of the future. Exemplifying the dramatic scale of political corruption, Yo reveals that even the authorities that are charged with protecting the nation's youth are the first to take advantage of them. Furthermore, as in *La leyenda de los soles* where Aridjis denounces the climate of violence against women in the capital, in this sequel the narrator emphasizes how the state contributes to the fragile conditions of urban security while also exploiting the powerless. The city of the future becomes a crude spectacle of perdition; as in Fuentes's *Cristóbal Nonato*, in Aridjis's two novels mass media is shown to foster the desensitization of human beings with its constant bombardment of televised images that transform the viewers into automatons and ultimately into unthinking beasts. In spite of all these circumstances, Aridjis's strong characters defy the politics of fear, offering a vision of self-reliance and mutual support to counter unethical and inefficient governmental entities and practices.

In a fashion similar to *Cristóbal Nonato*, where the protagonists are presented with the opportunity to leave the decadent "Makesicko City" and "Acapulcalypse" for the utopian Pacífica, in *¿En quién piensas?*, Baltazar asks Yo to accompany him to the paradisiacal island of Antigua in order to escape the hellish dwellings of Moctezuma City. Nevertheless, like Fuentes's Ángel and Ángeles Palomar, Yo refuses to abandon the capital and chooses to weather the havoc of the city and the constant tremors that shake its foundations. Yo's decision to remain in the country highlights the hope and confidence in the future of the residents of the capital to resolve the economic and cultural roots that have led to the ecoapocalypse. As in the previous novel, at the end of *¿En quién piensas?*, a massive earthquake hits Moctezuma City but instead of signifying the annihilation of human civilization, it symbolizes the beginning of an alternative, balanced way of life, where nature and humanity can live together in harmony, again invoking the promise of the Aztec myth of renewal through destruction. Happily, as in *La leyenda de los soles,* Aridjis closes his sequel with a sense of new beginning and a possible rebirth of nature and nation as Baltazar and Yo rejoin forces, opting to build a new life atop the recent ruins of Moctezuma City.

In the following pages, we will discuss how in *Leyenda* and *¿En quién piensas?* Aridjis questions the utopian ideal of the city as an emblem of modern life by depicting the ecological damage and decline of standards of living in the Mexican capital; following this, we will engage the representation of modern government in which the state through violent force and the use of mass media contributes to the degeneration of the country; and finally, we will address how women become a key component of what Aridjis calls a biosophical principle, that is, "un código de conducta responsable para vivir en armonía con la Tierra y con las criaturas que habitan en ella" (*Apocalipsis* 354). As will be apparent in the following discussion, his representation of female characters as positive forces of ecological consciousness positions Aridjis at the center of ecofeminist debates that aim to deconstruct the traditional patriarchal paradigm of women that uncritically associates women with nature.

Industrialization, Hyperconsumption, and Ecocide

As Tom Moylan proposes in *Scraps of the Untainted Sky,* "Dystopia's foremost truth lies in its ability to reflect upon the causes of social and ecological evil as systemic. Its very textual machinery invites the creation of alternative worlds in which the historical space-time of the author can be re-presented in a way that foregrounds the articulation of its economic, political and cultural dimensions" (xii). The narrative frame of dystopia opens up the possibility for exploring the roots of the conditions of contemporary living by identifying the persistence of sociopolitical problems as structural. The excesses of the metropolitan nightmare depicted in Aridjis's novels allow for the discussion of specific limitations of Mexican modernity. The two narratives examined here combine the Aztec notion of the end of the Fifth Sun with the political and environmental issues prevailing at the turn of the millennium, expressing concern for the erosion of the project of modernity and its effect on the cultural, political, environmental, and economic fabric of Mexican society.

The themes of globalization, environmental pollution, and the future of humanity, expressed in Aridjis's previous poetic and prose works, take a definitive step forward in *La leyenda de los soles* and its sequel. These novels also continue the apocalyptic images of ecological damage on both the regional and national levels presented in the previous decade by Fuentes's *Cristóbal Nonato*. Moving to a global scale, Aridjis portrays the destruction of the earth's atmosphere in a hypothetical year 2027 due to the dramatic combination of natural and man-made disasters that assail the planet, forcing nations of the "Fourth World" to engage in ecological wars among themselves in order to secure access to basic resources for their survival.[15] In Aridjis's version of this highly volatile future, natural reserves such as the Amazon basin and the Lacandon Jungle have disappeared, becoming instead large deserted areas. In the novels, environmental emergencies are repeatedly declared in several parts of the world and volcanic eruptions have decimated whole countries around the globe. To make matters worse, entire oceans such as the Mediterranean have dried up, converting the cradle of Western civilization into a desert.

In this ecoapocalyptical future, several marine and terrestrial species have perished because of the destruction of their ecosystems. As a result of industrialization and the excessive use of motor vehicles, the hole in the ozone layer widens over Antarctica, causing massive tidal waves and consequently depleting the coastal areas of vital plankton. In addition, global warming and a severe drought have led to famine and plagues in several developing countries, causing an exodus from the countryside to the already overcrowded cities. As in Fuentes's *Cristóbal Nonato*, the only precipitation in Aridjis's futuristic megalopolis is "una lluvia ácida y gris, una lluvia triste que irritaba los ojos y el ánimo, ensuciaba el pelo y hacía toser" (*Leyenda* 30). Increasing the realm of destruction, the lack of water and the dome of smog that surrounds Mexico City create a continuous heat wave, heightening the already acute sensation of oppression in the capital. In both novels, the city formerly surrounded by lakes has become a tragic testimonial to industrialization, which has resulted in a massive ecological and human disaster.

Situated in the early twenty-first-century, *La leyenda de los soles* begins with the painter Juan de Góngora reminiscing over a map depicting the Mexican capital in the year 1550. Through the painter's perspective, Aridjis laments the disappearance of the last traces of the ancient Aztec capital of Tenochtitlan and its transformation into the contemporary megalopolis of Mexico City: "Corría el año 2027, la ciudad se estaba hundiendo y los volcanes se habían perdido de vista en el paisaje del altiplano. Y no sólo las montañas legendarias ya no se veían, del paisaje original del valle ya no quedaba ni huella" (*Leyenda* 15). The narrator refers to the Anahuac Valley's most prominent landmarks and symbols of national cultural identity, the active volcanoes Popocatépetl and Iztac Cíhuatl, which, obscured by the high levels of pollution, have disappeared from plain view, increasing the feeling of alienation and despair in the urban desert. Through the image of a rapidly vanishing nature, *Legend* depicts the pronounced decay of the Mexican capital in this hypothetical future, illuminating the paradox of development by erasing the signs of cultural identity. The narrator's comments highlight the nostalgic perception of the capital and the volcanoes as emblems of the nation and voice Juan de Góngora's dream of recovering the past for the future through the artistic representation of Mexico City and the surrounding area.

The narrator goes on to describe the colonial map, presumably painted by a native *tlacuiloque,* that adorns the walls of painter Juan de Góngora's apartment in a middle class neighborhood in the modern capital: "[Juan] supo que ésta no siempre había sido esa inmensidad irrespirable que hacía llorar los ojos y raspaba la garganta, sino un valle luminoso cubierto de lagos resplandecientes y verduras inmarcesibles" (*Leyenda* 15). This passage reminds the reader of the former utopian setting of Tenochtitlan, whose abundance of water contrasts sharply with the dry and desolate circumstances of the landscape depicted in the novel. Through the comparison of the past with the present, Aridjis emphasizes how the conquest of the New World began a domino effect of ecological damage to the Americas that by 2027 has caused the collapse of several ecosystems in Mexico.

In addition to emphasizing this contrast between past and present, the narrator also uses the representation of the map to reconstruct the archetypal image of the earthly paradise that fueled the exploration and settlement of the Americas:

> [Juan] pasó los días observando la isla en 1550, cuando la ciudad era apenas un corazón que comienza a latir y un cerebro que empieza a imaginar. Cuando el caserío español era blanco, los lagos verde pálido, los caminos de agua verdes y los indios de carga y servicio, los *tamemes*, arreados por sus amos extremeños, iban vestidos por caminos melosos. (*Leyenda* 15–16)[16]

This reference to the pristine white houses and crystal clean waters of the capital of colonial New Spain contrasts with the conditions of acute deterioration in Aridjis's projected future. While the image of utopia is present in the description of the colony, the narrator also emphasizes how the city was constructed literally on the backs of the native Mesoamericans, who were forced to carry heavy loads, thus linking both the destruction of the environment and the subjugation of the indigenous population to the enterprise of imperialism. By associating the utopian image of Mexico with the exploitation of indigenous communities, Aridjis calls the reader's attention to the unbalance created by the pursuit of utopia dating back to the time of the foundation of colonial Mexico. Step by step, the narrator describes how the construction of the modern city—and the ensuing model of culture—displaced nature as well as giving birth to a system of exclusion and subjugation of the Amerindians. Through the juxtaposition of the colonial origins of Mexico City with the dystopian representation of the future megalopolis, then, Aridjis criticizes the project of modernity that has caused the ecological decay of the Anahuac valley.

Aridjis uses the literary image of the city as a sick body to highlight the impact of industrialization, describing twenty-first-century Mexico City as the epitome of degeneration where the foul odor of human waste and dead animals worsens the quality of an already unbreathable air and "los ríos de aguas negras y los basureros líquidos, reminiscencias viles de lo que un día fue la Venecia americana" (*Leyenda* 19).[17] In both novels, the transformation of the former Aztec capital into an ecological nightmare stands as a resounding criticism of the results of

modern industrialization. Shopping malls are built atop lands
formerly used for farming, and stagnant rivers mix their stench
with the smell of fast food and industrial waste. Because of the
lack of water, the canals have dried up: "La ciudad de los lagos
[. . .] ya no tenía agua y se moría de sed. Las avenidas desar-
boladas se perdían humosas en el horizonte cafesoso y en el ex
Bosque de Chapultepec la vegetación muerta se tiraba cada día
a la basura como las prendas harapientas de un fantasma verde"
(*Leyenda* 17). Once again the personification of the capital en-
ters into the discussion, this time in the form of the city dying
of thirst.

Most people living on the periphery of the thirty-square-
mile city lack the most basic resources for survival: "En pleno
siglo XXI, los habitantes de Ciudad Moctezuma parecían estar
viviendo en una época anterior a la electricidad y al agua potable" (*¿En quién piensas?* 186). In *Leyenda*, the government
is described as corrupt and inefficient, attempting to hide from
the urban population information regarding the lack of basic
resources for survival, and ultimately declaring itself incapable
of supplying the forty million residents of the megalopolis
with water and electricity. In *¿En quién piensas?*, the narrator
observes that the lakes, rivers, and canals that used to provide
Mexico City with the precious liquid have long ago dried up,
and as a result popular demonstrations protest the lack of water.[18] While the project of modernity offers the appearance of
growth across broad areas of the capital, Aridjis points to the
widespread scarcity of water and energy as evidence of overpopulation and underdevelopment resulting from unplanned
urbanization. Hence, in spite of the promises of modernity,
Moctezuma City represents regression, as the advances promised by the Revolution do not make their way to the majority.

Alongside the scarcity of clean, potable water, the most serious environmental problem confronting the metropolis is air
pollution. Since global warming has virtually eliminated the
difference between the seasons, one month is just like another,
and every day the sky is gray and people suffer from headaches
and burning eyes. Because of the deplorable air quality, the bird
migrations that once marked the transition between the seasons
have ceased altogether: "De un tiempo para acá los pájaros
migratorios ya no se caían muertos en la ciudad, porque ya no

había pájaros" (*Leyenda* 36). Residents of the capital no longer even know where the sun rises and sets, since they never see it. Adapting to their surroundings, the citizens learn to tell time based on the airborne contaminants that vary throughout the day. In addition, they develop a whole new vocabulary to describe contaminants, replacing former conversations about the weather: "Antes aquí las gentes platicaban de las tolvaneras de febrero, de los aguaceros de mayo, de la luna de octubre y de los fríos de diciembre, ahora hablan de las partículas suspendidas, de las inversiones térmicas y de las concentraciones de ozono" (*Leyenda* 42). Because decision-makers place the values of industrial modernization above the preservation of the natural environment, the gods no longer smile upon the capital: "el dios de la lluvia ya no lloraba sobre México, una sequía aérea agrietaba el cielo atormentado y no nos bendecían los aguaceros ni los rayos" (*¿En quién piensas?* 159). As the narrator of *Leyenda* observes, virtually the only thing the inhabitants of the capital share in common is the adulterated air they breathe.

In contrast to the other authors examined in the present study, Aridjis's ecological consciousness does not end with the effects of air pollution on human health, but leads to a deeper meditation on the perils faced by the continent's flora and fauna. For example, in *¿En quién piensas?*, Yo Sánchez sees a monarch butterfly for the first time since her childhood, and it appears to her "como sobreviviente de la extinción biológica y como fantasma de migraciones pasadas, fuera de lugar y de tiempo" (25). Paradoxically, pet stores feature for sale the last remaining specimens of disappearing species alongside novelty items made from the tails, feet, and fur of extinct animals. In the face of an absence of live flora and fauna, throughout the metropolitan area there are streets named for extinct flowers and dried-up rivers.

In both novels, Aridjis systematically deconstructs mankind's neglect of the environment in order to promote his biosophical principles of respect for nature and its creatures. His protagonists are so estranged from the natural world that they barely notice its disappearance:

> Los habitantes de Ciudad Moctezuma, que habían perdido desde hacía décadas el hábito, o el masoquismo, de ver el cielo, el Sol y la Luna, no lo advirtieron, como tampoco

> habían advertido años atrás el silencio extraño que reinaba
> en los campos y los bosques del país. (*¿En quién piensas?*
> 199)

Too preoccupied with their dehumanized existence to appreciate what little natural beauty remains in the urban jungle, the residents of the metropolis do not take the time to admire the occasional oasis where nature finds refuge: "Como un prodigio de la fertilidad de la Naturaleza, unas plantas verdísimas crecían en medio de un arroyo tan pútrido y espeso que había perdido todo movimiento" (*Leyenda* 42). On the rare occasion that *Leyenda*'s Juan and Bernarda see a sunset untainted by air pollution, it happens that "más cuidadosos de no caer en una alcantarilla abierta ni en ser atropellados por un vehículo que circulaba con exceso de velocidad, Juan y Bernarda apenas tuvieron tiempo para indulgencias estéticas" (*Leyenda* 42).

The only beauty Aridjis's protagonists can admire is ironically the result of the chemical by-products of industrialization itself: "El día era hermoso, no por límpido, sino por las posibilidades estéticas de la contaminación. El día era aromático, no por los perfumes del campo, sino por las combinaciones aéreas de sustancias innombrables" (*¿En quién piensas?* 28). Air pollution colors the urban sky:

> Como perlas dentro del gran molusco que era Ciudad Moctezuma, las lámparas del alumbrado público daban a la parte superior de la avenida un tono anacarado. [. . . .] [E]l resplandor rojizo de un anuncio luminoso reverberaba en una ventana del piso de cemento, aún vacío, de un edificio en obras. La infición color fresa se adhería en el vidrio [. . .].
> (*¿En quién piensas?* 185)

When Moctezuma City's corrupt mayor contemplates the beauty of the sky tinted by gases and metallic particles that approximate the rainbows of pre-industrial Mexico, he refers to the smog as progress a hundred meters tall (*¿En quién piensas?* 28). As the narrator of *¿En quién piensas?* comments, there is little difference between Mexico and Moctezuma City, as their respective mayors "se dedican igualmente, afanosamente a tumbar árboles, aplanar montículos, rellenar barrancas, entubar ríos, derrumbar monumentos históricos y a desaparecer ruinas arqueológicas" (42). Through examples of how industrialization creates only pale imitations of natural beauty, Aridjis points to the questionable achievements of a pseudomodernity sustained by a corrupt government.

In an effort to deflect attention from the ecological damage resulting from a poorly planned urbanization, in *Leyenda* the government fills the parks with grotesque artificial plants and turf: "En el Paseo de la Malinche no había ni un árbol, ni una planta, sólo pasto pintado de verde, arbustos de plástico, fuentes secas" (29).[19] In *¿En quién piensas?*, the narrator describes how in downtown Moctezuma City, humanity reproduces nature through industry not only in terms of flora but fauna as well: "En el centro de la plaza surgió un árbol de metal. En sus ramas tubulares estaban cantando pájaros autómatas, que abrían y cerraban el pico y las alas a cada trino. Flores artificiales, iluminadas por dentro, fosforecían. Turistas y niños rodeaban ese *novísimo árbol de la vida*" (48; emphasis mine). Schoolchildren become familiar with nature only through these synthetic imitations in parks and zoos:

> Miles de pupilos deambulaban aquí y allá comiendo alimentos chatarra y mirando los árboles de plástico y las estatuas de concreto de los próceres de la historia oficial. Árboles y próceres no sólo ofendían los ojos con sus colores chillones, eran una agresión material a la estética y a la ecología. Aunque los delfines en el lago artificial eran de hule, el espectáculo hechizo que representaban cada dos horas tenía sus admiradores y los mozalbetes ya hacían largas filas para presenciarlo. (*¿En quién piensas?* 163)

Here we observe how the devastation of the environment goes hand in hand with the loss of a historical consciousness as citizens are spoon-fed a single distorted version of history.[20] Thus, Aridjis's novels call attention to the fragile character of both history and the ecology, as both are vulnerable to potential manipulation and annihilation in the name of state-sponsored consumerism.

Moctezuma City's unscrupulous mayor goes so far as to make the manmade trees gray and depressing, encircled by grates with peeling paint, in order to make them seem more realistic in a city deprived of water and direct sunlight. Significantly, this representation of the rapid extinction of both animal and plant life and their substitution with synthetic replicas calls attention to the insidious goals of contemporary consumer culture where nature is transformed into an object of veneration precisely at the same time that industrialization destroys the ecosystem: "Desnaturalizamos la vida, matamos a la Naturaleza mientras hablábamos de salvarla" (*Leyenda* 121). Ironically, industrialization ravages nature and then takes its place as an object of consumption and as a sign of a more developed society, in the form of eco-industry.

As a poignant reminder of the imposition of "civilization" over nature, on top of the newly built buildings of Moctezuma City, a neon sign announces the extinction of plant and animal species and the destruction of habitats across the globe: "En el noveno piso de un edificio, las noticias del día daban vueltas en una banda luminosa. Una y otra vez notificaban los últimos obituarios: la extinción del lobo mexicano, el fin de la palmera nakax en Sian Ka'an, la desaparición de una orquídea en los Tuxtlas, la muerte del Río de las Mariposas" (*¿En quién piensas?* 48). The cause of these extinctions is none other than man himself; when one of her companions observes that no bird falls to the ground unless it is the will of God, Yo Sánchez adds that no bird falls to the ground unless man has a hand in the matter. When some grassroots activists attempt to release domesticated animals into the wild, they note that the animals fail to thrive, pointing out that "muchos ya están muertos de hambre y de hombre" (*Leyenda* 145).

These novels highlight how along with the theme of utopia, with the rise of modern science there emerged the concept of controlling and modifying nature for humankind's benefit. Aridjis criticizes the genetic modification of botanical specimens, since the alteration of nature fails to prevent the disappearance of various species needed for human survival: "Los ingenieros genéticos cruzaron plantas incompatibles entre sí. Buscaban hacerlas resistentes a los insectos, a los virus, a los herbicidas y a la contaminación. *Pero no pudieron hacerlas resistentes a la mano del hombre*" (*Leyenda* 121; emphasis mine). This genetic manipulation and the pursuit of biotechnology thus do not amount to progress, as the attempt to modify nature ultimately causes the deterioration of biological diversity.

While the entire planet's ecosystem sees its future endangered, the narrator of *Leyenda* points to how the commodification of nature and the pressures of modern living produce the alienation of individuals like the painter Juan de Góngora:

> Buscó su peine desdentado en un cajón del buró y halló recibos de luz, cuentas de videófono, notas de tintorería, facturas pagadas y no pagadas, y pares de mancuernillas en forma de delfines, tortugas, mariposas y abejas. *La Naturaleza en el puño, para quien pudiera dudarlo.* (*Leyenda* 35; emphasis mine)

Here we see how the defamiliarization of humankind with the natural world contributes to the overwhelming sense of alienation associated with the experience of modernity. As nature becomes an object of consumption, industry replaces it with bizarre simulacra that estrange the individual from the natural and cultural environment. Pointedly, nature is displaced and ironically becomes a commodity within the very modern lifestyle that has destroyed it.

Along with the gradual extinction of several living species, Aridjis points to the degradation of human quality of life as a by-product of the objectification of nature for consumption. Since virtually all vegetation has died, young people are forced to become acquainted with nature through photographs and historical documentaries[21] or at best in ecological sanctuaries, such as the ones where characters like Natalia and Arira live, as will be discussed below. *Leyenda*'s narrator clearly marks how the loss of humankind's natural habitat has a direct negative effect on human experience in the future: "En todas partes se sentía el exilio, la inminencia del fin de una época, la nostalgia de un mundo que se había ido de las manos y los ojos sin que nadie lo hubiera vivido plenamente" (123). The following section will discuss the representation of Mexico City in which Aridjis emphasizes the combination of ecological and moral degeneration affecting the residents of the most populated city in the world.

Urban Nightmares: Mexico City and Moctezuma City

As has been examined in previous chapters, during the nineteenth and twentieth centuries the city represented the ideal of modernization for developing elites throughout Latin America.

Like Fuentes's *Cristóbal Nonato*, Aridjis's *La leyenda de los soles* and *¿En quién piensas cuando haces el amor?* dismantle the principal tenets of the Latin American project of modernity such as the city being the emblem of progress and cosmopolitanism. Aridjis addresses two different issues in his portrayal of an apocalyptic megalopolis: first, the image of urban space as representative of national identity exemplified by the transformation of the Aztec capital of Tenochtitlan into modern Mexico City; and second, the contrast between the modern idea of viable cities and the chaos, crime, and dysfunction that plague the contemporary capital. While in *Leyenda* Aridjis focuses on the fragmentation of Mexico City, offering the image of the labyrinth as the quintessential metaphor for the negative impact of industrialization, in *¿En quién piensas?*, he emphasizes how the fictional Moctezuma City does not represent the harmonious growth and order associated with modernity but rather exemplifies the chaotic effects of a lack of urban planning as well as the corruption of the political system. Ultimately, these futuristic cities embody the uncertainty and anxiety produced by the collapse of the model of the modern nation and its institutions as a result of the problems posed by a globalized Mexico.

Like Fuentes's *Cristóbal Nonato*, both of Aridjis's novels portray the metropolis in corporeal terms as a sick body or as a contagious plague inscribing its degenerating marks over the once immaculate nature of the Anahuac Valley. This negative depiction of urbanization as a malady calls into question the actions of politicians pursuing the rapid industrialization of Mexico leading to a nightmarish city without order or design. In both *La leyenda de los soles* and *¿En quién piensas cuando haces el amor?*, Aridjis elaborates on how the living conditions in the capital have decayed beyond the possibility of survival. Through the comparison of Mexico City to a diseased body, Aridjis makes more graphic the image of an unfinished modernity: "Los primeros rayos del Sol se posaron sobre los escombros de la ciudad como sobre un vasto organismo herido" (*Leyenda* 195). As in Fuentes's *Cristóbal Nonato* and Morales's *The Rag Doll Plagues*, the capital falls ill in the future because of the massive emissions of three million cars that daily cross the enclosed Valley of Mexico:

> Un polvo gris llovía en la ciudad, formaba charcos cenicien-
> tos, ensuciaba los cristales de los coches, los vidrios de los
> lentes. El cielo se quebraba en una sequía ubicua y la urbe
> daba la impresión de sufrir una enfermedad del futuro, pero
> ya presente en sus monumentos y avenidas. *Los ladrillos ca-*
> *carañados, las ventanas caturrientas, las paredes fitulosas,*
> *el aire purulento* eran manifestaciones de ese mal venidero.
> (*Leyenda* 127–28; emphasis mine)

At the end of *Leyenda*, Mexico City appears as a wounded body
whose guts are being torn out as earthquakes announce the
end of the Fifth Sun: "Uno tras otro, los edificios se abajaron,
mostraron sus entrañas y sus cicatrices. Las casas tenían voz y
gritaban" (*Leyenda* 181). The precarious construction of these
buildings exemplifies the disjointed connection between the
system of government and the community, thus pleading for a
better integration in order to improve conditions in the capital.

In both novels the cities of the future expand from demographic necessity and without design and planning. As an example, Moctezuma City—"ese conglomerado de miseria al pie
de una barranca, que un día sin fecha un ciudadano anónimo
bautizó con el nombre del último emperador azteca" (*Leyenda*
41)—also appears as a living organism that stands out for its
uncontrolled growth: "Situada al norte del río Nuestra Señora la
Coatlicue, *una mañana había nacido como un hongo de cartón*
y lámina, y al paso del tiempo se había extendido sobre cerros
y llanos como una aberración urbana" (*Leyenda* 41; emphasis
mine). Aridjis captures the relentless movement of modernity,
describing urban sprawl in zoomorphic terms as a living organism with its own rules, independent from humankind's control:
"La megalópolis había entrado, ciertamente, a la época de los
grandes desastres, *los grandes catarros, las grandes hemor-*
ragias, los grandes centros comerciales, los grandes burdeles y
las grandes contaminaciones, pero seguía siendo un pueblote"
(*¿En quién piensas?* 200; emphasis mine). Urban growth is represented graphically in terms of contagion and the decomposing
body: "Ciudad Moctezuma es fea sin remedio. Ciudad Moctezuma no es un cataclismo social ni un drama geográfico, es
un chancro" (*Leyenda* 41). As in Fuentes's *Cristóbal Nonato*,
here the city appears as an infectious sore that grows and

spreads without regard for authority, transgressing boundaries and highlighting the unpredictable character of urbanization.

In addition to representing the metropolitan area as a source of degeneration, Aridjis focuses his critical eye on the ill-defined and contradictory project of Latin American modernization through the metaphor of the labyrinth. *Leyenda*'s Mexico City is represented as constantly and chaotically being demolished and reconstructed, a veritable spectacle of underdevelopment:

> Un México de calles en reparación sin previo aviso, cloacas sin tapadera, señalamientos de tránsitos mal colocados o desorientados, fachadas acribilladas por la última granizada de partículas metálicas, puertas fuera de quicio, ventanas que ningún ingenio humano podía cerrar bien, obras públicas inconclusas o mal hechas, aberraciones de arquitectos y escultores chafas, ruinas contemporáneas no producidas por los desastres naturales sino por la mano inepta y corrupta del hombre. (*Leyenda* 143; emphasis mine)

In *¿En quién piensas?*, in like manner, the narrator describes Moctezuma City as an elaborate urban puzzle that no resident can master because of the chaotic system of numbering, differing streets with the same name, and streets with no name. Like neighboring Mexico City, it appears as a work in progress, always under construction, an intricate interweaving of boulevards and back alleys. The labyrinth is emblematic of urban chaos: "Era un laberinto sin entradas ni salidas, sin centro ni Minotauro, hecho de inmovilidad y movimiento, de soledad y promiscuidad, y bastante feo" (*¿En quién piensas?* 27).

This description of the metropolis of the future contradicts the notion of the utopian city with goals of planned growth, harmony, and individual satisfaction. In the second novel, the fantastic Moctezuma City in particular is described as a labyrinth in which the avenues intertwine without order: "Avenidas de circularidad sin centro, arterias entretejidas en desorden, periféricos y circuitos con cientos de entradas y salidas [. . .] conformaban el embrollo, *el mapa de la confusión*" (*¿En quién piensas?* 111). Instead of the capital representing the accessibility of services and opportunities for everyone, the intricate design of the city encapsulates Mexico's failure to manage development because of its wasteful administration of resources.

As this image reveals, the uncontrolled growth of the capital represents the problematic character of Mexican modernity, since the constant redrawing of the urban map exceeds the aims of planned expansion.

Through the metaphor of the labyrinth, Aridjis thus deconstructs notions of order and progress, pillars of the projects of nation proposed by postrevolutionary Mexican regimes. While industry and technology have benefits for First World nations, for Latin America they can lead to disorder:

> Los habitantes de otras capitales gozaban de las visiones urbanísticas de nuestro tiempo, el laberinto era una creación de osados avances tecnológicos; en Ciudad Moctezuma el laberinto era una suma de desórdenes pretéritos. No era un sueño futurista, era un delirio actual. (*¿En quién piensas?* 27; emphasis mine)

Here the contrast with more developed nations highlights the image of Mexico as the consequence of an unfinished modernity and abandoned utopian dreams. Aridjis's megalopolis represents the catastrophe of growth without order; sadly, this chaos becomes the face of the future.

In *La leyenda de los soles*, through the eyes of the painter Juan de Góngora, Aridjis questions the constant transformation of the city, which is compounded by the state's avoidance of a critical analysis of the relationship between the cultural and natural environment and its effect on the everyday citizen: "Las máquinas de construcción hacían agujeros, hacían demoliciones, levantaban edificios baratos, altos y flacos. Ruinas contemporáneas. *El y su pasado, pensaba [Juan], eran expulsados sin cesar de una ciudad sin memoria, en la que el automóvil era el dueño de las calles y del presente*" (*Leyenda* 16). As is clear here, the industrial age's widespread use of machinery radically affects the former utopian aims of the city as historical buildings are demolished and human life is devalued in favor of maintaining the circulation of vehicles. Ironically, while the concept of the modern city was imagined to foster communication among individuals with a common past, the model of development adopted by Mexico leads to the loss of a sense of community and historical consciousness, thus presenting challenges for the future of the national patrimony and cultural heritage.

Aridjis dramatizes how the blind pursuit of modernity through the accumulation of technology without regard to environmental impact has a soundly negative effect on the people of the Mexican labyrinth, producing alienation and loss of identity. Noticeably, in the overcrowded metropolis, the individual becomes a minuscule object juxtaposed against the massive monster that is the city. *Leyenda*'s Juan de Góngora experiences panic attacks in the metro and suffers nightmares about falling through a hole in the ozone layer, while his bookshelves are populated with self-help texts on how to survive in a world filled with paranoia, neurosis, and anxiety. In order to confront the urban jungle, residents of Mexico City in 2027 arm themselves with protective gear such as face masks, personal alarms, bulletproof and antiviral clothing, water and air purifiers, and sunglasses to prevent damage from ultraviolet rays that penetrate the depleted ozone layer. These items protect the citizens from harm but also significantly isolate them from their fellow humans.

Adding to the decadence, confusion, and alienation that the intricate mapping of the city offers, Aridjis also criticizes the cultural contamination that assails the urban dweller as billboards and badly painted signs attest to the influence of the English language on Mexican culture as a phenomenon of globalization. In a fashion similar to the depiction of the futuristic Makesicko City of Fuentes's *Cristóbal Nonato*, Aridjis describes the influence of English as a direct attack on Mexican national autonomy, depicting it as another form of pollution: "[Juan], leyó los letreros de las tiendas; El New Hippy, La Bunnie, El Nursery, La Nymphet, Los Unhappy Many, El pasaje de las Boutiques, Hacia el Lobby, Solo Women, Tienda de Ready Made, El Edificio Blue. [. . .] Harto de recorrer la contaminación del idioma [. . .]" (133). This idea is reiterated in *¿En quién piensas?*, when Yo, Arira, María, and Facunda wander through Moctezuma City:

> Nosotras leíamos los letreros de las tiendas, los restaurantes y los bares, ejemplos lucientes de la contaminación del idioma: Chicken Rápido, Century Veintiuno; Speak con Propiedad: Escuela de Spanglish; Latinoamerican Institute: Conserve la Tradition; Parking aquí; Pregnant? Nueve Meses sin Intereses, Café Mejor Lazy que Crazy; Jóvenes Encueradas, Mujeres sin Panties. (235)

The globalization of a culture of consumption undermines the notion of local communities as is evident in the names of neighborhoods like Palmolive and in the fact that throughout the metropolitan area manufacturers of cheap disposable goods have replaced repair shops, while family-owned small businesses have ceded to international fast food chains. As in futuristic narratives such as Philip K. Dick's *Do Androids Dream of Electric Sheep*, on which the film *Blade Runner* is based, here fiction serves as an apt instrument for detecting changes on the cultural level that call attention to the unpredictability of the globalized culture of the future.

From his apartment, Juan witnesses the rapid modernization of the city while at the same time losing all contact with nature and with his sense of self: "Desde su estudio, él había sido testigo infiel y perezoso de los cambios que estaban ocurriendo delante de sus ojos y no se había dado cuenta que *la pérdida gradual de suelo, de aire y de agua a su alrededor era la pérdida gradual de su propio yo*" (*Leyenda* 17; emphasis mine). Along the same lines, Yo Sánchez, the narrator of *¿En quién piensas?*, observes that when man presumes that he has the right to determine whether other species on the planet may live or die, he also forfeits his own future. Here we observe the loss of human identity associated with the destruction of nature, as industrial mechanization, rapid urban growth, and the demands of modern daily life are detrimental to the symbiotic relationship between the individual and the natural environment.

Leyenda and *¿En quién piensas?* coincide with films such as *Metropolis* and *Blade Runner* in their emphasis on the effects of overcrowding in the megalopolis of the future. In spite of being surrounded by fellow humans, Juan and his companion Bernarda Ramírez experience alienation in the oppressive atmosphere of the subway system whose entrance is crowded with street vendors:

> La explanada del metro Chapultepec era un mercado de ruidos. Nadie estaba solo, podía andar solo, rascarse a solas la cabeza, en cualquier sitio alguien caminaba, compraba, vendía, miraba, estorbaba. Los vendedores callejeros bloqueaban las entradas, las salidas de la estación, se peleaban por el control de las aceras, de los escalones, de las puertas, ofrecían zapatos, camisas, calcetines, sombreros, sacos, máscaras, guantes, lentes de sol. (*Leyenda* 30)

Resorting again to the zoomorphization of inanimate objects, the narrator describes the metro in terms of a living organism: "Entre los cuerpos que surgían de todas partes como por creación espontánea, luchó por ganar un espacio, por avanzar, por no ser manoseada" (30). Walking around the city, the individual becomes lost: "Bernarda Ramírez trató de perderse en el gentío. Y el gentío se la tragó. Sus pasos se mezclaron a los de otros andantes y la oscuridad confundió los perfiles" (143–44).

Lacking personal space, Bernarda loses her very identity: "Bernarda Ramírez, como si no tuviera rostro propio, nombre ni dirección fija se dejó llevar por ese presente indeterminado, por ese anonimato colectivo que representaba el metro" (32). The crowd takes on a life of its own: "Miles de gentes andaban en el Paseo de la Malinche, más como un organismo múltiple que como cuerpos independientes" (*Leyenda* 46). As a result, Bernarda is unable to separate her sense of self conceptually from the city falling apart around her: "Al cabo de un rato de caminar, Bernarda vislumbró el fin de la ciudad. En su temor, ésta no terminaba en el tiempo ni en el espacio, sino en ella misma. Ella misma, quien se había vuelto una metáfora ruin, una memoria insegura de la urbe que se desmoronaba" (*Leyenda* 143).

When perambulating around Moctezuma City, the narrator of *¿En quién piensas?*, Yo Sánchez, also describes the alienation of life in the world's most densely populated urban center: "En cualquier parte uno tenía la sensación de hallarse fuera de lugar, fuera de sí mismo, fuera de época. Lo urgente era irse lejos de la calle, lejos de su propio cuerpo" (27). She also describes the multitude as a living being: "Desde mi ventana [. . .] me ponía a observar al gentío como a un organismo monstruoso, pero animado, de dos mil patas y mil cabezas" (113). In the midst of the crowd, Yo nevertheless experiences loneliness and anxiety: "Cientos de individuos salían de un cine, de tiendas, de bocas del metro, de autobuses. Todos, rápidamente, se esparcían, inundaban las calles, las aceras [. . . .] Yo, a medida que me fundía más en la muchedumbre tenía la sensación de quedarme más sola" (119). Yo Sánchez is overwhelmed by feelings of alienation in a modern world that was proposed as a utopian dream but turned out to be a technological nightmare: "Yo me sentía inerme ante la fantasia abrumadora de mi época, inerme ante ese orbe desalmado que suplantaba el mundo de mis ancestros y conformaba una realidad ajena en donde los objetos familiares se convertían poco a poco en las invenciones frías de una tecnología anónima" (179). Thus technology, rather than improving human life, only seems to increase the alienation the individual experiences in the modern city.

While the urban jungles depicted in these two novels are fictionalizations of a potential future, the conditions Aridjis represents are not far from the present realities described by Mexican cultural critic Carlos Monsiváis in *Los rituales del caos*. In his 1995 collection of essays, Monsiváis illustrates the effects of overcrowding on the psyche of people living in the world's largest capital:

> En el terreno visual, la ciudad de México es, sobre todo, la demasiada gente. *Se puede hacer abstracción del asunto, ver o fotografiar amaneceres desolados, gozar del poderío estético de muros y plazuelas, redescubrir la perfección del aislamiento.* Pero en el Distrito Federal la obsesión permanente (el tema insoslayable) es la multitud que rodea la multitud, la manera en que cada persona, así no lo sepa o no lo admita, se precave y atrinchera en el mismo sitio que la ciudad le concede. Lo íntimo es un permiso, la "licencia poética" que olvida por un segundo que allí están, nomás a unos milímetros, los contingentes que hacen de la vitalidad urbana una opresión sin salida. (17; emphasis mine)

The following observation by one of the characters in *¿En quién piensas?* echoes Monsiváis's sentiment:

> "En nuestra época, una muchedumbre móvil y ubicua rodea instantáneamente al individuo, a todos los individuos, y lo sofoca, los sofoca," replicó María. "Esa muchedumbre quita las fuerzas y frustra los ánimos. Cualquier persona, por insensible que sea, se siente anonadada entre tanto hijo de familia desesperado y agresivo." (187)

The massive concentration of human population in a reduced space presents an ambiguous situation for the *capitalinos* since even though there are tens of millions of people in Mexico City's metropolitan area, the residents experience isolation, alienation, and loneliness. As Arira observes in *¿En quién piensas?*, "Qué curioso, en medio de todo ese ruido me encuentro terriblemente sola" (37). While the current model of development favors industrialization, urbanization, and cosmopolitanism, Aridjis's novels denounce the consequences of these factors on the psyche of the inhabitants of the most populated urban area on the planet.

Ultimately, the protagonists of Aridjis's 2027 see their city as contemporary ruins, and themselves as an object of study for anthropologists. Curiously, the narrator of *¿En quién piensas?* observes how the "Mexican labyrinth" becomes tremendously appealing to the gaze of the outsider:

> El laberinto mexicano era sumamente atractivo para la vista, el oído, el tacto y el olfato, y para la fotografía, el cine vérité, la antropología social, el turismo sexual, y para aquellos interesados en realizar informes sobre violaciones a los derechos humanos, tener experiencias o elaborar dossiers sobre abusos a la mujer, al niño, al hombre, al árbol y al animal. (112)[22]

Here Aridjis pointedly critiques the neoimperialistic discourse of Western cultures that treat Latin American cities as laboratories for elaborating theories of under-development. Noticeably, the failure to fully achieve modernity becomes a vicious cycle leading Mexican reality to be used as a case study, rendering human suffering as an object of global consumption. This deterministic view of Mexican reality thus points to the breakdown of programs of modernization and utopias of national development.

In *¿En quién piensas?*, Moctezuma City in particular represents a criticism of the lack of urban planning and emphasizes the loss of the ideal of a prosperous balanced future. Through the representation of an urban sprawl perpetually under construction, Aridjis deconstructs the image of the city as a utopian emblem of Mexican modernity, pointing to the simultaneous destruction of tradition and the erection of a confusing project of growth with deleterious effects for the citizens, specifically the most marginalized members of society such as Amerindians and women.

While *La leyenda de los soles* focuses heavily on the theme of violence against women, in *¿En quién piensas cuando haces el amor?*, the author delves more deeply into the moral and material corruption of the capital, signaling that because of the economic crisis of the 1990s and the lack of educational opportunities, many women have become prostitutes in order to survive. In *Leyenda*, Aridjis describes Mexico City as the modern incarnation of Sodom and Gomorra where cosmopolitan areas such as the affluent Zona Rosa have turned into red light districts. While the corrupt police look on, taking their bribes in cash or in kind, women as well as young children from all parts of the globe are exhibited in glass cages to be sold as sex slaves:

> La Zona Rosa se había vuelto roja y en los últimos años se había convertido en la carnicería humana más grande del país. Competía con las ciudades fronterizas con sus variados productos carnales, procedentes de las tres Américas. Pues en el mundo se había establecido un nuevo mercado de esclavos, el de las hembras para la prostitución. (*Leyenda* 77)

The Zona Rosa, an area currently known for its trendy connection with the global market and international fashion, in the future has regressed into a slave market for prostitutes of all ages and genders, thus reminding the reader of the dark side of globalization. In *¿En quién piensas?*, the fictional Moctezuma City is likewise portrayed as having the largest sexual marketplace in Latin America, inaugurated by the corrupt President Huitzilopochtli, where "se vendían productos femeninos y masculinos nacionales y de importación" (13). Emphasizing the international nature of this commerce, advertisements for sexual tourism appear in English: "'Babylonian style massage.' 'Susi. Exciting fantasy, active company. Try it, male/female.' 'Exquisite night with Pretty and Young models. Full body massage. Anytime. 24 hours'" (*¿En quién piensas?* 19).

In addition to sexual exploitation, women and children on the streets risk being kidnapped and murdered so that their organs can be sold for transplants. This representation of rampant international prostitution and organ trafficking constitutes a serious criticism of current patterns of development, since in Aridjis's projected future women—and in particular indigenous women—have been excluded from the governing structures of society and do not partake fully in the benefits of globalization, a situation that is not remedied but rather intensified with the widespread adoption of neoliberal agendas. By making literal the selling of human flesh, Aridjis questions the notion of economic progress that has fueled the political campaigns of neoliberal governments during the 1980s and 1990s.

As an example of how globalization excludes the least protected members of society, in both *Leyenda* and *¿En quién piensas?* women and children are victimized by sexual predators in the decadent Mexico City of 2027. Specifically, young women are kidnapped, raped, murdered, and then dumped on the outskirts of the cities, reminding the reader of the actual gendered violence in the border town of Ciudad Juárez since the 1990s.[23] Notoriously, the primary agents of violence and corruption in Aridjis's fictions are police officers and "narcopoliticians," who in addition to assaulting young women are guilty of drug trafficking, white slavery, and trading in the international black market in human organs. Residents of the capital feel they can protect themselves better from thieves than the ostensible guardians of public safety, as the police academy is little more than a training ground for delinquents. The citizens feel impotent reporting such abuses, since the commission on human rights is supervised by the same corrupt politicians who kidnap women and children in broad daylight. The neoliberal project of development thus not only fails to produce opportunities in terms of education, employment, and security for the feminine sector of Mexican society, but rather it worsens their conditions as the national economy and its social structures degrade.

Through the depiction of Mexico and Moctezuma City as the ultimate urban dystopias, Aridjis points to the failure of the Mexican Revolution and postrevolutionary administrations to create a viable system of democratic government. Both *La leyenda de los soles* and *¿En quién piensas cuando haces el amor?* dramatize how the foundation of Mexico City marks the beginning of the end as the utopian Venice of the Americas gives way to the rapidly sinking megalopolis. To advance his inquiry into the indiscriminate cloning of Western modernity by Mexican elites, Aridjis critiques the state's failure to facilitate a rational program through which Mexico could create its own sustainable growth capable of incorporating all sectors of society. As the following section will address, Aridjis's critical assessment of Mexican modernity includes an appraisal of the state's manipulation of history and the influence of mass media, pointing to the need to improve government through the democratic principles of civil society.

Image Is Everything: Mass Media and the Dictatorial Use of Power in Dystopia

As in Fuentes's *Cristóbal Nonato*, in both *La leyenda de los soles* and *¿En quién piensas cuando haces el amor?* the crisis on the ecological level coincides with the disintegration of the political structure, compromising Mexico's territorial and political integrity.[24] In Aridjis's 2027, southern states such as Chiapas have declared their independence—with the assistance of military forces from neighboring Guatemala—while to the north, the mighty United States has escalated its policy of deterring the waves of economic refugees from south of the border through the deployment of military force, ultimately annexing the northern states of Mexico. Surprisingly, the northern states have offered no opposition to the foreign invasion, opting instead to submit to US domination. Citizens harbor little fear that the incursion could extend as far as Mexico City, since the web of impenetrable traffic would block any foreign invader from attacking the capital. Nevertheless, Mexican sovereignty is threatened from all sides in this futuristic vision.

In both novels, Aridjis attacks the dictatorial character of Mexican leadership which promises economic development and improved living conditions for all sectors of society but in fact has been primarily responsible for the deterioration of the environment and the fragile conditions of security. Like Fuentes, Aridjis criticizes a government incapable of sponsoring ideals of democratic order, economic growth, and ecological conservation for Mexico's future. Aridjis's novels emerge during a critical moment in Mexican history as a result of the changes set in motion by the decline of the official party in a period known as the "transition to democracy." The assassinations of political figures such as PRI candidate Luis Donaldo Colosio and the Secretary General of the PRI, José Francisco Ruiz Massieu, threatened the stability of the system and the continuity of the neoliberal agenda of national development supported in the early 1990s by the Salinas regime. In *Leyenda* and *¿En quién piensas?*, when political figures are assassinated, no real effort is made to investigate; instead, the "usual suspects" are rounded up and executed summarily to close the case, since it is known that the facts would ultimately point toward President Huitzilopochtli and General Tezcatlipoca as the guilty parties. Significantly, Aridjis's fictional President José Huitzilopochtli and General Carlos Tezcatlipoca constitute none-too-subtle references to Mexican presidents José López Portillo and Carlos Salinas de Gortari, primary figures of two of the most dramatic periods of economic and political crisis in twentieth-century Mexico.[25]

Similar to the state's omnipotent control in the science fiction works of Zamyatin, Huxley, Orwell, and Bradbury, both *Leyenda* and *¿En quién piensas?* represent how Mexican politicians employ a wide gamut of resources such as the rewriting of history for the fostering of official ideology, the manipulation of reality through mass media, and the deployment of violent paramilitary forces for the suppression of dissidents. Both novels highlight how the dystopian state trains and supports special forces such as the aforementioned *nacotecas*, as well as the Sanitary Police, and even death squads called the Mano Armada to maintain control over the citizens. In Aridjis's apocalyptic future, the mass media conglomerate goes by the name Circe of Communication as a reminder of the seductive goddess who lured Ulysses's sailors to her den and turned them into swine.[26] This representation of modern mass media contradicts the assumption that technology will improve public awareness about the problems of society, as the function of the Circe of Communication is to keep the citizens occupied through degrading TV programs in order to prevent them from developing a social consciousness.

The state's manipulation of the nation's past also encompasses the erection of monuments to the leaders of official history in the streets of the decadent Mexico City and the burgeoning Moctezuma City. Both novels point to how the historic landmarks of the two cities function as a parody of nationalism as they pay homage to the dubious deeds and heroes of post-revolutionary governments, being named after economic crises, national disasters, and questionable heroes such as the Plaza of the Devaluated Peso, Monument to the Unknown Bureaucrat,

Avenue of the Only Party of the Revolution, Monument to Hernán Cortés,[27] and the Hotel Maximiliano,[28] in addition to the aforementioned Paseo de la Malinche.[29] One of the characters in *¿En quién piensas?* refers to the index of a city map as a veritable who's who of official history, since the boulevards are named after the ineffective and unethical politicians who "ungovern" the citizens. Hence, the metropolis itself becomes a monument to a dysfunctional government that has proven unable to foster a true modernity.

In Aridjis's version of 2027, then, Mexican history has been reduced to a series of landmarks recording the misdeeds of corrupt politicians. Significantly, President Huitzilopochtli is depicted personifying several heroes of Mexico in a series of statues adorning Moctezuma City's decadent Paseo de la Malinche. In addition:

> En la Avenida del Partido Único de la Revolución, la cual llegaba hasta Ciudad Moctezuma, Bernarda Ramírez *observó la hilera de los bustos mutilados y rostros cacarizos de la historia patria.* Contempló los monigotes de concreto (de héroes anónimos y personajes ceremoniosos) que conformaban la *epopeya trivial de los políticos en turno.* (*Leyenda* 143; emphasis mine)

The former Aztec capital becomes a mirror of the distorted history that those in power manipulate to maintain control of the nation's cultural heritage. Aridjis promotes a holistic biosophical principle by representing the way unscrupulous politicians not only destroy the environment but also erode the memory and moral core of the citizenry. Instead of the ruling elites representing an agent of change and progress, these groups embody adulterating elements of a decaying social order.

While politicians manipulate the past in order to legitimize their autocratic control, the utopian rhetoric of the future is also amply used by the state. For instance, *La leyenda de los soles* relates how General Tezcatlipoca takes over the government after killing President Huitzilopochtli and, like the leaders of many Latin American countries, promises a new installment of the utopia of urban modernity, in the shape of a spectacularly affluent metropolis:

> El nuevo presidente, en su discurso de toma de posesión,
> reveló sus sueños de crear *una nueva grandeza mexicana.*
> Prometió abrir grandes avenidas [. . .] manifestó sus planes
> de levantar torres de cincuenta pisos donde ahora existían
> pajareras de cemento y vidrio. En Ciudad Tezcatlipoca, ex
> Ciudad Moctezuma, erigiría la urbe del orbe: *una ciudad del
> futuro sin pobres, sin familias numerosas, sin prostitutas,
> delincuentes ni mendigos.* (*Leyenda* 159; emphasis mine)

General Tezcatlipoca's allusion to the "grandeza mexicana"
or splendor of Mexico reveals the presence of the concept of
the modern city as a model of development.[30] Reminiscent of
Cristóbal Nonato's corrupt politician Ulises López, whose wife
has Bloomingdale's department store reproduced in their Mexico City home, the usurping President Tezcatlipoca orders his
Minister of Public Works to expeditiously construct shopping
malls with luxurious boutiques, a glass stock exchange, Aztec
pyramids, and ample promenades, projecting the image of the
capital as a spectacle of modernity and consumerism.

Like other corrupt politicians, the macabre leader promises
an urban zone free from poverty and marginalization, not as a
result of the implementation of social programs and job creation
but rather because the state systematically eliminates the destitute, prostitutes, delinquents, and homeless people from the
city through the use of death squads.[31] As one of his first acts
of government, President Tezcatlipoca orders his Secretary of
Health to limit the number of children per family and control
access to the capital from rural areas by checking passports
at airports, bus and train stations, and freeway entrances. This
series of dictates highlights how the project of nation in Mexico
favors urbanization and industrial development while at the
same time excludes both the rural and urban poor from its plans,
thus condemning those living in the countryside to poverty and
isolation. From its inception, Aridjis's fictional Moctezuma City
was constructed on top of anthropological sites, with shopping
malls built over fertile farm land. Perniciously, with this model
of development, the countryside fails to produce sufficient grain
or animal stock for the survival of the cities, thus opening the
door for increased dependency on more developed nations for
basic staples.

In *¿En quién piensas?*, in the interest of projecting an image
of order in the capital, General Tezcatlipoca organizes para-

military groups—such as the Mano Armada and the Sanitary Police—whose function is to rid the streets of "undesirables":

> Para limpiar la ciudad de esos pequeños delincuentes, comandos de nacotecas exterminadores y escuadrones de la muerte habían conformado el grupo de la Mano Armada [. . .] [cuyos miembros] operaban al amanecer, sorprendiendo a las víctimas dormidas, los venadeaban y los abandonaban torturados, violados, desmembrados, desfigurados en la vía pública, para intimidación y escarmiento de los vivos. (202)

These death squads impose a reign of terror as they patrol the streets, doing away with disenfranchised members of society. Pointing to how the project of modernity has a clearly classist and racist agenda, this systematic violence mainly targets the lower classes and dark-skinned individuals: "La mayor parte de los chamacos eran varones y sus edades fluctuaban entre los siete y los doce años, aunque había mujercitas. En general, *eran mestizos y procedían de las ciudades y los pueblos paupérrimos de provincia, de los barrios populares y de los cinturones de miseria de la Zona Metropolitana*" (*¿En quién piensas?* 202; emphasis mine). Aridjis points to the discriminatory nature of Western modernity as the forces of "order and progress" in reality serve to repress and exclude. The author juxtaposes the ostensible affluence of the capital with the violent backdrop of genocide at the hands of the authorities. Significantly, in a scene reminiscent of the Tlatelolco massacre of 1968, at the end of *Leyenda* Aridjis depicts how President Tezcatlipoca endeavors to suppress the will of the population by ordering the *nacotecas* to attack the people who gather in Mexico City's main plaza to celebrate the end of the Fifth Sun. In addition to describing armed repression, Aridjis scrutinizes more insidious aspects of the state's apparatus, underscoring how through their control of the media, the ruling classes weaken the public's will to participate in society, thus limiting the possibilities of demand for social change.

Similar to classic science fiction novels such as *We, Brave New World, Nineteen Eighty-Four*, and *Fahrenheit 451*, as well as the previously discussed *Cristóbal Nonato*, *¿En quién piensas cuando haces el amor?* highlights the connection between the state and mass media as one of the key elements of the dictatorial aspect of dystopia:

> La Circe de la Comunicación había convertido a los seres
> humanos en puercos mentales. [. . .] El prójimo puto y caní-
> bal pasaba las horas y los años dormido con los ojos abiertos
> devorando las imágenes y los sonidos que la Circe le arrojaba
> a él y a su progenie sin cesar. En su cuarto, los proyectiles de
> las batallas intergalácticas encendían las paredes, los mutan-
> tes irradiados iluminaban los rincones oscuros y los cuerpos
> decapitados, bañados en sangre, caían momentáneamente al
> piso. En ese mundo de luces y ruidos, que formaban paisajes
> horripilantes y escenas ilícitas, se despertaban los deseos y
> las anxiedades sexuales. (*¿En quién piensas?* 176)

Aridjis addresses the decisive role of television in manipulating
public opinion as citizens occupy most of their time incessantly
flipping channels and passively witnessing the degradation of
humanity. Just like Circe of Homer's *Odyssey*, the Circe of
Communication resorts to sensuality to dissuade the spectators
from taking an active role in their society. The reference to the
viewer as cannibal reminds us that in this dystopian world, mass
media does not improve the quality of life but instead causes
regression by appealing to the lowest common denominator.
Through the creation of a virtual reality in which the public
continually plays video games or watches denigrating talk
shows, the state fails to raise the citizenry's levels of education
or culture.

As in Bradbury's *Fahrenheit 451*—where literature has been
banned and mass media is used to promote complacency—in
Aridjis's novels the state keeps its citizens occupied as actors
in interactive reality shows and soap operas: "La Circe de la
mente buscaba cautivar a ese prójimo cada día más, hacién-
dolo participativo, parte y centro de la acción, el drama y la
comedia" (*¿En quién piensas?* 176–77). In this dystopian
information medium, televised spectacles present images of
violence and degeneration, feeding the voyeuristic gaze of the
spectator. The disturbing images of modern media emphasize
a sadomasochistic pleasure that dehumanizes the viewer: "Los
conductores, convertidos en sacerdotes y médicos sociales,
decían investigar los casos, pero más bien hurgaban hasta sacar
sangre en el corazón de las víctimas, inflingiéndoles una violen-
cia verbal pública, además de la corporal que ya habían sufrido"
(*¿En quién piensas?* 178). Here mass media desensitizes individuals, implicating them in their own moral debasement, as

television presents a depraved exhibition that calls into question the advances of modernity and technology. This spectacle of human degradation—comparable to the Aztec ritual of human sacrifice—reveals the dark underbelly of progress, thus questioning the rhetoric of modernity, a pillar of the ruling elites.

In this apocalyptic world, viewers' potential to contribute to society is reduced to the role of being spectators. Rather than exercising real power, they can only exert power through the manipulation of the remote control and interactive joystick:

> En una pieza oscura, él (ella) podía manipular el control a su antojo, hablar con el actor, bailar con la cantante, salvar al niño en peligro, dar puñetazos al malvado o al bueno e intervenir en los debates políticos y sociales. Fascinado por la nada hasta el día de su muerte, cuando la pantalla de colores se vaciaría de imágenes y de sonido, el puerco cautivo bien podía exclamar: "El medio me ha hechizado." (*¿En quién piensas?* 177)

This representation of the Circe of Communication accentuates how televised propaganda precludes modern individuals from engaging actively in their own reality: "En este paraíso de imágenes fugitivas, el prójimo desrostrado desperdiciaba sus años, vivía entregado a un realismo más irreal que el de su vida" (*¿En quién piensas?* 178). Rather than acting as a means of communication, television isolates individuals in a universe of passivity: "La Circe de la Comunicación había incomunicado a la gente entre sí y frente a sus cientos de canales había pocas posibilidades de defensa" (177). Notably, mass media is described in *¿En quién piensas?* as antithetical to the formation of a historical consciousness, since the broadcast of current events promotes what Aridjis calls a culture of oblivion, in that both advertisements and news of wars, murders, and natural disasters are presented in rapid succession to viewers with an ever shorter attention span. The retired actress Arira laments the fact that her career was dedicated less to the development of the enduring arts and more to product endorsements, in "el medio más olvidadizo de todos, el de la Circe, donde el nuevo comercial borra el anterior" (57). Like the mythical goddess who seduced sailors into oblivion, the Circe of Communication lulls the denizens of Mexico into a forgetful stupor.

Through the depiction of voyeuristic images, the Circe of Communication alters the viewer's perception of reality:

> Una lujuria teledirigida entraba gratuitamente por las paredes apantalladas a millones de ojos, fomentando la masturbación visual y el sadismo. Infantes pintarrajeados, putas africanas, busconas piramidales, rusas emigrantes, *starlets* californianas, vikingas nórdicas, enanos españoles y transvestidos neoyorquinos y brasileños [. . .] ocupaban los muros de extremo a extremo, cubrían con movimientos soeces los espacios aburridos de un cuarto perdido en la noche urbana. (*¿En quién piensas?* 178)

Instead of technology serving as a means to foment communication, disseminate information, and provide instruction aiming toward personal improvement, the ruling classes use the media to seduce the viewer, reaffirming hierarchies of sexual exclusion as women's bodies serve as the primary focus of the male gaze.

Postmodern critic Jean Baudrillard observes that the culture of consumerism demonstrates how the "real world" and the imagined world of mass media are "simulations" that notoriously resemble one another:

> [T]he truth of the mass media: it is their function to neutralize the lived, unique, eventual character of the world and substitute for it a multiple universe of media which, as such, are homogenous one with another, signifying each other reciprocally and referring back and forth to each other. In the extreme, they each become the content of the others—and that is *the totalitarian "message" of a consumer society.* (123; emphasis in the original)

According to Baudrillard, television reinforces the idea that the world is visible and malleable, making it easy to promote consumption. This conceptualization is key for the understanding of the role of media in postmodern society as it renders individuals unaware of how their quality of life has diminished.

As Phillip Wegner writes in *Imaginary Communities*, one of the most important aspects of classic science fiction novels lies in the representation of the state's monopoly over the means of communication and its manipulation of propaganda to consolidate power and promote official ideology (190). In dystopian novels, the representation of mass media becomes a critical site for the evaluation of models of government and society. Representing the intersection between a repressive state's ideology and modern technology, Aridjis's Circe of Communication does not contribute to the creation of a rational public sphere but rather hinders the possibilities of human social interaction, making the citizens lose their critical awareness of the miserable conditions of their surroundings both on the material and the moral level. Although it is called the Circe of Communication, the verb *incomunicar* is used to describe its effects, as it isolates individuals in their own fantasy worlds. This version of Big Brother thus powerfully dulls the senses and precludes individuals from being able to form alliances to resist the omnipresent power of the state.

In *La leyenda de los soles* and even more emphatically in *¿En quién piensas cuando haces el amor?*, Aridjis depicts an apocalyptic universe where the advances of technology are used to arrest the possibilities of fostering a democratic society. While the majority of the population is described as victims of alienation and hopelessness, as will be evident in the following section, Aridjis presents women as the principal actors in the creation of alternative projects of modernity, capable of linking nature and humanity through the development of an ecological consciousness and the resurgence of the arts.

Art, History, and Ecofeminism at the Dawn of the New Millennium

A key element of Latin American dystopian writing examined here has been the critical assessment of the causes for the exclusion of traditionally disenfranchised sectors that are perceived as impeding the realization of Latin American modernity. In his novels, Homero Aridjis calls the reader's attention to the systematic marginalization of women and indigenous peoples from the mainstream, depicting, for example, the way that women are continually kidnapped, raped, and murdered in the crumbling megalopolis of Mexico in 2027. This violence is a constant reminder of the shortcomings of Mexico's government in fulfilling the Revolution's promise to create a just society guaranteeing the peace and safety of its citizens. In spite of this gendered and racialized violence, both *La leyenda de los soles* and *¿En quién piensas cuando haces el amor?* offer strong female and indigenous characters who resist the status quo, aiming to re-humanize society and formulate an ecological agenda. Vital to this project of linking nature and culture is the use of the arts and humanities, specifically history and drama, in the search for a balance between humankind and the environment.

Aridjis thus positions gender and race at the core of the discussions of the project of nation and modernity in Mexico during the years following the signing of NAFTA and the concurrent Quincentenary of the encounter between Old and New Worlds. *La leyenda de los soles* and *¿En quién piensas?* point to the crucial issue of the inclusion of indigenous and women's history in the reorganization of social agendas aimed toward rethinking the relation between humans and their environment. Through characters like *Leyenda*'s Cristóbal, Juan, Bernarda, and Natalia as well as Arira, María, Rosalba, Facunda, and Yo in *¿En quién piensas?*, Aridjis outlines an aesthetic and ecological program coinciding with his concept of "biosophy," which he defines as an ethical code through which human beings can live in harmony with nature, representing a needed element for the renovation of the biological world and the cultural sphere of the nation.

Through his juxtaposition of dystopian science fiction with the appropriation of the pre-Columbian past by the ruling elites, Aridjis presents an alternative vision of the future of the native societies of the Americas. The incorporation of indigenous cultures as an alternative for the future is represented by two main events in *Leyenda*: first, the appearance of the sixteenth-century *tlacuilo* Cristóbal Cuauhtli in twenty-first-century Mexico and the final triumph of the Blue Goddess, an incarnation of nature. After traveling from the past, Cristóbal informs the protagonist Juan de Góngora of the existence of a sixteenth-century manuscript, the *Codex of the Suns*, narrating the first days of the creation of the world according to Aztec tradition. The manuscript bears the secret of the future of humanity as it predicts that on the last day of the Fifth Sun, the possessor of the codex will determine the path of the new age either as the sun of nature, represented by the Blue Goddess, or as the dark sun of the god of pestilence and war headed by Tezcatlipoca. The *tlacuilo* warns Juan that he must recover the missing document before the *tzitzimime* descend to devour humankind, thus underscoring the importance of preserving history in order to save the future.

Thanks to his admirable memory, Cristóbal Cuauhtli is able to re-create in his mind the image of Mexico's past before its dramatic transformation caused by the violence of the conquest: "En su imaginación vio los lagos, los canales, los puentes, las calles de agua de aquella Venecia abolida que un día fue Mexico Tenochtitlan" (*Leyenda* 94). Cuauhtli thus represents the preservation of oral history as a link with the ecological system. As a representative of the defeated Aztec class in charge of safeguarding history, the *tlacuilo* becomes a symbol of indigenous peoples' need to preserve their cultural memory before it is engulfed by globalization. This effort to bring forth both the indigenous past and present as key elements of the future is reinforced when at the end of *La leyenda de los soles* the Blue Goddess, representative of nature, rises from the ancient volcanoes overlooking the Anahuac Valley, implying a return to a more balanced order. While the politicians and Tezcatlipoca represent a violent and repressive face of the pre-Columbian past, through Cristóbal Cuauhtli and the Blue Goddess, Aridjis presents a harmonious link between native people and the ecology.

One of the most original aspects of Aridjis's novel is the incorporation of an ecofeminist perspective in the creation of a constructive alternative to the ecological and social devastation of Mexico City. In both novels, Aridjis portrays female characters who wage a war against the biological extermination of several animal and plant species as well as denounce the widespread climate of political corruption and violence of Mexico in the year 2027. In *La leyenda de los soles,* Aridjis introduces positive models such as the photographer Bernarda Ramírez, who searches tirelessly for her kidnapped daughter Ana Violeta, as well as Natalia, sister of the sadistic Carlos Tezcatlipoca. Natalia maintains a sanctuary for endangered animals in the Desierto de los Leones in the foothills of the volcanoes surrounding Mexico City. Although Natalia is not a fully developed protagonist since she is murdered by her own brother soon after the reader is introduced to her character, the connection between women and the environment as a response to the chaos resulting in part from globalization is clearly established in *Leyenda* and further explored in the sequel. *¿En quién piensas cuando haces el amor?* in particular singularizes how the active female protagonists Yo, Arira, Facunda, and María offer hopeful solutions for the future of national development, outlining an aesthetic agenda in which the arts and humanities as well as a concern for the environment provide a creative option to the ecological destruction and human alienation associated with modern urban life.

¿En quién piensas? emphasizes that a revalorization of the history of women and indigenous peoples is vital for the understanding of the roots of contemporary social problems. While Fuentes's *Cristóbal Nonato* highlights how Cristóbal's mother, Ángeles, does not have a history or memory, Aridjis also points to how traditionally women's perspectives on society have been disregarded or interpreted as a form of underdeveloped consciousness through the gaze of male historians. Notably, *¿En quién piensas?*'s Luis Antonio, husband of the recently deceased Rosalba, is writing a book about the trinity of goddesses of destruction and earth renewal, Coatlicue, Kali, and Freya.[32] Through Luis Antonio's eyes the order of the world is represented by a connection between women and nature: "Las diosas representan el tiempo primordial, que se ha desplegado en horas, en días, en siglos, en árboles, en pájaros, en montañas, en hombres" (*¿En quién piensas?* 34). This character identifies the roots of the chaos of contemporary industrial society in the loss of an ancient matriarchal order.

As discussed in the introduction to the present study, in recent decades feminist scholarship has developed a current that examines patriarchal society's problematic association of women with nature. While some feminist scholars reject the connection with nature as demeaning to women, ecofeminists choose to build on this link to address the ecological destruction that has resulted from industrial capitalism. Since culture aims to dominate both nature and women, ecofeminist critics have endorsed measures that protect the natural environment as a key component of a new liberating project. Aridjis's novels can be called ecofeminist in the sense that they present female characters working to preserve the environment not only as mediators but as active agents of social change.

Throughout both novels, the return to nature is related to the myth of the Fifth Sun, emphasizing a cyclical reordering where death and rebirth are considered as stages of a corresponding evolutionary logic. The widower Luis Antonio believes that the future depends on a coming together of the mother goddesses during the earthquakes that announce the end of the Fifth Sun. Notably, his fascination with these goddesses of earth renewal is inscribed under the spell of the destruction of patriarchal culture: "Reduciremos a los hombres a su condición de carroña y los devoraremos. Toda la tierra será nuestra" (32–33). While the resurgence of these avenging mythic female figures representative of the creative and destructive powers of nature evokes the fear of castration, it also invokes the power of nature to radically transform a flawed project of civilization, as the return of the goddesses signals a cleansing of the earth and its creatures according to the millennial belief that holds that the regeneration of social forces is only possible through the erasure of the past.

While official Mexican history legitimizes the subordination of women and nature to the interests of modernization, Aridjis significantly offers female characters who create alternatives for the future through the formation of what he would call biosophical consciousness. Beginning with Natalia, Tezcatlipoca's sister in *La leyenda de los soles*, the author focuses on how women become agents of environmental protection by raising awareness about ecological issues at the grassroots level. We are told how Natalia constructs a sanctuary on the outskirts of Mexico City to protect the meager fauna that is being decimated throughout the country. Notably, this work is not supported by the state, and is even perceived as subversive: "Sin apoyo de nadie y con poco dinero, logró reproducir monos aulladores, jaguares, guacamayas, teporingos, quetzales, zopilotes y chachalacas. Ha dedicado quince años de su vida a la labor secreta, subversiva, de construir un santuario con las sobras del paraíso" (*Leyenda* 69; emphasis mine). Natalia is devoted to the conservation of species that the pursuit of the utopia of modernization has placed in peril of extinction. As her brother observes: "Mi hermana tiene animales que ya sólo se hallan en la memoria de los hombres o disecados en los museos de historia natural o cosidos en un abrigo" (*Leyenda* 70). Exemplifying how consumer culture encompasses a simultaneous subjugation of nature and women,

General Tezcatlipoca invades the sanctuary, kills the remaining animals, and even murders his sister, thus putting an end to her efforts to preserve endangered species.

While Natalia's attempt to salvage nature in *Leyenda* ultimately fails, the characters of Arira, María, Rosalba, Facunda, and Yo in *¿En quién piensas?* point to women's critical involvement in the creation of solutions for the future. Rosalba, in particular, is linked to the healing powers of nature: "En la noche, con los ojos cerrados, Rosalba podía percibir en la distancia a los pájaros por el tamaño de su cuerpo y por la grandeza de su silencio" (257). Rosalba even has the power to return life to animals: "Con sólo pasarle la mano por la cabeza hizo que se movieran sus ojos apagados, que las patitas tiesas se estiraran y abriera el pico pidiendo alimento" (50). Rosalba is successful in her endeavor to preserve nature and even after her death, her twin, María, continues this work herself by rescuing hundreds of birds and housing them in their sister Arira's home in polluted Moctezuma City. The twins represent a formidable pair that reinforces the regenerating powers of nature; as María observes: "Rosalba tenía buena mano para los pájaros, como yo la tengo para las plantas" (56).

Whereas individual citizens make an effort to rescue nature, the Mexican state does little to help. For instance, Arira's garden is full of empty holes waiting for trees that the Secretary of Agriculture has failed to send. However, in spite of the lack of state support, marginal forces strive to create an alternative community, seeking to save both nature and culture from oblivion. Like her sisters Rosalba and María, Arira sees her urban garden as a potential birthplace for new growth: "Desde este ombligo vegetal Arira había creído que la Naturaleza renacería un día en el valle de México y al pasear sus ojos por ese yermo vislumbraba en su centro el árbol futuro: su raíz, su tronco, su copa, su racimo, su vástago, su caducidad, su muerte" (*¿En quién piensas?* 245). Through her art and her garden, the former actress labors to foment cultural and natural renewal. Referring to Arira's dramatic talent, a theater critic affirms, "Con esa voz ella podría hacer cantar los pájaros y hacer crecer las plantas" (60). In Arira's garden, plant life finds a sanctuary that leads to a partial renaissance of nature: "Detrás de su fachada ruinosa palpita un organismo consciente" (*¿En quién piensas?* 243).

The allusion to a conscious organism highlights a change of mentality regarding nature, from being considered as an inanimate object that is subject to modification by humans to being recognized as an organic and even "thinking" source of life.[33]

In addition to environmental activism, artistic expression becomes a significant form of resistance to the status quo in both novels, since it serves as a means of combating the loss of Mexico's cultural and natural history. For example, *Leyenda*'s Bernarda Ramírez is a photographer who uses her art to preserve a record of the natural environment prior to the damage wrought by industrialization:

> [Bernarda] Se dirigió a su cuarto oscuro. Tenía urgencia por trabajar, por revelar sus fotos, por precisar en el papel las imágenes inasibles de la época que estaba viviendo. Al minuto, se fue a sentar en el estudio con un vaso vacío en la mano. Se puso a observar en la pared una de las primeras fotos que había tomado, un retrato del mar, cuando el mar era el mar.
> —Ese mundo se ha acabado—se dijo. (*Leyenda* 168)

In this passage, we see the sense of urgency with which Bernarda undertakes this important task. The concern for the ephemeral nature of human memory and the desire to preserve the landscape through photography constitute means of resistance against the official rewriting of history that has been deployed in Mexico throughout the postrevolutionary period.

Bernarda's companion, the painter Juan de Góngora, also significantly uses his art to safeguard the memory of the panorama of central Mexico as it stood prior to the devastation that ultimately finds its roots in the European conquest of the Americas. Juan labors just as intensely as Bernarda toward the goal of preserving a document of the transient past: "Juan de Góngora se puso a pintar. No pensó en otra cosa que en terminar su cuadro. Con frenesí colocó en la tela mujeres, caminos, árboles, volcanes, la luz corpórea de una figura azul" (*Leyenda* 180–81). As Juan and Bernarda attempt to ward off the apocalypse with the help of painting and photography, they realize that their effort faces severe limitations considering there is little hope for the future: "Por esa avenida venía un río, ¿cómo pintar ahora su ausencia, su cuerpo entubado, su carga de aguas negras?, ¿cómo pintar la desesperación de un río, el grito silencioso de la

Naturaleza en agonía? [. . .] ¿cómo pintar la soledad del último conejo teporingo que se extingue en la falda de un volcán?" (*Leyenda* 164). Juan and Bernarda's actions and reflections regarding the role of art underscore the need for artists to create awareness of the pitfalls of industrial globalization.

Juan's specific focus is on the two volcanoes that can no longer be seen from Mexico City through the smog, but which in previous centuries formed an important point of historical significance, since in Aztec mythology they represent the guardians of the Valley of Mexico: "Los volcanes Popocatépetl e Iztac Cihuátl han desaparecido de la ciudad desde hace décadas. Durante mi vida, una sola vez los he visto, y eso ha sido desde el Paso de Cortés" (*Legend* 64). For Juan, painting the volcanoes becomes symbolic of his effort to rescue both the past and the future of Mexico, since through his art the volcanoes are reborn as signs of cultural identity that form a link with nature and with the indigenous past, both of which have been suppressed by modernization and more recently by globalization.

In *La leyenda de los soles*, then, art functions as a form of regeneration accentuating the power of imagination and creativity over destruction and erasure: "[Juan] sentía el deseo de volver a su estudio para acabar el paisaje del Valle de México, antes de que desapareciera el Valle de México" (*Leyenda* 64). *Leyenda*'s protagonist attempts to recover the past by foreshadowing a future in which the Valley of Mexico is once again guarded over by the two volcanoes: "De pronto, Juan de Góngora vislumbró las siluetas borrosas de los volcanes. Admiró la cima color castaño del Popocatéptl, la ola blanca en forma de cuerpo femenino del Iztac Cihuátl. Pero se dio cuenta que sólo eran imágenes de su mente, porque el neblumo creaba montañas y animales en el aire" (*Leyenda* 164). Juan's painting becomes a form of resistance against the destruction of the past, reinforcing the link between humankind and the environment: "Si uno no anima las montañas que ama no sería hombre, no crearía dioses" (*Leyenda* 64). Hence, Juan and Bernarda's efforts to record images of nature through art become a way to preserve a national history threatened by the politicians that modify it in order to remain in power.

As mentioned above, *La leyenda de los soles* begins with the painter's meditation on a sixteenth-century map of Mexico City.

Like *Leyenda*'s Juan, Facunda of *¿En quién piensas?*, a former schoolteacher, is inspired by geography to contemplate Mexican history: "[Facunda] trae colgado en la cabeza el mapa de una geografía imaginaria, donde el Imperio Mexicano se extiende hasta la América Central y penetra en los Estados Unidos como un hacha" (36). Thanks to her formidable memory, Facunda is able to evaluate the social and environmental conditions of the country's history relative to its present fragmentation. Her memory allows her to contrast the past with the possibilities for the future, as Facunda asserts: "Soy una experta en la historia de la ilustre y leal Ciudad Moctezuma y puedo comparar su degradación actual con su esplendor pasado, haciendo uso de una topografía de la memoria" (*¿En quién piensas?* 36). Through her historical consciousness Facunda is capable of offering a critical point of view regarding the present state of degradation of the Mexican metropolis.

Facunda's memory is equated to other forms of preservation of experience such as art and literature: "Sus paisajes son mentales, son como portadas de libros y fotos de época que el sol decolora en las vitrinas de una librería de viejo" (*¿En quién piensas?* 36–37). While the state and the ruling classes erase history, destroying the historical buildings of downtown Mexico City and erecting new populations over archaeological sites, narrator Yo Sánchez and her friends become the living memory of a disappearing nation; as Facunda observes: "Del México antiguo nos queda una patria moral, la única que no pueden echar a perder nuestros presidentes ni nuestros conciudadanos, ni pueden explotar ni invadir nuestros adversarios históricos" (37). Facunda and her peers at the National Theater Company blame corrupt politicians for the moral degradation of the capital and point to how only the memory of the past survives the systematic violence imposed by the state. For these characters the concept of the fatherland—a centerpiece of official post-revolutionary rhetoric—represents a propitious critical location from which to scrutinize national projects of development and offer sound and viable solutions for the future.

While Facunda, the modern version of Mnemosyne,[34] salvages the past as an ethical point of contrast to the present, throughout *¿En quién piensas?*, the use of artistic expression as a form of resistance is evident primarily through the medium of theater, in which all of the protagonists are involved. In the case of narrator Yo Sánchez, her profession as a lighting technician at the National Theater Company enables her to illuminate and shade the dramatic stage as a utopian escape from a fragmenting and decadent reality. Through the manipulation of artificial light, Yo makes the sun rise or set and take poetic tones for a public desperately in need of an escape from reality. With the assistance of technology, Yo is able to complement Arira's acting, adding her own subjectivity to the performance. Thus, like Bernarda Ramírez and Juan de Góngora of *La leyenda de los soles*, both Arira and Yo use artistic expression to transmit their culture to posterity.

¿En quién piensas? also denounces the ineptitude of the educational system and cultural agencies of Mexico in 2027, such as the National System of Culture, a bureaucratic organization that serves merely as a façade since its public buildings are recognizably empty. As in Fuentes's *Cristóbal Nonato*, in which major landmarks are reproduced in the Mexican capital, Aridjis's megalopolis features cardboard facsimiles of buildings representing cosmopolitan cities from around the globe. Numbed by mass media and the values of a consumer society, the citizens lose their awareness of the transformation of their city into a monstrosity of metropolitan mimicry. Notably, Moctezuma City's corrupt mayor cuts the ribbon in inauguration ceremonies for libraries without books, theaters without seats, and archaeological museums without artifacts to exhibit. As the narrator of *Leyenda* observes: "[Juan] entró en una biblioteca repleta de autores del siglo XX: Marcel Proust, Franz Kafka, James Joyce, Jorge Luis Borges, Fernando Pessoa . . . Los volúmenes (en libreros, en cartones y en desorden) cubrían el suelo, las paredes, subían hasta el techo. Pero, desgraciadamente se veían abandonados, que no habían sido abiertos en muchos años" (86).

In contrast to utopian novels, which favor literature as a representation of imagined communities, dystopian novels underscore the decadence of the anti-intellectual model of a consumer culture that fails to foster the literary acumen of its citizens. For instance in Aridjis's future, the state constructs simulacra of agencies of culture—empty museums, libraries, theater halls—replacing their real counterparts with instruments of consumption such as shopping malls:

> En este dédalo singular, la vida vegetal y animal, y la vida
> cultural, habían sido casi exiliadas, las librerías, las bibliote-
> cas, los jardines, las salas de conciertos y los teatros casi no
> existían. Había en cambio edificios de gobierno, conjuntos
> comerciales y ejes viales, semejantes a otros edificios, con-
> juntos y ejes viales en otras partes de la Zona Metropolitana,
> otros lados de la nación y del mundo. (*¿En quién piensas?*
> 111)

Here we see that the state creates the illusion of progress but re-
linquishes autochthony, as the dominant order is not interested
in creating an authentic national infrastructure but rather in
cloning the façade of foreign projects of modernity.

Significantly, in the Mexico of 2027, there is no real democratic debate about any political matter, since the intellectuals who report for the various metropolitan newspapers write
only propaganda in support of President Huitzilopochtli. As
evidence of the lack of interest in the humanities, in *¿En quién
piensas?* the public does not attend theater functions nor does
the state support the intellectual and cultural development of
the citizens:

> Hubo un tiempo en el que asistía a los estrenos de las
> obras de Arira el presidente de la República, licenciado
> José Huizilopochtli Urbina. [. . .] El talento de espectador
> de Huizilopochtli no era grande, pero la noche del estreno
> de *La Celestina* se retiró en silencio, visiblemente decep-
> cionado. Al día siguiente, quitó el subsidio a la Compañía
> Nacional de Teatro y los locales destinados al arte dramático
> del gobierno cerraron sus puertas, los actores se quedaron sin
> empleo. El teatro no le interesaba más. (*¿En quién piensas?* 70)

Here Aridjis critiques the Mexican government's limited notion of progress and specifically the lack of funding for the arts
and humanities, which are subordinated to the goals of global
consumption.

After state agencies cease promoting art and culture, Arira
devotes herself to the living theater: "Sin escatimar gastos ni
energía personal, se entregó a producir la obra de Fernando de
Rojas como si fuera a crear un organismo vivo, su organismo,
y a jugarse en él la vida" (63). Through the actress's cultural
activism we see how art becomes not only a vehicle to preserve
the memory of the past but also a vital organism capable of

surviving on its own terms in spite of society's disregard. When the state-sponsored National Theater Company ultimately closes its doors to the public, Arira dedicates her life to exploring alternative ways to resuscitate her dramatic passion for future generations: "Muerto el teatro, he plantado en el jardín de la casa algunas obras como *La Celestina, Antígona, Las Bacantes, La tempestad* para ver si florecen en el futuro" (56). Thus, like Bradbury's *Fahrenheit 451,* where as a response to the state's burning of books members of an underground resistance group each memorize one literary work in order to save literature from oblivion, Aridjis's characters each rescue an aspect of natural or artistic life for future memory.

In *¿En quién piensas?*, all of the female characters have some role in the preservation of art and history as well as the conservation of nature. Because in 2027, theater is extinct, Yo, Arira, Facunda, and María devote their time to recording the memory of the dramatic performances that formerly took place in the National Theater Company, which now serves as a historical archive:

> Nosotras le ayudamos [a Arira] a clasificar los recuerdos, las fotos, las reseñas. En vida recibió homenajes oficiales necrofílicos, provenientes de un gobierno acostumbrado a premiar a los artistas muertos, físicamente o en su capacidad creativa. Vivos los intelectuales rebeldes eran enemigos del Estado, difuntos los burócratas de la cultura los colmaban de honores. (*¿En quién piensas?* 71)

Arira in her new role as archivist devotes herself to preserving the memory of cultural traditions by bringing history and literature to life for posterity.

Significantly, Arira's Moctezuma City house becomes an emblem for a change in mentality toward both the environment and the arts. Serving as a rudimentary theater where she can perform dramatic pieces for her peers, her home symbolizes the return to community-based organization as an antidote to the alienation and lack of security that characterize the dystopian society that Mexico has become. Arira's resolve to create a grassroots option to the hegemonic state also highlights the need for civil society to participate in the formation of alternatives to a corrupt government that fosters models of development that destroy both the community and the environment. In spite of the pacific means employed by these characters to reform the project of nation, the narrator warns the reader that the changes coming in the future will be accompanied by violence.

Coinciding with the millenarian views of the Aztecs, Aridjis describes the destruction of the present world as a necessary step for the foundation of a future society. As a reminder that humankind is only one member of the ecological world, at the end of both novels mother nature in the shape of an earthquake destroys the capital and forces a reordering of society. As in Fuentes's *Cristóbal Nonato*, where the destruction of Make-sicko City implies a return to grassroots forms of communal living, the earthquake of the Fifth Sun in *Leyenda* and *¿En quién piensas?* becomes an emblem for the emergence of spon-taneous forms of solidarity signaling a rebirth of civil society. Importantly, the birth of each new sun entails an improvement over the limitations of the previous stages of development. Mexican historian Miguel León-Portilla observes, in *Los anti-guos mexicanos*, "Para el pensamiento indígena el mundo había existido, no una, sino varias veces consecutivas. [. . .] En esas edades llamadas 'Soles' por los antiguos mexicanos, había tenido lugar una evolución 'en espiral,' en la que aparecieron formas cada vez mejores de seres humanos, de plantas y de alimentos" (15). In the Aztec philosophical tradition, then, the death of the previous sun did not imply the end of humanity but rather a form of evolution in which both natural and human life improved and adapted to the environmental and social changes that continually reshaped Mesoamerica prior to the arrival of the conquistadors.

Highlighting the reference to the pre-Hispanic past in *¿En quién piensas cuando haces el amor?*, critic Hélène de Fays concludes:

> Aridjis resorts to Aztec myths in *¿En quién?* as a warning
> to Mexicans. [. . .] Fulfilling the myth, the ending of the
> novel predicts the end of the Fifth Sun—the technological
> era—by showing the destruction of Moctezuma City. [. . .] In
> other words, Aridjis reasserts Mexico's heritage and future
> through the use of Aztec myths. ("Neo-Luddism" n.pag.)

By framing the ecoapocalypse as part of the Aztec paradigm of destruction and re-creation, Aridjis critiques the Western notion of progress, which imposes a linear logic in which global industrialization and hyperconsumption appear as the most desirable attributes for a society. By interpreting Western modernity as another stage and not the most perfect in human development, Aridjis subordinates the dominant paradigm of unlimited progress to an indigenous cosmovision that recognizes nature as an organizing principle.

La leyenda de los soles and *¿En quién piensas cuando haces el amor?* end with a return to nature and the possibility offered by a regeneration of humans, the natural world, and the relation between the two. At the close of *Leyenda*, after a massive earthquake has leveled the majestic buildings of Mexico City, Juan de Góngora and Bernarda Ramírez abandon the demolished capital and travel toward the state of Michoacán. As they depart, in the foothills of the volcano Iztac Cíhuatl (Sleeping Woman, in Nahuatl), they gaze upon the awakening of the Blue Goddess, announcing a balance between humanity and nature under the Sixth Sun:

> Bernarda y Juan dejaron atrás las calles destruidas, salieron a la carretera a Toluca, camino al estado de Michoacán. Al cabo de un rato, perdieron de vista la ciudad de México. En la punta, sobre un tunal vieron la *figura azul de una mujer que tenía los brazos extendidos hacia el Sol, como si quisiera tomar de él el calor y el esplendor de la mañana. En su mano se posaba un pájaro dorado de plumas luminosas. Era el primer día del Sexto Sol. (Leyenda* 198; emphasis mine)[35]

Like Fuentes's *Cristóbal Nonato*, *La leyenda de los soles* and *¿En quién piensas?* close with a promising note regarding the future, as Iztac Cíhuatl reigns over earth with renewed energies. The Blue Goddess represents a return to natural cycles, to an autochthonous order and a re-inscription of both women and nature for the future. At the moment of major destruction of the environment, then, there occurs an epiphany where the possibilities of a new world order are radically revealed, suggesting the use of alternative energy sources such as solar energy.[36]

At the end of *La leyenda de los soles* we observe the return of nature to a pristine state representing a time prior to the conquest of the Americas:

> Cerca de las veinte horas, se propaló el rumor de que se habían llenado de agua los lagos desecados y que en adelante no escasearía el líquido precioso. También se propagó la

> noticia de que unos visionarios habían visto la arquitectura
> sagrada de la vieja ciudad en el lugar mismo que ocupaba
> cuando a la llegada de los españoles y que los dioses se po-
> dían ver difusos, pero se podían ver. (*Leyenda* 160)

Amidst this atmosphere of broad-scale disaster the ancient pre-Columbian order returns to the city:

> Este espectáculo alucinante no podía ser gozado por nadie
> más que por los creyentes en las deidades prehispánicas y
> por los visionarios mismos. Indígenas, vestidos de caballeros
> águila y de guerreros muertos en batalla [. . .] danzaban en
> círculo bajo el sonar de los atabales y el arder del copal. Una
> mujer hincada copaleaba hacia la dirección de los santuarios
> en el Templo Mayor. Los ruidos ventrales de la tierra se con-
> fundían con el tamborileo. (*Leyenda* 161)

As is evident here, native cultures are fundamental to the new world order envisioned in Aridjis's novels, as Mexico's future necessarily must incorporate its indigenous roots.

Foreshadowing the dawn of a new age where ecological concerns will be a top priority, at the end of *La leyenda de los soles,* the air and the sky clear up over the formerly contaminated city:

> El Popocatépetl y el Iztac Cíhuatl se precisaron en la distan-
> cia con la limpidez original. Más viejos que el tiempo y que
> los dioses, los volcanes flotaban en el presente indiferentes a
> las eras y a los calendarios humanos. Para Juan de Góngora,
> una sola cosa era cierta, el sol cotidiano que lo había mirado
> durante los últimos mil años los seguiría mirando mil años
> después. O, ¿quizás, no? Porque las montañas, como las pie-
> dras y los soles, también mueren. (*Leyenda* 198)

After the colossal earthquake, while preparing his exodus, Juan discovers that his painting depicting the Valley of Mexico has miraculously survived nature's fury: "Cubierto con mugre y desazón, Juan de Góngora buscó el cuadro que pintaba cuando su estudio se vino abajo. Con alivio, lo halló misteriosamente intacto. La pintura tridimensional era tan viva que tuvo ganas de [. . .] morar en su interior" (*Leyenda* 196). Importantly, Juan leaves his painting behind in Mexico City, since the world that originally inspired it has died.

¿En quién piensas cuando haces el amor? ends with a massive earthquake that destroys Moctezuma City, reminiscent of the real 1985 tremor that devastated Mexico City. For Yo and her friends, there is no doubt that this seismic activity is the announcement of the end of the world as they know it. Yo searches for her friends as the city falls to pieces around her, but can only find her boyfriend, Baltazar, with whom she pledges to construct a new future. As this conclusion indicates, all of the predictions of the end of the Fifth Sun were correct, but significantly, it is not the end of human life itself. This becomes clear when in Yo's words: "Lo más curioso de todo es que en ese momento de destrucción masiva, de confusión general, de estremecimiento y estruendos, animados por las luces confundidas, *todos los pájaros se pusieron a cantar, creyendo que era el alba*" (*¿En quién piensas?* 273; emphasis mine). As Hélène de Fays observes in reference to this ending: "This final comment reminds the reader of the cyclical concept of time in the Aztec culture" ("Neo-Luddism" n.pag.). While the era of the Fifth Sun has ended, the singing of the birds announces the dawn of the Sixth Sun as a rebirth of nature.

During the seismic eruptions there is a moment of epic proportions where citizens spontaneously organize to preserve history without the intervention of the state:

> Entonces imaginé oír, arrastradas por el tumulto de la tierra, *miles de voces* (entre ellas, la de Arira y la mía) dialogando entre sí, *hablando en el suelo nombres de personas y lugares*, cada vez más rápido, más rápido, más fuerte, más fuerte, *como si quisiesen decirse la historia humana, la individual y la colectiva*, en unos cuantos segundos fugitivos; *tratasen de explicarse nuestro pasado entero* antes de que las ondas sísmicas, que viajaban a la velocidad de la muerte, *lo borrasen para siempre*. (*¿En quién piensas?* 272; emphasis mine)

Here the polyphonic voices achieve a dialogue, transcending the silence and isolation that the urban experience of modernity promotes. In this passage, at the moment of crisis the voices that have been repressed from history by the Western model of development return to signify a radical change for Mexico. While the nation has failed to achieve a democratic modernity, the earthquake and the spontaneous irruption of history create an alternative future where everyone is heard.

As demonstrated in the above, both *La leyenda de los soles* and *¿En quién piensas cuando haces el amor?* criticize postrevolutionary agendas of national development for their exclusion of women and indigenous peoples from their plan for the implementation of modernity in Mexico. Even when these fictional pieces paint a pessimistic picture of the nation's future, however, Aridjis illuminates how marginalized sectors can overcome their historical exclusion by addressing the future of the ecology as well as the role of women and indigenous peoples within the culture of the nation. At the end of both novels, it is clear that the author both questions the indiscriminate imposition of the Western concept of progress, and points to a return to nature not as a bucolic escape but as a modern necessity. Significantly, at the moment of greatest destruction, the isolated sectors of Mexican society find a common dialogue in which to consolidate their own future leading to the emergence of a more democratic society. In contrast to the Western conception of the apocalypse that implies the death of all life, Aridjis adopts an Aztec logic that perceives the end of successive suns as a necessary step toward perfection, thus implying that the next generation will be better fit to save the planet.

Conclusion

The Angel of History and
the Postapocalyptic Consciousness

As I write the final lines of this book, a decade has gone by since NAFTA went into effect and the Zapatista insurrection in Chiapas began; as Josefina Saldaña-Portillo observes: "The Zapatista uprising has brought the Mexican nationalistic project to a crisis and has challenged *mestizaje* as its dominant trope for citizenship" (405). Following the PRI's loss in the 2000 elections, Mexico has been governed by a right-wing presidency watched over by a wide range of political parties, leading to the realization of many of the political developments anticipated by Carlos Fuentes in his 1987 futuristic dystopia.

In this study we have traced the different concepts of utopia that have shaped Latin American history since its "discovery" or "invention" in relation to programs of colonization and later self-rule. The utopian ideals of the perfect society, the modern city, and the use of technology to enhance quality of life have had a direct impact on developing societies such as Mexico, shaping their national identity, their socioeconomic goals, and their environmental policies. Nevertheless, the dream of unlimited progress has had its dark side as modernity has installed its hegemony over those who were perceived as Other. The effect of the signing of NAFTA on Mexico's sovereignty has unmasked the contradictions of an indiscriminate adoption of the Western model of industrialized development, leading the writers discussed here to scrutinize the promotion of globalization as a panacea for the national crisis of the 1990s. In their novels, dramatic images of the ecoapocalypse emerge as a criticism of both the mega-projects of trading blocks that fail to address the impact of neoliberal policies on indigenous communities and also of the detrimental effects of industrialization on the environment. While the discovery of the New World originally inspired utopian dreams of an earthly paradise, late twentieth-century Mexican and Chicano writers draw on the trend of dystopian science fiction to project the long-term consequences of colonization, modernization, and globalization.

Through the use of apocalyptic images, Fuentes, Morales, Boullosa, and Aridjis reflect on Mexico's future, studying the political, economic, and cultural characteristics of the country's makeup to suggest alternative models of development. Whereas traditionally in Mexico the state has been the premier motor of the nation, as Néstor García Canclini illuminates, globalization relocates this role in that entities can trade in the global market without state intervention. In the novels examined in the preceding chapters, we saw how the authors suggest grassroots movements as a means of local resistance both to the state's hegemony and to the forces of globalization.

In chapter 1, we discussed how the "Mexican Miracle" collapsed in its totality during the late 1980s. Through the use of dystopian narrative techniques, Carlos Fuentes emphasizes the failure of the *indigenista* project alongside the moral and ecological degeneration of the city. Nevertheless, in the midst of this chaos, *Cristóbal Nonato* ends with hope for the future, emblematized by the refusal of the unborn protagonist's parents to abandon the country. Thus, on the eve of the signing of NAFTA and on the day of the five hundredth anniversary of Columbus's first landing on American soil, Cristóbal is born destined to remain in Mexico to examine its future role in the new global marketplace.

Alejandro Morales also looks to the history of colonization for answers about both Mexican and Chicano identity, predicting a post-NAFTA world that falls victim to an epidemic for which residents of Mexico City offer the only hope of a cure. *The Rag Doll Plagues* points to the need to understand the origins of marginalization in past, present, and future time frames as it examines the possibilities and limitations of racial and cultural *mestizaje* as a response to the ecoapocalypse in a borderland characterized by phobias of contact.

Like Morales, Carmen Boullosa highlights the importance of an historical perspective in her prediction of future devastation as she presents us with three utopias that each fail, evolving into apocalyptic nightmares of dehumanization and ultimately leading to the destruction of all living creatures. Each of the utopian societies described in *Cielos de la tierra* neglects to listen to the lessons of history, representing humanity's folly in its search for perfection in an imperfect world.

Homero Aridjis's novels likewise predict environmental ruin in their portrayal of a futuristic megalopolis in which the ecological destruction is equaled only by the ethical degeneration of its leaders. However, amidst a climate of political chaos and moral bankruptcy, women and indigenous communities are represented as harbingers of a better future. Both *Leyenda de los soles* and *¿En quién piensas cuando haces el amor?* therefore end on a positive note, reclaiming the national and natural space, which, despite constant assault, continues to thrive.

While the novels studied here represent notable examples, they are not the only narratives that employ the dystopian mode and the techniques of science fiction to express concern for a fragmenting nation that seems unprepared to face the challenges of a global society. The themes examined above are also expanded in several other literary works depicting the ominous situation of Mexico City in the late 1990s, such as those by detective fiction master Paco Ignacio Taibo II and cultural critics Guillermo Sheridan and Hugo Hiriart. Taibo's *Máscara Azteca y el Doctor Niebla* (1996) takes place in a decrepit capital where political and ecological abuses have greatly diminished the quality of life. Based in part on the real story of a wrestler named Superbarrio who in the 1990s gained influence over large popular sectors of the city to denounce political corruption, Taibo's novel centers on the ability of common folk to resist a repressive regime by adopting elements of popular culture. Corruption is also the theme of Guillermo Sheridan's *El dedo de oro* (1996) in which a deteriorating Mexico City forms the background for an exposé of legendary labor boss Fidel Velázquez. Hugo Hiriart has a novel entitled *La destrucción de las cosas* (1992), which combines the invasion of Tenochtitlan with an alien takeover. In addition to novels there are also novellas and short stories—such as those compiled in Guillermo Samperio's *Gente de la ciudad* (1986), Cristina Pacheco's *La última noche del tigre* (1987), Gabriel Trujillo Muñoz's *Laberinto* (1995), Sandro Cohen's *Lejos del Paraíso* (1997) and *Los hermanos Pastor en la corte de Moctezuma* (2003), Malú Huacuja del

Toro's *Un dios para Cordelia* (1995) and *Herejía en contra del ciberespacio* (1999), Mauricio Molina's *Tiempo Lunar* (1993) and *Mantis Religiosa* (1996), Ana García Bergua's *El umbral* (1993), Héctor Chavarría's *El mito del espejo negro* (1997), Ramón López Castro's *El salmo del milenio* (1998), Alejandro Alonso's *Ceroniverso* (2000), and Luciano Pérez's *Cuentos fantásticos de la ciudad de México o aventuras en Mexicópolis* (2002)—that merit recognition for their use of dystopian elements to depict the alienation of humanity in the world's most densely populated capital. Ricardo Guzmán Wolffer's *Bestias de la noche* (1998), in turn, represents the transition to cyberpunk, a current that also employs elements of science fiction. The theme of the apocalypse has served to launch Mexico's newest generation of writers known as *El crack,* who launched their careers employing dystopian motifs: see Pedro Ángel Palau's *Memoria de los días* (1995); Ignacio Padilla's *Si volviensen sus majestades* (1996); Jorge Volpi's *Temperamento melancólico* (1996); Eloy Urroz's *Las Rémoras* (1996); and Ricardo Chávez Castañeda's *El día del Hurón* (1997).

Incipient yet insistent, the bibliography of critical studies of Mexican science fiction has been accumulating since the 1970s, when Ross Larson's *Fantasy and Imagination in the Mexican Narrative* (1977) identified early works with this focus. The end of the 1980s and the beginning of the 1990s saw the explosion of science fiction publications and the presence of science fiction literary prizes such as the Premio Puebla as well as the use of the Internet as a new means to disseminate dystopian writing. Critics and authors Gabriel Trujillo Muñoz, Paco Ignacio Taibo II, Ramón López Castro, Federico Schaffler, Miguel Ángel Fernández, Gonzalo Martré, and Mario Trejo have made a solid contribution with the publication of their anthologies and critical volumes solely dedicated to the study of this genre. As can be expected, science fiction has been the impulse behind several web pages such as the ones developed by Miguel Ángel Fernández Delgado and José Luis Ramírez. In recent years, Latin American science fiction has generated a great deal of scholarly attention as there have been numerous conferences with this theme as well as critical anthologies such as the work of Andrea Bell and Yolanda Molina Gavilán and Libby Ginway and the doctoral dissertations of Hélène de Fays and Miguel Ángel Estrada.

While Mexico City continues to be a focal point of much contemporary apocalyptical writing thematizing globalization, recent literature stresses the importance of incorporating all regions into any definition of national identity. Significantly, the dream of a Mexican modernity has also been contested by border writers, whose work comprises one of the most prolific and promising contributions to literary production in recent decades. Notably, Mexico's entrance into NAFTA has had a particularly direct effect on border cities, where the 1990s saw a vast increase in migration and a proliferation of maquiladora factories. Gerardo Cornejo's *Al norte del milenio* (1989) and Luis Humberto Crosthwaite's *La luna siempre será un amor difícil* (1994), among others, utilize a dystopian and parodic mode to critique the effect of globalization on national life.

Sonora native Gerardo Cornejo's *Al norte del milenio* addresses from a regional perspective the problems of centralism and nepotism that have vexed Mexico since the 1920s, as he represents the fragmentation of the nation and the dispossession of Mexican territories that have fallen into the hands of unscrupulous capitalists. The action takes place in northern Mexico where what Cornejo calls the Owners have taken control of the economic, political, and cultural life of the region. While the "Center-City" ignores the rest of the country, which has fallen victim to the Great Alienation, the nation witnesses a return to right-wing politics where businessmen allied to the church manipulate public opinion and have a stranglehold on education. In the face of utter disillusion, however, the surviving tribes of Guarajíos organize a resistance movement to dethrone the political might of the reactionary Trinity of Regression comprised of the Catholic Church, the Owners, and the National Restoration Party, which is reminiscent of the real-life conservative National Action Party.

While Cornejo may be the border writer most closely allied to the vein of science fiction employed by the authors discussed above, Tijuana author Luis Humberto Crosthwaite's *La luna siempre será un amor difícil* uses time travel to similarly forge a link between colonial history and globalization. This novel depicts two sixteenth-century characters, an Aztec noblewoman Florinda/Xóchitl and her companion the Conquistador Balboa—representatives of Hernán Cortés and his indigenous consort Malintzín—who cross a spatial and temporal border into the modern Northern Empire in search of the "American Dream," only to discover maquiladora factories that exploit immigrant laborers. These border works merit separate study because they engage the emergence of alternative centers of cultural production far from the centralist vision of Mexico City.

The recent rise in speculative narrative—including science fiction and the detective novel—has seen an ample contribution by border writers. These writers produce local views of national and international issues through subgenres such as the *narconovela*, of which Cornejo's *Juan Faustino Judicial* (1996) and Everardo Torrez's *Narco* (2004) are recent examples of a literary trend that encompasses both sides of the border. Homero Aridjis's *La zona del silencio* (2002), in turn, utilizes a combination of fantasy, detective novel, *narco-novela*, and science fiction in his depiction of the historically silenced border zone.

The term *postapocalypse* has recently emerged in literary and cultural circles to document the daily struggles, attitudes of perseverance, and fortitude of the Mexican people. Now, in the early years of the new millennium, the doomsday predictions of the total *americanización* of Mexico have come and gone. The national economy grows steadily even in meager years. NAFTA continues to be in effect but its impact on Mexico is far from the sweeping changes forecast in the novels discussed above. While the Chiapas rebellion continues to be a national issue, the state has made an effort to avoid open conflict. Nevertheless, the conflict inherent in a model of society that ignores indigenous communities and their environment continues with no apparent solution.

Within the context of postapocalyptic visions, it is important to note that the most populated city in history continues to survive and indeed to thrive, since for every disaster, there is also hope and faith as a new form of citizenship emerges from the rubble of the single-party system that for seventy years ruled the country. In fact, in spite of air and water pollution, high levels of unemployment, and urban violence, Mexico continues moving toward a more inclusive society. The demise of the great Western master narrative of unlimited progress is clear, as the movement toward local responses to national and global problems has added a critical edge to the projects of national development. While the negative aspects of political corruption and ecological decay permeate these novels, their endings express confidence in the Mexican people's ability to use the knowledge of history to transcend their differences and join together to forge a new future.

Notes

Introduction
Utopian Dreams, Apocalyptic Nightmares:
Rewriting Mexican History in the Times of NAFTA

1. The study of science fiction as a critique of society has flourished in recent years, as demonstrated by the fact that in May 2004 the *PMLA* published its first issue dedicated solely to the discussion of this literary genre. While this is an important contribution to critical approaches to science fiction and utopian studies in general, notably, the issue does not include any reference to Latin America, Mexico, or the borderlands where this genre is thriving.

2. The event of the quincentenary in 1992 provoked a transatlantic discussion regarding the appropriateness of the term *discovery* for representing what occurred in 1492 on the shores of the Caribbean islands. As a result, the term *encounter* has been adopted in order to represent a less Eurocentric spin on these events. However, *encounter* also tends to downplay the violence of the conquest. In the light of the lack of an appropriate term without problematic ideological implications, both the new *encounter* and the traditional *discovery* will be used here.

3. Scholar Enrique Dussel identifies these historical developments as the chief pillars for the evolution of Western modernity (25).

4. The classical literary utopia encompasses a collection of myths of perfect societies such as the Golden Age, expounded in the notion of Arcadia; the image of the ideal city present in Plato's *Republic*; and the motif of the Garden of Eden based on the Judeo-Christian tradition of paradise. While the myth of the Golden Age implies the return to an untouched pure state of humanity as it existed at some time in the past, in the modern literary utopia this notion is replaced with projections toward the future in the form of a hypothetical ideal state, which in some narratives takes shape in American lands (Manuel and Manuel; Kumar; Pastor).

5. Utopia presupposes a non-existent place, a "nowhere" whose conceptualization varies according to the historical period that creates a particular utopian vision. Critic Krishan Kumar points out that utopianism is mainly a Western cultural construction and adds that, "Thomas More did not just invent the word 'utopia,' [. . .] he invented [. . .] a new literary form or genre [. . .] a novel and far-reaching conception of the possibilities of human and social transformation" (23–24).

6. Several scholarly works such as Edmundo O'Gorman's *La invención de América,* José Rabasa's *Inventing A-M-E-R-I-C-A,* Beatriz Pastor's *El jardín y el peregrino,* and Stelio Cro's *The American Foundation of the Hispanic Utopia* have focused on the reactivation of the ancient Greek tradition of utopian discourse after the discovery of America, describing how it was employed in the New World chronicles. For the historian O'Gorman, America "did not suddenly emerge full-blown as the result of the chance of discovery by Columbus of a small island on October 12,

1492; it developed from a complex, living process of exploration and interpretation which ended by endowing the newly-found lands with a proper and peculiar meaning of their own" (*Invention* 124). In *Myth and Archive*, González Echevarría adds, "The entire European archive of imaginary representations of a fantastic geography is evident and, at the same time, provides many of the categories and images that articulate their expression during the exploration and conquest of the Americas" (73).

7. As Pastor observes: "El impulso mitificador, la determinación individual y colectiva de descubrir o crear una realidad a la medida de los sueños se manifestaron en la Conquista con una intensidad sin precedentes. Todo un repositorio de imágenes del deseo acumuladas durante siglos en el archivo de la cultura occidental cobró vida, flexibilizó sus formas frente a una realidad desconocida que, por lo mismo, parecía capaz de albergar cualquier quimera" (26).

8. Of all the myths emerging from this violent juxtaposition, perhaps the most important is the legend of El Dorado, which depicted the New World as paved with gold. Literary critic Bart Lewis has documented the impact of this myth on contemporary narrative in *The Miraculous Lie: Lope de Aguirre and the Search for El Dorado in the Latin American Historical Novel.*

9. Peruvian sociologist Quijano singularizes colonial violence as the root of modernity, asserting, "The history of modernity itself began with the violent encounter between Europe and America at the end of the fifteenth century. From then on, there followed, in both worlds, a radical reconstitution of the image of the universe" ("Modernity" 202).

10. Scholar Santiago Castro-Gómez agrees: "Modernity is an alterity-generating machine, that in the name of reason and humanism, excludes from its imaginary the hybridity, multiplicity, and contingency of different forms of life" (269).

11. Hayden White in *Tropics of Discourse* elaborates on this aspect of Western discourse.

12. Literary critic José Rabasa studies the nuances of representing America as a naked female body. He concludes that "the naturalness [understood as nakedness] of America is a mere mirage of European culture and its exploits. The emergence of America marks its loss of identity. It becomes merely a 'naked body' for the inscriptions and longings of European imagination" (27).

13. Although Guerra's explicit intention is to condemn Latin American homosexuality and to lay the blame for its existence at the feet of the Amerindians, his book is nevertheless useful to scholars for its compilation of an astounding number of citations referring to sodomy, cannibalism, and human sacrifice in colonial documents.

14. As Sharona Ben-Tov writes: "Feminist historians and philosophers of science explore how the Scientific Revolution changed the Western perception of nature from that of an animate, semidivine mother to inert, dead matter" (10).

15. Françoise d'Eaubonne coined the term *ecoféminisme* in *Le féminisme ou la mort* (1974). Among the best known literary works in the twentieth century in this trend, Bartkowski cites Charlotte Perkins Gilman's *Herland* (1979), Monique Wittig's *Les Guerrillères* (1971), Joanna Russ's *The Female Man* (1975), Ursula LeGuin's *The Dispossessed* (1974), Marge Piercy's *Woman on the Edge of Time* (1976), Suzy McKee Charnas's *Walk to the End of the World* (1974), Margaret Atwood's *The Handmaid's Tale* (1986), Kim Stanley Robinson's *The Gold Coast* (1988), Marge Piercy's *He, She, and It* (1991), and Octavia Butler's *Parable of the Sowers* (1993) and *Parable of the Talents* (1998). In the Latin American context, themes, motifs, and narrative techniques related to this current have been cultivated by Gioconda Belli's *Waslala: memorial del futuro* (1996), Malú Huacuja del Toro's *Un dios para Cordelia* (1995), and *Herejía en contra del ciberespacio* (1999), and Carmen Boullosa's *Cielos de la tierra* (1997).

16. Jules Verne's early works, which include *From the Earth to the Moon, Twenty Thousand Leagues under the Sea,* and *The Clipper of the Clouds,* demonstrate a confidence in science as a facilitator of human happiness.

17. For example, *Brave New World* depicts a "hatchery" where humans are mass produced *in vitro,* and in Margaret Atwood's *The Handmaid's Tale* the politics of reproduction is the central focus.

18. In his representation of censorship, Zamyatin anticipates key aspects of Soviet Socialist Realism.

19. H. G. Wells's *The Time Machine* (1895) had earlier expressed this fear through the representation of a future society in which two separate species have evolved from capitalism's division of labor between owners and workers.

20. William Rueckert has been quoted as one if not the first to utilize this concept to refer to this academic instance in his 1978 essay "Literature and Ecology: An Experiment in Ecocriticism." One of the principal priorities of Green Cultural Studies has been the defamiliarization of the relations of exploitation between humankind and the environment. Since relations between humanity and the environment are heavily coded, ecocritical studies look at the construction of nature in the humanities, underscoring the manipulation of nature and the construction of nature as a discourse of appropriation. Green Cultural Studies deconstruct nature's representation in the mass media and as an object of consumption in order to build upon a public sphere able to reflect upon environmental protection. Ecocritics problematize representations of nature as wild, barren, disposable, malleable, and empty space for the realization of the Western project of modernity and for the epiphany of the "human subject." Some of the most influential works in this vein are: Leo Marx's *The Machine in the Garden* (1964), Alfred Crosby's *Ecological Imperialism: The Biological Expansion of Europe* (1986), Carolyn Merchant's *The Death of Nature* (1980), Lawrence Buell's *The Environmental Imagination: Thoreau, Nature Writing, and the Formation of American Culture* (1995), Patrick

Murphy's *Literature, Nature, and Other: Ecofeminist Critiques* (1995), and Cheryll Glotfelty and Harold Fromm's *Ecocriticism Reader: Landmarks in Literary Ecology* (1996).

In Latin America, ecological concerns have been present since the colonization from fray Bartolomé de Las Casas's *Brevísima destrucción de las Indias* to Pablo Neruda, Gabriela Mistral, Nicanor Parra, Octavio Paz, Oscar Hahn, Miguel Angel Asturias, Eduardo Galeano, José Emilio Pacheco, Ernesto Cardenal, Mario Vargas Llosa, José María Arguedas, Gioconda Belli, Homero Aridjis, and Carmen Boullosa.

21. In continental Spanish America, the wars of independence began in 1810 and continued until their resolution in 1821 (Mexico and Central America) and 1824 (South America). The struggle for Spanish American self-determination continued until 1898 with the independence of Cuba, Puerto Rico, and other island territories.

22. Post-structuralist critic Michel Foucault in his essay "What Is Enlightenment?" points to how this philosophical revolution consolidated the role of the subject as agent of history. Both Hegel and Kant defined this process as marking a period of maturation of society and individuals in which the intellectual and physical efforts were aimed to improve human existence through the use of reason. This "rationalization of human experience," in Max Weber's words, produced the first intellectual project to radically transform the relationship of the individual with society and its administrative arm the nation-state in a way that would guarantee the protection of each individual's universal rights.

23. Based on Auguste Comte's conception that social reality is discernible under scientific principles and subject to experimentation and observation, positivism was a highly influential philosophy in Mexico and throughout Latin America. Positivism led to a spirit of social reform, as it was believed that citizens' lives could be improved through the implementation of public sanitation, health, and education. The dark side of positivism, as seen here, was that it excluded traditionally marginalized groups from sharing in the fruits of modernity.

24. Some of the essays from *Tiempo mexicano* have been revised and have reappeared as part of an updated volume entitled *Nuevo tiempo mexicano* (1995), which has been translated into English as *A New Time for Mexico*. This citation is from the translated essay "On Mexican Time: Kierkegaard in the Pink Zone."

25. "Order and Progress" is the slogan of the Latin American positivists. Positivistic views supported the creation of an economic and political elite to rule society, which in Mexico accounted for the ascent to power of a group called "los científicos" (the scientists). The "científicos" promoted progress and modernization at any cost, even sacrificing democratic principles and rationalizing the use of military force, thus contributing to Porfirio Díaz's three decades of rule (1876–80; 1884–1911).

26. On the topic of political fraud, see Enrique Krauze's *Mexico: Biography of Power: A History of Modern Mexico, 1810–1996* and Kevin

Middlebrook's *The Paradox of the Revolution: Labor, the State and Authoritarianism in Mexico.*

27. Regarding the history of the PRI, see Wayne Cornelius and Ann L. Craig's *Mexican Politics in Transition: The Breakdown of a One-party Dominant Regime,* and Dale Story's *The Mexican Ruling Party: Stability and Authority.*

28. In the colonial period, the *encomienda* was an indigenous community assigned by the king of Spain to work for Spaniards on a plot of land known as a *repartimiento.* The system in theory demanded that the *encomendero* seek both the physical and spiritual wellbeing of the Amerindians, but in practice, the indigenous workers were treated as virtual slaves.

29. For additional sources on the role of anthropology in national discourses in Mexico, see William Rowe and Vivian Schelling, Ricardo Pérez Montfort, Guillermo Bonfil Batalla, Néstor García Canclini, and Claudio Lomnitz.

30. Novelists responded to the reformist policies of Cárdenas with an indigenist trend of literary production, an early example of which is *El Indio* (1935) by Gregorio López y Fuentes. The novel represents human beings assailed by real social problems such as lack of education, land, and economic opportunities, emphasizing the need for state intervention in promoting indigenous integration.

31. For more information on land reform, see John Womack's *Zapata and the Mexican Revolution.*

32. Meyer et al. observe that whereas the Cárdenas administration had distributed over 49 million acres of land, Ávila Camacho's government distributed fewer than 12 million (604).

33. The population of the country doubled between 1940 and 1964 to about 40 million. The booming of industry and the policies of industrialization directly affected the population of cities such as Mexico City, Monterrey, and Guadalajara with massive migration from the countryside amounting to as much as three million (Meyer et al. 589–94).

34. For more information on the Tlatelolco massacre, see Elena Poniatowska's *La noche de Tlatelolco,* translated as *Massacre in Mexico,* and Carlos Monsiváis and Julio Scherer García's *Parte de guerra.*

35. While foreign investors were not allowed to own the majority of a company in Mexico, there were loopholes, since the Mexican government fomented a corrupt system that allowed the national elites to become titular owners of international corporations (Meyer et al. 582).

36. Critics of globalization, such as Anthony Giddens in *The Consequences of Modernity,* define the phenomenon as a new form of relation between the local and the global. According to Giddens:

> Globalisation can thus be defined as the intensification of the worldwide social relations which link distant localities in such a way that local happenings are shaped by events occurring miles

away or vice versa. [. . .] Local transformation is as much a part
of globalization as the lateral extension of social connections
across time and space. (181)

In Giddens's assessment, globalization redefines the relationship between
periphery and metropolis in radical ways.

37. For a comprehensive study and a chronology of the negotiations
surrounding the signing of the trilateral treaty, see Maxwell A. Cameron
and Brian W. Tomlin, *The Making of NAFTA: How the Deal Was Done*.

38. In 2001, President Vicente Fox announced the end of agrarian reform as there was no more land to distribute.

39. In September of 2003, President Fox was quoted as saying that
remittances "are our biggest source of foreign income, bigger than oil,
tourism or foreign investment" (Lugo).

40. Neil Harvey points out that the "[a]verage yields in Mexico are 1.7
tons per hectare, compared to 6.9 tons in the United States" (181).

Chapter One
The Brave New World of Carlos Fuentes's
Cristóbal Nonato: A Critique of Mexican Modernity

1. Carlos Fuentes (1928–) is the most prolific writer and essayist in
Mexico in the twentieth century. His literary works have been published
in translation in many languages. *Cristóbal Nonato* has been translated
into English by Alfred Mac Adam and Carlos Fuentes and published in
1989 as *Christopher Unborn*. Fuentes has also published several books
of essays, of which the most important are *Cervantes o la crítica de la
literatura, Tiempo mexicano* and *Nuevo tiempo mexicano*, translated as *A
New Time for Mexico*.

2. *Cristóbal Nonato* has been the subject of more than two dozen critical articles, discussing diverse aspects such as the novel as an allegory of
the nation; the image of Christopher Columbus and the discovery; intertextuality with Laurence Sterne's *Tristram Shandy;* a comparison with
Ramón López Velarde's "Suave patria"; the role of the reader; and the use
of postmodern techniques.

3. Since the publication of his collection of essays *Tiempo mexicano,*
Carlos Fuentes addresses the role of the nation state as main promoter
and sponsor of modernity. More recently he has updated his own personal
view of the nation incorporating his perception of its biggest challenges
for the future in *Nuevo tiempo mexicano* (1996), and in *This I Believe*
(2005).

4. The narrator's father, Ángel Palomar, was himself conceived on the
historically significant October 2, 1968, the day that the Mexican government ordered the use of deadly force in the repression of students demonstrating in the Plaza of Tlatelolco. Contrastingly, the female protagonist,
Ángeles, does not have a history; as the narrator observes: "Pero mi

madre compensaba esta abundancia de símbolos: ella no sabe ni cuándo nació, mucho menos cuándo fue gestada" (63).

Significantly, Ángeles appears as altogether lacking in historical context and memory, a reflection on Mexican women's role as abnegated, silenced subalterns.

5. There is a clear intertextuality with Laurence Sterne's *Tristram Shandy* in that Fuentes's protagonist narrates his conception and gestation; this connection is reinforced by several references to the eighteenth-century British novel within the text of *Cristóbal Nonato*. See Ilán Stavans, "Tristram Shandy regresa de nuevo" and Debra Castillo's "Fantastic Arabesques" for further discussion of this link.

6. Fuentes foretells the real economic disaster of 1994 in which the Mexican peso dramatically declined in value relative to the dollar.

7. This reminds the reader of the French invasion of 1862, in which because of Mexico's debts to France, Napoleon III took over the country and made the Hapsburg Maximilian of Austria emperor of Mexico from 1864 until he was executed in 1867.

8. The reference to this fictitious incursion is reminiscent of the real 1916 invasion of Mexico in which US Marines captured Veracruz in the midst of the Mexican Revolution.

9. As discussed in the introduction, since its formation and throughout the twentieth century the PRI dominated Mexican politics. From his 1987 perspective, Fuentes anticipates the victory of the conservative PAN, which did in fact prevail in the 2000 elections when Vicente Fox became the first president representing a party other than the PRI to be elected in three-quarters of a century. As Fuentes predicted, however, the change has not meant the loss of the longtime dominant party's ample influence, as the PRI continues to exercise considerable power through members of congress and other state officials during Fox's presidency.

10. As will be discussed in further detail below, for García Canclini, "cultural reconversion" enables both hegemonic and subaltern sectors to appropriate one another's cultural capital, diminishing the state's role as intermediary and holder of the national patrimony ("Cultural Reconversion" 30–32).

11. As discussed in the introduction, the Mexican Revolution of 1910–17 represented the country's most radical reform of the project of nation since the war of independence (1810–21). The Revolution was brought on, among other factors, by the concentration of land and wealth among a select group of families after thirty years of dictatorial rule by General Porfirio Díaz (1876–80; 1884–1911). Although there were various ideological platforms, most revolutionary groups such as the agrarian-based factions commanded by Emiliano Zapata and Francisco Villa demanded land redistribution, the right to education, and democratic elections. As examined above, in the postrevolutionary decades, there were various attempts to implement these goals, notably under the presidency of Lázaro Cárdenas (1934–40), but none was entirely successful.

12. According to Elliot: "But the simultaneous discovery of the world also represented a discovery of man—the European discovery of non-European man, a creature whose strange, varied, and frequently repulsive habits proved to be a source of consuming curiosity" (42).

13. Castro-Gómez affirms that: "Without the aid of the social sciences, the modern state would not be in a position to exercise control over people's lives, define long- and short-term collective goals, or construct and assign to its citizens a cultural 'identity'" (271).

14. Responding to the ideological divide between Mexican intellectuals in the wake of the 1968 Tlatelolco massacre, several anthropologists, among them Arturo Warman, Guillermo Bonfil Batalla, and Margarita Nolasco Armas, questioned anthropology's relation to the state apparatus in *De eso que llaman antropología mexicana* (1970). For these critics, anthropology lost its critical edge by siding with the state in adopting a logic of assimilation, instead of providing indigenous communities with the tools for their own cultural survival.

15. As scholar Marianna Torgovnick observes, the appeal of the primitive—which in the early twentieth century was perceived as the key to the origins of human nature—ultimately constituted another maneuver of colonialism to justify the West's hegemony over subaltern cultures.

16. A decade and a half prior to writing *Cristóbal Nonato*, Fuentes had dedicated his collection of essays *Tiempo mexicano* to Fernando Benítez. The figure of the anthropologist is key in Fuentes's essays as well as his fiction, as in other novels such as *Cambio de piel* (1967), which also includes a character who is an anthropologist.

17. Michel Foucault expands on this concept of the panopticon in *Discipline and Punish*.

18. As Tzvetan Todorov observes, the reduction in the Native American population can be attributed to two factors: as a direct consequence of violence and warfare, and indirectly as a result of the spread of European diseases to which Amerindians had insufficient resistance. The "demographic catastrophe" that Fuentes's narrator refers to includes the infamous plagues of smallpox and measles that wiped out the greater portion of the native population of the New World. As a result of colonial contact, the indigenous population of Mesoamerica declined from some twenty-five million to a mere one million over the course of the first fifty years following the conquest as the research of medical historians such as Woodrow Borah and S. F. Cook, George Raudzens, Noble David Cook, Suzanne Austin Alchon, and Donald B. Cooper, among others, supports.

19. As will be further elaborated in the following chapter, the expression "transculturation" was coined by Cuban social ethnologist Fernando Ortiz, who in *Contrapunteo cubano del tabaco y el azúcar* (1940) employed this term to contradict the hegemonic notion that acculturation was the only possible future for multicultural societies. Transculturation refers to the mutual influence among Amerindian, European, and African cultures that defines Latin American society. After Ortiz, scholars such as

Ángel Rama and Antonio Cornejo-Polar have adapted this term to literary and cultural studies, refashioning it as "transculturación narrativa" and "heterogeneidad conflictiva" respectively, adding social concerns and matters of cultural survival to the original definition. Mary Louise Pratt, in turn, has elaborated on the concept of transculturation in ethnography and travel writing.

20. *Deep Mexico* defines the nation in terms of absolutes, representing the real Mexican as the Amerindian, which has provoked several criticisms. In his *Exits from the Labyrinth*, for example, Claudio Lomnitz criticizes Bonfil Batalla's essentialist conceptualization of the indigenous Mexican as the center of the nation, on the basis that it denies the identity of the mixed-race urban classes as equally representative of Mexican culture.

21. Fuentes discusses Benítez's contribution to the study of the native populations of Mexico in the section "Indian Mexico" in his book *A New Time for Mexico*.

22. Fuentes's representation of migration to the United States addresses the question of the search for origins, since according to oral history the first tribes to settle Mesoamerica migrated from the north. Ironically, Fuentes suggests that contemporary migration has created the conditions for the "re-Mexicanization" of the territories once belonging to Mexico that were lost with the Treaty of Guadalupe Hidalgo in 1848. In his recent collection of novellas *La frontera de cristal* (1995), Fuentes refers to the growing presence of Mexicans in the US Southwest as a "chromosomic reconquest" of the United States.

23. Several critics discuss Fuentes's intertextuality with Ramón López Velarde's poem "Suave patria." Among them, Santiago Juan-Navarro rightly notes: "La situación de México expuesta en la novela de Fuentes es la anti-utopía del poema de López Velarde" ("En busca de la utopía" 26). Leticia Reyes-Tatinclaux, in turn, has categorized the parody of this text as a form of demystification: "Al retomar estos versos, la novela nostálgicamente evoca la noción idealizada y sobrepasada de la patria que nunca fue y al confrontarla con una realidad aberrante, termina desmitificándola" (102).

24. The verses that are parodied here read as follows in López Velarde's "Suave Patria": "Patria: tu superficie es el maíz / tus minas el Palacio del Rey de Oros / y tu cielo, las garzas en desliz / y el relámpago verde de los loros. / El Niño Dios te escrituró un establo / y los veneros de petróleo el Diablo" (156–57).

25. In his article "En busca de la utopía," Santiago Juan-Navarro has examined the image of urban degeneration in Fuentes's novel, focusing on aspects of national identity.

26. Mumford traces the urban manifestation of utopia back to the Greek city-state: "The first utopias we know were fabricated in Greece; in spite of their repeated efforts at confederation, the Greeks were never able to conceive of a human commonwealth except in the concrete form of a city" ("Utopia, the City, and the Machine" 3).

27. The analysis of the roots of Mexico's economic underdevelopment from colonial times has been a recurrent theme in Fuentes's essays since his *Tiempo mexicano* (1971) and *Cervantes o la crítica de la lectura* (1976). In the latter essay, Fuentes introduces the idea that Mexico's developmental trajectory was determined to a great extent by Spain's dependence on gold, which did not foster the conditions for the development of capitalist production but instead extended feudalism, paradoxically underdeveloping Spain's own society as well as that of Spanish America for centuries to come.

28. Salman Rushdie's *The Satanic Verses* (1988) describes in similar terms the effects of globalization in the postmodern world: "The tide was in when the Ayesha Pilgrimage marched down an alley beside the Holiday Inn, whose windows were full of the mistresses of film stars using their new Polaroid cameras, when the pilgrims felt the city's asphalt turn gritty and soften into sand, when they found themselves walking through a thick mulch of rotting coconuts abandoned cigarette packets pony turds non-degradable bottles fruit peelings jellyfish and paper, on to the mid-brown sand overhung by high leaning coco-palms and the balconies of luxury sea-view apartment blocks, past the teams of young men whose muscles were so well-honed that they looked like deformities, and who were performing gymnastic contortions of all sorts, in unison, like a murderous army of ballet dancers, come to take the air or make business contacts or scavenge a living from the sand, and gazed, for the first time in their lives, upon the Arabian Sea" (514).

29. The Aztec deity Xipe Totec is associated with the earth cycles, thus Fuentes's representation of the band member Hipi Toltec suggests an implicit alliance between the Aztec gods and the subaltern entities of the Mexican port. According to Mary Miller and Karl Taube: "At the time of the Conquest the Xipe Totec festival fell during the month of March, and much of its imagery suggests agricultural renewal: as a seed germinates, it feeds off the rotting hull around it, finally letting the new shoot emerge" (188).

30. In Fuentes's fiction, these same coyotes were originally trained to drive the native inhabitants from the coast toward the hills and further inland.

31. As Ignacio Trejo Fuentes underscores, throughout his literary production, Carlos Fuentes's depiction of the city combines references to the pre-Hispanic past; the long-term consequences of the projects of the Mexican Revolution; and the image of the urban center as the microcosm of the nation (28).

32. The Aztecs erected Tenochtitlan over an island of Lake Texcoco. The propensity toward lung diseases and other respiratory maladies in residents of Mexico City has been common since colonial times, as a result of the geographic location of the city. As medical historians Woodrow Borah and S. F. Cook, Donald B. Cooper, and Noble David Cook propose, the city's orientation toward the west eventually made life difficult as the waste deposited in Lake Texcoco made its way into the densely populated urban area in the form of contaminated air and rain.

33. Mexico's water system faces a severe crisis in reality; in 2000, the precious fluid was brought from other areas of the country to augment Mexico City's scarce water supply. This aspect of the ecological crisis is further elaborated in Homero Aridjis's novels examined in chapter 4 of the present study.

34. This concept derives from Jürgen Habermas, who develops the notion of the "unfinished project of modernity" in *The Philosophical Discourse of Modernity*.

35. Both Jules Verne and H. G. Wells criticized in numerous novels the abuse of science and technology by unscrupulous autocratic leaders.

36. In Mexican political culture, the term *revolutionary family* refers to the nepotistic practices of the revolutionaries and to the alliances with private sectors established by postrevolutionary governments. Fuentes has taken up this theme previously in novels such as *La muerte de Artemio Cruz* (1962) and *Las buenas conciencias* (1959).

37. In Orwell's *Nineteen Eighty-Four*, the Party orders the celebration of national contests to keep the people immersed in an atmosphere of illusion:

> It was probable that there were some millions of proles for whom the Lottery was the principal if not the only reason for remaining alive. It was their delight, their folly, their anodyne, their intellectual stimulant. [. . .] There was a whole tribe of men who made a living simply by selling systems, forecasts, and lucky amulets. [. . .] (indeed everyone in the Party was aware that the prizes were largely imaginary). (73)

At the core of the dystopian novels *Nineteen Eighty-Four* and *Brave New World* lie the themes of the negation of human interaction and the fierce policing of the private sphere by the state.

38. I base my comments on the reading of Barbara Creed's *The Monstrous-Feminine* and Donna Haraway's "A Manifesto for Cyborgs." I further develop the analysis of this association between women and technology in my chapter on the narrative of Alejandro Morales.

39. The creation of Mamadoc also evidences the conceptualization of women deeply ingrained in modernist aesthetics, which as Andreas Huyssen examines, tends to conceive of mass culture as feminine and high culture as masculine (47).

40. In this representation of mass media, from his 1987 perspective Fuentes anticipates the impact of the "reality shows" that currently form a national pastime, as Mexican TV mimics US programs along the lines of "Big Brother." In fact, on Mexican television, the expression "reality shows" is used in English rather than translated into Spanish, and the Mexican version of "Big Brother" has this English title copied directly from US TV.

41. This concern with elite notions of prestige is parodied when Fuentes depicts how minister Ulises López's wife has the lobby of Bloomingdale's department store reproduced in their ostentatious Mexico City home—complete with escalators—while at the same time she secretly orders the burning of shantytowns that occupy her lands.

42. In *Hybrid Cultures*, García Canclini observes how the longtime ruling party has organized Mexico's National Museum of Anthropology in a way that represents the PRI as the inheritor of national history while relegating the living Amerindians to secondary halls. In Mexican history even prior to the Revolution, nationalism created a genealogy based on pre-Columbian cultures but as demonstrated above, the indigenous peoples have always been conceptualized as Other and their presence inscribed in the nation on a primarily symbolic level. In a manifestation of the contradictory nature of nationalism, modernizing sectors have perceived the Amerindians as valuable symbolic raw material while at the same time preventing the articulation of their political demands.

43. According to oral history, the god Huitzilopochtli gave the Aztecs a sign to settle in the place where an eagle was devouring a snake above a cactus plant. The Mexican state has inherited that myth and uses it as a symbol of the nation, as is apparent in the images on the flag, coins, and all official iconography.

44. The loss of national territory to the United States and the trauma associated with this event was predicted in one of the early works of science fiction in Juan Nepomuceno Adorno's 1862 short story "México en el año 1970."

45. Inspired by the German philosopher Jürgen Habermas's *Die Postnationale Konstellation*, the term *postnationalism* has been used by Mexican thinkers such as Roger Bartra in his *La sangre y la tinta*, translated as *Blood, Ink, and Culture: Miseries and Splendors of the Post-Mexican Condition*, to refer to the crisis of modern institutions in Mexico and to their adaptations to modern globality.

46. As in Alejandro Morales's *The Rag Doll Plagues* discussed in the following chapter, in *Cristóbal Nonato* we do not see an equitable distribution of wealth in the United States under globalization.

47. In 1988, California passed the infamous Proposition 187, which aimed to deny illegal immigrants access to health and educational services.

48. As Jorge Hernández notes in *Carlos Fuentes: Territorios del tiempo*, Fuentes recognized in an interview with journalist Bill Moyers that some of the ideas for describing the border region that he used in *Cristóbal Nonato* were inspired by Joel Garreau's *The Nine Nations of North America*.

49. In *Brave New World*, Huxley depicts a borderless zone where the character known as the Savage lives; this world is characterized by its lawlessness and primitive forms of living.

50. Fuentes anticipated the near future in that border towns such as Ciudad Juárez and Tijuana did indeed explode with a massive migration as a result of the real economic crisis of the 1990s, causing overcrowding in those cities.

51. As discussed in the following chapter, Alejandro Morales in *The Rag Doll Plagues* develops a similar notion of the border in his futuristic post-national territory called LAMEX. Homero Aridjis in *Leyenda de los soles* also has an intertextual relationship with Fuentes's novel as some of his twenty-first-century Mexican citizens read the *Diario de Mexamérica*.

52. The characters involved in the truck drivers' rebellion remind the reader of the role of the *pochtecas* (Aztec merchants), whose routes Cortés exploited for the colonization of Mesoamerica.

53. In *A New Time for Mexico*, Fuentes emphasizes the experience of travel as a main constituent of the modern novel, echoing Mikhail Bakhtin's *Dialogic Imagination*. Fuentes's preference for the highway as a site of an emerging response to modernity coincides with Bakhtin's description of the open road as an ideal setting for the novel: "Encounters in a novel usually take place 'on the road.' [. . .] On the road ('the high road'), the spatial and temporal paths of the most varied people—representatives of all social classes, estates, religions, nationalities, ages—intersect at one spatial and temporal point" (243–44).

54. See Jacques Lafaye's *Quetzalcoatl and Guadalupe*, D. A. Brading's *The Origins of Mexican Nationalism*, Francisco de la Maza's *El guadalupanismo mexicano,* and Serge Gruzinski's *Images at War* regarding this syncretism. In 2002, Juan Diego was canonized as a saint by the Catholic church.

55. García Canclini elaborates, "Instead of the death of traditional cultural forms, we now discover that tradition is in transition, and articulated to modern processes. Reconversion prolongs their existence. Briefly, to reconvert cultural capital means to transfer symbolic patrimony from one site to another in order to conserve it, increase its yield, and better the position of those who practice it" ("Cultural Reconversion" 31–32).

56. Both Debra Castillo in "Fuentes fronterizo" and George Yúdice in "Postmodernity and Transnational Capitalism" have observed in Fuentes's writing a clear predilection for urban sectors as the agents capable of transforming and negotiating modernity, whereas both the rural and the indigenous populations tend to be represented as helpless and hopeless victims of underdevelopment.

57. This act of official violence reminds the reader of the actual Mexican government's aforementioned repression of 1968 when hundreds of dissidents were massacred in the Plaza of Tlatelolco a few days before Mexico City hosted the Olympic Games.

58. Anecdotally, Fuentes dedicates one of the novellas in his collection *La frontera de cristal* to Jorge Castañeda, who at the beginning of the new millennium served as Mexico's minister of foreign relations under Fox's presidency until his dismissal from that post in January 2003.

59. In his now classic *El laberinto de la soledad*, Nobel laureate Octavio Paz underscores the importance of colonial history in the Mexican imaginary in terms of "un conflicto secreto, que aún no hemos resuelto" (95). In her novel *Cielos de la tierra*, Carmen Boullosa cites José Emilio Pacheco as affirming the need for Mexico to resolve the issues surrounding the conquest and colonization before being able to truly enter the new millennium: "México se soñaba moderno y modernizante y quería verse ya entrado en el impensable Siglo veintiuno sin haber resuelto los problemas del Siglo dieciséis" (68).

60. Quetzalcoatl (feathered serpent) is the ancient god that the Aztecs believed would return to rule Mexico at the end of the cycle known as the Fifth Sun. It is widely believed by scholars today that the myth of the return of Quetzalcoatl was instrumental to Cortés's conquest of Mexico as the Aztecs mistakenly took the conquistador for their mythic deity.

Chapter Two
Cultural Identity and Dystopia in
Alejandro Morales's *The Rag Doll Plagues*

1. Seymour Menton's *Latin America's New Historical Novel* catalogs historical novels on all topics, while Kimberle S. López's *Latin American Novels of the Conquest* specifically examines historical novels thematizing the colonization of the Americas.

2. Alejandro Morales has published several novels both in English and Spanish such as *Caras viejas y vino nuevo* (1975); *La verdad sin voz* (1979); *Old Faces and New Wine* (1981); *Reto en el paraíso* (1983); *The Brick People* (1988); *Death of an Anglo* (1988); *Barrio on the Edge* (1990); *The Rag Doll Plagues* (1992); and *Waiting to Happen* (2001). Morales is also a literary critic and a professor of Chicano Studies at the University of California, Irvine.

3. *The Rag Doll Plagues* has attracted the critical attention of several scholars, including María Herrera-Sobek, Antonio C. Márquez, Manuel M. Martín-Rodríguez, José Pablo Villalobos, Miguel López-Lozano, Michele Botallico, Dean Franco, and Marc Priewe.

4. In reference to the nature of the representation of epidemics in Morales's novel, Antonio C. Márquez notes: "The plague has no etiology; like Camus's *The Plague*, it suggests a transhistorical trope for the human capacity to create pestilences and also heroically try to eradicate them" (83).

5. In her article "Epidemics, Epistemophilia, and Racism," María Herrera-Sobek draws the connection between the representation of race and ecological criticism in Morales's novel. Herrera-Sobek asserts that Morales is "the first Chicano novelist to systematically sustain an ecological perspective throughout his novel *The Rag Doll Plagues*. [. . .] Morales's work is not merely one concerned with ecological problematics but one in which the ecology of the planet intersects directly with issues of racism, oppression, discrimination, and dehumanization" (100).

6. In "The Global Border: Transnationalism and Cultural Hybridism in Alejandro Morales's *The Rag Doll Plagues*," critic Manuel Martín-

Rodríguez discusses the topic of deterritorialization and transnationalism in Morales's novel (86–88). José Pablo Villalobos in "Border Real, Border Metaphor: Altering Boundaries in Miguel Méndez and Alejandro Morales" further elaborates on the theme of spatial displacement in *The Rag Doll Plagues* (134–36).

7. See Robert C. Young and H. L. Malchow.

8. For an insightful comparison of contemporary appropriations of the theme of *mestizaje* by Mexican American literati, see Juan E. de Castro's comparison of Vasconcelos's theory of a "cosmic race" and Richard Rodriguez's notion of "the browning of America," the centerpiece of Rodriguez's 2002 book, *Brown: The Last Discovery of America.*

9. In *La raza cósmica,* José Vasconcelos declares: "El indio no tiene otra puerta hacia el porvenir que la puerta de la cultura moderna, ni otro camino que el camino desbrozado de la civilización latina" (25).

10. Ortiz opened this dialogue by coining the term *transculturation* as an alternative to the sociological term *acculturation,* since he found transculturation to embody a more accurate description of the cultural dynamic between different ethnic groups in Cuba. In his 1982 book, Ángel Rama applies Ortiz's concept to literature using the term *transculturación narrativa.*

11. Martín-Rodríguez observes how *mestizaje* in *The Rag Doll Plagues* emphasizes the process rather than the product: "What *Plagues* celebrates is continuous *mestizaje*: between Mexicans and Spaniards (in part one), between Mexican Americans and Jews (in part two), and between Mexican Americans and Asian Americans (in part three). But this *mestizaje* [. . .] no longer stems from the notion of an eventual product, Vasconcelos's *raza cósmica*. Rather, the emphasis is on the process [. . .]" (94).

12. As discussed in the previous chapter, in *Cristóbal Nonato,* Fuentes uses a play on words in English, "Makesicko City," to refer to a dystopian future metropolis.

13. Morales grounds his description of a colonial plague in the history of various epidemics that affected New Spain since the beginning of the conquest. From the moment of initial Euro-American contact, there began a decrease in the population of native communities caused by the introduction of Old World viruses, a phenomenon that has been studied in depth by scholars Woodrow Borah and S. F. Cook, and more recently by Noble David Cook, Suzanne Austin Alchon, and George Raudzens. Smallpox and other epidemics decimated the population of the urban centers, making it easier for the Europeans to appropriate the land. Tzvetan Todorov observes how both *mestizaje* and epidemics changed the face of Mesoamerican reality and facilitated the process of conquest and colonization. Mexico City in particular was prone to plagues because of stagnant waters in canals in which rubbish and human waste were exposed, as described in *The Rag Doll Plagues*. In the later colonial period various infectious diseases constituted a concern for the viceregal administrations; from 1733 to 1792 there were epidemics that caused a decline in the population of Mexico City. Although the plagues that Morales describes in his text are fictitious, the threat of epidemics caused by diverse factors such as lack of public hygiene and a diet poor in vitamins was a constant in colonial Mexico.

14. Morales comments that he was inspired by John Tate Lanning's book on the Royal Protomedicato in New Spain when he wrote this section of *The Rag Doll Plagues* ("Dynamic Identities in Heterotopia" 21). Luis Leal further elaborates on the influence of Lanning's book on Morales's medicalization of the colony (41).

15. The use of scientific discourse as a disciplinary apparatus indicated by the reference "immoral racial mixtures" is not new in the territorial space known now as Mexico. The narrator's listing of different races as part of a degenerate rabble is reminiscent of late seventeenth-century scholar Carlos de Sigüenza y Góngora's essay on the riots in Mexico City that protested repeated shortages of corn. Sigüenza's "Alboroto y motín" summarizes the uprisings that occurred as a result of the scarcity of food—and also the plagues—in colonial Mexico City:

> [. . .] preguntaráme Vmd. cómo se portó la plebe en aqueste tiempo y respondo brevemente que bien y mal; bien, porque, siendo plebe tan en extremo plebe, que sólo ella lo puede ser de la que se reputare la más infame, y lo es de todas las plebes, por componerse de *indios, de negros criollos y bozales de diferentes naciones, de chinos, de mulatos, de moriscos, de mestizos, de zambaigos, de lobos y también de españoles* que, en declarándose zaramullos (que es lo mismo que pícaros, chulos y arre-batacapas) y *degenerando* de sus obligaciones, son los peores entre tan ruin canalla. (181; emphasis mine)

Both the seventeenth-century Mexican scholar and Morales's fictional narrator express their fears of contamination in their descriptions of the heterogeneous body of colonial society.

16. In reference to the context of colonial India, David Arnold describes how medical science was used as a means of legitimizing imperial enterprises, keeping the "superiority" of Western medicine unquestioned.

17. The figure of Catalina de Erauso, better known as the "Monja Alférez," or Lieutenant Nun, has been the subject of several contemporary novels, among them *Duerme* (1994) by Carmen Boullosa, which is loosely based on her story.

18. This same pattern is further emphasized in the other two sections of the novel as Gregory and Sandra Spear travel to Tepotzotlan to look for a cure for AIDS in the book entitled "Delhi," and Gregory and Gabi Chung visit the population of a lumpen area of Mexico City in "LAMEX."

19. It is hard to avoid drawing a parallel between this plague and the AIDS epidemic, which was first associated with homosexuals and drug addicts before being recognized as a threat to the general population. In this context, it is revealing that the character who is afflicted by AIDS in the second book of Morales's novel is neither a homosexual nor a drug addict, but rather a woman from an affluent background who contracts the disease as the result of a transfusion. Like the plague in the first section, Sandra's illness in the second part points to the need to avoid associating epidemics with certain races, classes, or sexual orientations.

20. There is a parallel between this description of Sandra's apartment and the portrayal in the colonial section of the home of don Gregorio's guide, Father Jude: "[. . .] it was seductively alive with Mexican colors, from handwoven blankets, pillows, rugs, tapestries, gabans and more native items" (48).

21. In the early stages of the AIDS epidemic in the 1980s, AIDS was attributed to "[t]he result of genetic mutations caused by 'mixed marriages'" (Treichler 13).

22. Although females can be carriers of hemophilia, only rarely are they themselves victims of the illness. Sandra resembles the title character of Colombian Jorge Isaacs's foundational fiction *María* (1867) in which the protagonist is also Jewish and carries a rare disease. As Sander Gilman analyzes, the association between contagious diseases and Jewish origin has played an important role in Western medical discourse since the Middle Ages, underscoring the anti-Semitic phobias of contact (21).

23. Reading about Sandra's struggle brings to mind the story of Ryan White (1971–90) who contracted AIDS as a result of treatment for hemophilia. Like Morales's fictional character, Ryan was treated with contempt by his classmates, but despite this harsh treatment, Ryan fought to educate people about living with AIDS.

24. The AIDS epidemic made Chicano/a communities aware of issues of sexual orientation within their own culture. Chicana poet and academic Cherríe Moraga highlights how Chicanos had not directly engaged sexuality and sexism before "the AIDS epidemic ha[d] seriously shaken the foundation of the Chicano gay community" (162).

25. María Herrera-Sobek discusses this representation of Sandra as Coatlicue in detail in her article "Epidemics, Epistemophilia, and Racism."

26. As Mary Miller and Karl Taube describe, "Coatlicue wears a dress of woven rattlesnakes. Her pendulous breasts are partially obscured behind a grisly necklace of severed hearts and hands. Writhing coral snakes appear in place of her head and hands, denoting gouts of blood gushing from her severed throat and wrists" (64).

27. For an analysis of the connection between gender and technology, see Donna Haraway's essay "A Manifesto for Cyborgs: Science, Technology, and Socialist Feminism in the 1980s."

28. The term "Triple Alliance" also evokes the pre-Columbian coalition between Tenochtitlan, Tezcoco, and Tlacopan.

29. In the film *The Day after Tomorrow* (2004), we see an ironic reversal of traditional migration patterns in that in order to escape a new ice age resulting from global warming, North Americans rush to cross the border into Mexico.

255

30. As discussed in the previous chapter on Fuentes's *Cristóbal Nonato*, García Canclini applies the term *cultural reconversion* to the process of adaptation of "traditional cultures" to modernization.

31. In his article "The Global Border," Martín-Rodríguez discusses the way in which the residents of El Mar de Villas reinvent their space with recycled objects (91–92).

Chapter Three
The Dream of Mestizo Mexico: Memory and History in Carmen Boullosa's *Cielos de la tierra*

1. Carmen Boullosa, born in Mexico City in 1954, has published numerous novels and poetry anthologies. She has been the recipient of the Guggenheim and other prestigious fellowships and has taught in universities in the United States. Among her best-known narrative works are: *Son vacas, somos puercos* (1991), *Llanto: novelas imposibles* (1992), *La milagrosa* (1993), *Duerme* (1994), *Cielos de la tierra* (1997), *Treinta años* (1999), and *De un salto descabalga la reina* (2002). Boullosa's fiction has been translated into English, French, and German. The works translated into English include: *The Miracle Worker* (1994), *They're Cows, We're Pigs* (1997), *Leaving Tabasco* (2001), and *Cleopatra Dismounts* (2003).

2. *Cielos de la tierra* has attracted the attention of several critics such as Gloria Prado, Javier Durán, Claire Taylor, Anna Reid, Alejandro Morales, Demetrio Anzaldo González, Verónica Salles-Reese, Christopher Domínguez Michael, and Margarita Saona.

3. In its representation of the language of the future, *Cielos de la tierra* incorporates many lexical items from the universal language of Esperanto. Boullosa uses Esperanto as a way to highlight the need for a universal language that transcends the limitations of time and culture. *Kestos* means "chest" and is used by Boullosa to refer to the archive containing the narratives of Hernando, Estela, and Lear.

4. Ernst Bloch, in *The Utopian Function of Art and Literature,* identifies three different kinds of utopias: social utopias that strive for a "transformation of the world to the greatest possible realization of social happiness" (4), whose best example is Thomas More's *Utopia* (1516); "technological utopias," which through humankind's ingenuity achieve new levels of perfection, a genre best exemplified by Tommaso Campanella's *Città del sole* (1615) and Francis Bacon's *New Atlantis* (1624); and the "medical utopia" that pursues the elimination of illness and death (5). As we will see, in *Cielos de la tierra* Boullosa builds on all three utopian modalities.

5. In her novel *Llanto*, Boullosa problematizes interpretations of the conquest of Mexico, focusing on the Aztec emperor Moctezuma's final days and examining different versions of major historical events. In their scholarship, Carrie Chorba, Anna Reid, and Veronica Salles-Reese have addressed Boullosa's manipulation of historical sources. Notably, in her article "Cities, Codes and Cyborgs in Carmen Boullosa's *Cielos de la Tierra*," Claire Taylor discusses the novel in relation to postmodern currents such as those represented by the work of Donna Haraway, Jean Baudrillard, and Judith Butler.

6. In the prologue to his *Sermonario en lengua mexicana* (1606), the priest Juan Bautista recognizes the collaboration of a certain Hernando de Ribas of the city of Tezcucu in the production of several documents referring to the culture of the Nahua communities of Central Mexico. This prologue is reproduced in Lino Gómez Canedo's *La educación de los marginados durante la época colonial*, 371–79.

7. The severity of the Franciscan educational system and its strict scholastic demands coincided with the aims of the native *calmecac* (school for nobles); as Serge Gruzinski discusses in *The Conquest of Mexico*, "Temple-schools reserved for sons of the *pipiltzin* prepared the future rulers. Within these calmecac, wise men—those called 'the owners of the books of paintings' [*amatlacuilos*], 'the knowers of hidden things,' 'the keepers of tradition'—dispensed to the young nobles an education as austere as it was sophisticated, which associated knowledge with modes of speaking and ways of being" (9).

8. Pilar Gonzalbo Aizpuru's *Historia de la educación en la época colonial: el mundo indígena* documents that as early as 1525 there were conversations about the instruction of Amerindians at higher levels. In 1526, Rodrigo de Albornoz proposed the idea of a school for native children to the Emperor. By 1532, the Franciscans were teaching Latin grammar with good results, gaining the interest and enthusiasm of Bishop Juan de Zumárraga. With the arrival of a new viceroy, don Antonio de Mendoza, all these measures took form and in January of 1536, the College of Santa Cruz de Tlatelolco opened its doors to indigenous children (Gonzalbo Aizpuru 111–12).

9. Mignolo further explores this concept of the colonization of memory in *The Dark Side of the Renaissance*.

10. *Amatlacuilos* refers to those *pipiltzin* (nobles) in charge of deciphering and interpreting the paintings contained in *amates*, which combined graphic representations with oral tradition.

11. The reference is to Ashcroft, Griffith, and Tiffin's *The Empire Writes Back*.

12. As outlined in the introduction, the *encomienda* system enabled Spanish settlers to exploit indigenous labor.

13. Hernando's father is Temilotzin Tlacatécatl, leader of Tlatelolco and companion of the last Aztec emperor, Cuauhtémoc. His fate is unclear as different versions conflict about his final days: some describe him as dying under colonial occupation; other versions have him escaping at sea after stowing away on a Spanish ship; yet others describe him ending up as a learned man who writes an apocryphal "Memorial de la casa de Moctezuma sobre la pretensión de grandeza de España al señor Felipe II," remaining in Spain until his death.

14. The official ordinance specified that noble indigenous children be sent to the colleges, but it was not clear if they would be allowed to rule their own communities in the future.

15. Boullosa's primary source for Hernando's transcription of pre-Columbian law is the compendium of native customs compiled by the sixteenth-century Franciscan friar Bernardino de Sahagún, who was himself a teacher at the College of Santa Cruz de Tlatelolco.

16. In *The Dark Side of the Renaissance*, Mignolo refers to the historians Diego Muñoz Camargo, Fernando de Alva Ixtlilxóchitl, and Hernando Alvarado Tezozomoc as members of the indigenous elite who tried to negotiate their own version of history during different periods in colonial Mexico.

17. As Serge Gruzinski elaborates in *The Conquest of Mexico*: "It was this education that from birth set the nobles apart from the plebeians, the *macehuale*s, by making them intellectually and morally superior beings [. . .]" (9). In other words, the nobles' status in society was justified because they were the guardians of the memory of the community.

18. Andrés de Olmos's notion of the New World as a land of giants coincides with indigenous visions of the first sun in which it is said that giants were the first to inhabit Mesoamerica. As discussed in the introduction, the representation of America as the home of giants has additional connotations, as the New World once was thought to be the lost continent of Atlantis.

19. There is a parallel between Hernando's use of Latin in colonial New Spain and Lear's later use of Esperanto in L'Atlàntide in that both are universal languages.

20. Hernando emphasizes that even the most enthusiastic supporter of the Franciscan colleges, Bishop Juan de Zumárraga, plays an important role in the unjust trial and execution of the noble Carlos Ometochtzin, since the bishop not only does not defend the nobleman of Tezcoco who in history had been one of the college's most apt pupils, but also allows his enemies to execute him. For details on the historical trial on which this portion of the novel is based, see Greenleaf's *Zumárraga and the Mexican Inquisition* and Gruzinski's *Conquest of Mexico*.

21. In a footnote to her article on *Cielos de la tierra*, scholar Anna Reid points out that Boullosa transcribes almost verbatim the accusations against the historical don Carlos (183).

22. According to Martin Lienhard, besides the accuser of Carlos Ometochtzin, a Chiconcuitla native named Francisco, there were other corroborating testimonies. Lienhard adds: "There are few known examples—that is, transcribed—of a discourse that rejects the Spanish conquest and colonization of Mexico in a straightforward manner like that of don Carlos" (16; translation mine).

23. Lino Gómez Canedo's *La educación de los marginados en la época colonial* documents some of the Franciscan prejudices against the Amerindians.

24. These references to the natives as parrots have as their source the dialogue of Jerónimo López as reproduced by Pilar Gonzalbo Aizpuru (295).

25. Both Rudi Bleys and Richard Trexler discuss how categories of sexual difference have been employed in the colonization of non-European societies to control the identity of the conquered communities. Trexler even insinuates that the expressions of hatred against homosexuality are in reality a reflection of the colonizer's secret desire to share in the colonized peoples' insurmountable difference.

26. This surveillance of the scribe and his self-censorship are reminiscent of the vigilance exercised by the Guardians over the narrator of Zamyatin's *We*: "He [the Guardian Angel] had obviously noticed that the book on my lap was now closed and my thought far away. Well, it was ready, there and then, to open all the pages of my mind to him [. . .]" (67).

27. Hernando's situation reminds us of the cases of nepantilism: the state of in-betweenness that the dominated communities experienced after the destruction of their work and during the emergence of the new society (Mignolo, *The Dark Side of the Renaissance*; Alberro, *Del gachupín al criollo*).

28. In her 2007 book, Carrie Chorba has written with lucidity about the theme of *mestizaje* in Boullosa's *Llanto*, comparing it to Fuentes's *El naranjo* and Ignacio Solares's *Nen, la inútil*.

29. Benito Juárez was the first indigenous president in Mexican history (1861–63 and 1867–76). His reforms had an ambiguous effect on the native communities because they eliminated the last measures protecting their lands, and without them, these lands became easy prey for outsiders to purchase, causing unemployment and a massive depopulation that later contributed to enlarging the *latifundios* of Porfirian Mexico.

30. During the 1990s, there was a widespread promotion of native languages as publishing houses began to publish books in Nahuatl, Chol, and Tzotzil written by authors belonging to these ethnic groups. In 2002, the National University (UNAM) opened for the first time a degree in indigenous languages and literatures.

31. The grandmother's remarks are similar to those of the narrator of *We*, as in Zamyatin's science fiction masterpiece, humans are separated from nature by the Green Wall: "But fortunately between me and the wild green ocean was the glass of the Wall. Oh, great, divinely bounding wisdom of walls and barriers! They are, perhaps, the greatest of man's inventions. Man ceased to be a wild animal when he built the first wall. Man ceased to be a savage only when we had built the Green Wall, when we had isolated our perfect mechanical world from the irrational, hideous world of trees, birds, animals . . ." (93).

32. The name of Boullosa's futuristic dystopia calls to mind the lost city of Atlantis. One of the earliest literary utopias, Sir Francis Bacon's *New*

Atlantis (1626) thematizes the finding of the lost continent. The name also recalls other literary dystopias such as Orwell's Oceania and Fuentes's Pacífica.

33. As noted above, *kestos* refers to an ark or chest in Esperanto.

34. Here Boullosa evokes classic utopias with societies living in the skies such as H. G. Wells's *The Shape of Things to Come* (1933). The description of the Atlántidos' dwellings is also reminiscent of those described in Zamyatin's *We*: "At all other times we live behind our transparent walls that seem woven of gleaming air—we are always visible, always washed in light. We have nothing to conceal from one another. Besides, this makes much easier the difficult and noble task of the Guardians" (18–19). In Zamyatin's novel, we see that the transparency of the walls facilitates the panoptic vigilance of the One State.

35. Zamyatin's *We* also takes place in a society created after a two-hundred-year war that reduced the earth's population to 2 percent.

36. The theme of artificially assisted human reproduction and high-tech indoctrination has been present since Huxley's 1932 *Brave New World* in which people are created in "hatcheries." A more recent depiction can be found in the film *The Matrix* (2001) in which a mechanical womb houses millions of individuals fed on virtual images of an alternative world while neglecting the ecological nightmare in which they exist.

37. The reference is similar to the film *Soylent Green* (1973), where at the end of life, elderly people receive tranquil images of nature before being euthanized.

38. Another parallel that the narrator of *Cielos de la tierra* establishes with the past is found in a quote attributed to Sir William Berkeley, seventeenth-century Governor of Virginia, in which history and literature are blamed for bringing about heresy and rebellion "against the best government":

> Doy gracias a Dios porque no tenemos ni escuelas ni imprentas,
> y ojalá no las tengamos en estos cien años, en vista de que las
> letras han engendrado rebeldía y herejía y sectas en el mundo,
> la imprenta ha divulgado éstas y también calumnias contra el
> mejor gobierno. Dios nos libre de ambas. (31)

This passage attributed to Berkeley reminds us of the Casa de Indias's 1531 prohibition of the importation of books to the Spanish territories, which originated in the fear of filling the minds of the Amerindians with alternative ways of thinking.

39. This is reminiscent of the Great Operation that attempts to suppress the resistance movement at the end of Zamyatin's *We*.

40. As in Jorge Luis Borges's short story "The Immortal," *Cielos de la tierra* has characters who cannot die, but also have no reason to live in a society that has extinguished all traces of humanity.

41. Javier Durán identifies this last scene as a reminiscence of Stanley Kubrick's *2001: A Space Odyssey*. Its origins can also be traced back to

H. G. Wells's *The Time Machine*, where in the distant future humanity has evolved into two separate races: the Eloi, a species that resembles the myth of the noble savage living in harmony with nature, and their nemesis the Morlocks, a savage clan that resorts to cannibalistic feeding on the Eloi and their fellow Morlocks.

Chapter Four
Surviving the Ecoapocalypse in Homero Aridjis's *La leyenda de los soles* and *¿En quién piensas cuando haces el amor?*

1. Born in Michoacán, Mexico, in 1940, Homero Aridjis published several books of poetry in the 1960s and 1970s, and since the 1980s has worked in fiction. Among his numerous artistic achievements are collections of poetry and drama such as *Antes del reino* (1961), *Perséfone* (1967), *Los espacios azules* (1968), and *Gran teatro del fin del mundo* (1989). His novelistic production can be categorized into two major veins: the historical novel rewriting the period of the conquest such as *1492: Vida y tiempos de Juan Cabezón de Castilla* (1985) and *Memorias del Nuevo Mundo* (1988); and apocalyptical works such as *La leyenda de los soles* (1993), *El señor de los últimos días: visiones del año mil* (1994), and *¿En quién piensas cuando haces el amor?* (1996). Aridjis has been twice the recipient of the Guggenheim Fellowship and has taught at several universities in the United States such as Columbia University, New York University, and Indiana University. He has served as ambassador from Mexico to the Netherlands and Switzerland, and he is the founder and president of the Group of 100, an international environmental organization of writers, artists, and scientists. He has published with Fernando C. Césarman a collection of essays related to the effects of industrialization on the environment entitled *Artistas e intelectuales sobre el ecocidio urbano* (1989). Since the publication of the two novels discussed in this chapter, he has published a collection of essays entitled *Apocalipsis con figuras* (1997), addressing his environmental and philosophical concerns. More recently he has added novels such as *La montaña de las mariposas* (1999) and *La zona del silencio* (2000) to his vast collection of literary works. Several of Aridjis's novels have been translated into English such as *1492: The Life and Times of Juan Cabezón of Castile*, *The Blue Spaces*, *Persephone*, and *The Lord of the Last Days: Visions of the Year 1000*. Neither of the two novels discussed here has been translated into English.

2. Apart from reviews, the two novels have received little critical attention. *La leyenda de los soles* and *¿En quién piensas cuando haces el amor?* have been the object of respective articles by James López and Hélène de Fays. López points to Aridjis's use of images of corruption and decay represented by the carnivalesque in *La leyenda de los soles*, while De Fays applies elements of ecocriticism focusing on *¿En quién piensas cuando haces el amor?*

3. The historical document *Leyenda de los soles* or *Códice Chimalpopoca* dates to the year 1558 and is believed to be a written translation of a Nahua *amate* (combination of writing and painting) made by one of the anonymous first pupils of the College of Santa Cruz de Tlatelolco. This historical document narrates the destruction of the previous four suns and serves as a genealogical account of the feats of Mexica kings.

4. In his collection of essays *Apocalipsis con figuras,* Aridjis underscores the importance of the year 2027 as the date when the Aztec ritual of re-igniting the fire would have taken place, and notes that for this reason he set his novel in that year (261).

5. The Aztecs identified planets, stars, and galaxies visible during eclipses with female demons called *tzitzimime* that attack the sun and destroy it.

6. In Aztec legend, Tlaloc, the rain god, required human sacrifice to make water available to human beings.

7. Tezcatlipoca (Smoking Mirror), brother of Quetzalcoatl, was associated in Aztec culture with pestilence, illness, and contagion, and according to Sahagún, this deity promoted war and famines (31). Besides appearing in Aridjis's poetry, this mythic figure has been a central theme in his fiction. In *Memorias del Nuevo Mundo*, the fictional conquistador Gonzalo Dávila becomes Tezcatlipoca after he finds the golden mask that reveals the future. It is not coincidental that Aridjis chooses this Aztec deity, since he is the God of sorcerers, rulers, and warriors, an elite caste that Aridjis implies must be reformed and reeducated to create a new relation with history and nature.

8. As mentioned in the previous chapter, the term *tlacuilo* or *amatlacuilo* refers to the Aztec chroniclers, members of the nobility who were in charge of recording memory through the use of glyphs and paintings.

9. In *La leyenda de los soles*, the narrator resorts to a metaliterary representation of the past by referring to the story of the historical manuscript: "*La leyenda de los Soles*, libro traducido del mexicano al castellano por fray Bernardino de Sahagún" (195). Juan de Góngora refers to himself as a participant in the history: "Francisco Javier Clavijero habla de mí en un lugar de su *Historia*" (101). And Cristóbal Cuauhtli refers to himself as the latest reincarnation of mythic Mesoamerican deity Quetzalcoatl: "Yo mismo el dios Quetzalcóatl, yo la culebra con plumas, yo el dios Matl [. . .]" (76).

10. General Tezcatlipoca's aggressive nature creates an association with the notorious Mexico City Chief of Police Arturo "El Negro" Durazo Moreno, who ruled with an iron fist under José López Portillo's administration. At the end of Durazo's term as chief of police, he was discovered to have embezzled large sums of money to build himself a palace in the hills of Acapulco.

11. The racist term *naco* refers to indigenous-looking inhabitants of Mexico City, associated with the lower social strata of Mexican society and connoting bad taste.

12. Huitzilopochtli, the Aztec god of war, guided the Aztecs to the island upon which they built Tenochtitlan.

13. Toci (Our Grandmother) is the patron goddess of *curanderas* (healers) and midwives and is also associated with war (Miller and Taube 169–70).

14. Rosalba's husband, Luis Antonio, is a scholar interested in the connection between nature and women. He is writing a book on goddesses of creation and destruction among different cultures around the world such as the German Freya, the Hindu Kali, and the Aztec Coatlicue, as will be discussed below.

15. The term "Fourth World" is used here to refer to countries that struggle for the basic means of survival. In *Apocalipsis con figuras*, Aridjis warns that hunger will become the dreaded Fourth Horseman of the Apocalypse:

> El Cuarto Jinete será el hambre. El futuro de los alimentos humanos estará vinculado a la condición ambiental de la tierra. Varios países que en el pasado fueron considerados utopías serán las Etiopías del futuro; Etiopías que sufrirán hambrunas periódicas y librarán guerras entre sí, no por territorios ni por riquezas fabulosas sino por la comodidad más apreciada en el tercer milenio, el agua. (375)

16. The Nahuatl term *tameme* refers to Amerindians charged with carrying burdens for the colonizers.

17. Beginning with the early chroniclers of the conquest, the Aztec capital of Tenochtitlan was compared to European cities. The conquistador Hernán Cortés in his *Segunda carta de relación* equated it to Seville, and in the seventeenth century, criollo poet Bernardo de Balbuena in his epic poem *Grandeza mexicana* compared it to Troy, Rome, and Venice.

18. In *Apocalipsis con figuras*, Aridjis describes the potential effects of ecological devastation for developing countries, similar to what *La leyenda de los soles* calls the wars of the Fourth World:

> Dependiendo por completo de la producción extranjera de alimentos y materias primas, los hombres de las megaciudades tercermundistas no sólo se pelearán por espacio físico, vivienda, comida y energía, sino por el agua: los vecinos de un barrio, los habitantes de un estado, de una región o de un país disputarán unos contra otros por la posesión y el uso del líquido más precioso del mundo en el futuro, el agua, la cual tendrá que ser racionada. (372)

19. La Malinche is the name by which Hernán Cortés's interpreter in the conquest of Mexico is best known. The figure of La Malinche is important in Mexican culture, since traditionally the indigenous woman who became Cortés's mistress has been regarded as a traitor (Paz, *Laberinto de la soledad* 72–97).

20. Significantly, this scene takes place at the National Park. Developed in the nineteenth century over an Aztec site of historical significance, Chapultepec Park with its forest, zoo, palace, and museums particularly since the mid twentieth century has been a staple of *capitalino* culture where people of all ages can learn about the natural and historical heritage of Mexico.

21. As the previous chapter developed, this theme of the artificial representation of a devastated nature is prominent in Carmen Boullosa's *Cielos de la tierra*.

22. *Cinema vérité* is a current of French cinema that developed to contrast with films produced in Hollywood with mega budgets, superstars, and special effects. In *cinema vérité*, the filmmaker's goal was to show life as it really is using the film as his artistic medium. Sets and props were never used, and everything was shot on location, often with a small, portable camera.

23. Since the early 1990s, more than three hundred young women ranging in age from the teens to early twenties have disappeared and later been found murdered in the outskirts of Ciudad Juárez. In *La leyenda de los soles*, the mysterious kidnapper is known as Tláloc, which is also the alias of one of the presumed perpetrators of the violent acts in Ciudad Juárez.

24. Aridjis indirectly acknowledges his debt to Fuentes's *Cristóbal Nonato* when some of his characters living in 2027 read the news from the *Diario de Mexamérica*.

25. As outlined in the introduction, the presidency of José López Portillo (1976–82) is notorious for being one of extreme corruption during which Mexico experienced an economic boom resulting from the large-scale exploitation of the country's oil reserves. Nevertheless, by the end of López Portillo's six years in office, the Mexican peso devalued in relation to the US dollar. Later on, Carlos Salinas de Gortari (1988–94) opened the doors for the deregulation of Mexican import tariffs and the opportunity to participate in the global market through NAFTA. The last years of the Salinato witnessed a profound political crisis when the above-mentioned assassinations were linked to Salinas's desire to remain in power to lead the country on a neoliberal path. Because of the political crisis and lack of guarantees of security after the murder of distinguished public figures, the peace and prosperity of the first years of the Salinas regime were followed by a wave of violence and public strife. On January 1, 1994, various indigenous groups in the southern state of Chiapas began an uprising in protest against the neoliberal policies of the Salinato. From the arrival to power of his successor, Ernesto Zedillo (1994–2000), until his exile to Ireland where he resides today, Carlos Salinas was the main figure named in accusations of corruption and the assassination of both Colosio and Ruiz Massieu. One of the most prominent figures of Salinas's administration, his brother Raúl Salinas de Gortari, was convicted of corruption and embezzlement and has been incarcerated in Mexico since 1996.

26. In Greek mythology Circe is the daughter of Helios (the Sun) and Perseis, daughter of Okeanos. In Homer's *Odyssey*, Circe is best known for using her seductive powers to detain Ulysses's sailors on their mission by bringing the seamen to her bed and then turning them into swine and later on serving them as supper.

27. Here Aridjis toys with the fact that no statue of conquistador Hernán Cortés exists on Mexican soil, a notable absence that has always been a source of great pride to Mexican citizens.

28. In the mid nineteenth century, when Mexico owed a huge debt to France, Napoleon III sent the Austrian Maximilian to be the emperor of Mexico. While some Europeanizing elites welcomed the Hapsburg ruler, the supporters of President Benito Juárez ultimately prevailed and Maximilian was executed. While Maximilian did make some significant contributions to Mexico such as the development of the buildings and grounds of Chapultepec, because of nationalistic sentiments, no major landmark in Mexico City would ever be named after the hapless emperor.

29. The traditional representation of Cortés's interpreter/mistress as a traitor has been questioned in recent years, in particular by scholars such as Norma Alarcón, Sandra Messinger Cypess, and Margo Glantz.

30. The reference is to Criollo poet Bernardo de Balbuena's epic poem *Grandeza mexicana* (1603), which describes the flourishing of colonial Mexican society in terms of a utopia in which the richness of the New World is complemented by the fruits of Western civilization.

31. Curiously, a few years after the publication of Aridjis's novels, in 2002, the Mexican government employed the services of former New York City mayor Rudolph W. Giuliani as a consultant to deter crime and indigence in Mexico City.

32. These three goddesses are related to the representation of women as capable of giving life but also of taking it away. In Norse mythology, Freya is a goddess of love and fertility, yet also a goddess of war. The Hindu Kali is a destructive mother goddess, frequently depicted as having blood-stained teeth and wearing a garland of human skulls. Kali's worshipers purportedly placated her in the past with human sacrifices, while today she is propitiated with the blood of mammals. As discussed in chapter 2, Coatlicue is the Aztec goddess of earth and mother of the gods, depicted wearing a skirt of snakes, symbolizing her relationship with the earth and the powers of destruction. Like Freya and Kali, Coatlicue represents the prototype of the devouring mother in whom are combined both the womb and the grave.

33. In *Apocalipsis con figuras*, Aridjis underscores this change of paradigm from culture considering nature as a passive object to a recognition of nature as a living entity (337). This coincides with J. E. Lovelock's Gaia hypothesis, which conceives of the ecosphere as a totality, a living system encompassing the interconnectedness of all living creatures.

34. In ancient Greek history, Mnemosyne, goddess of memory, was the mother of the muses of art.

35. The Mexican state's image of the eagle, which harks back to the Aztec legend of the foundation of Tenochtitlan, has been adopted by Mexico's version of the Green Party, Partido Verde Ecologista de México (Ecologist Green Party of Mexico, PVEM).

36. In *Apocalipsis con figuras,* Aridjis expresses his confidence in a resolution to the problems of industrialization through the widespread application of solar energy:

> El tercer milenio será el milenio del Sol, del Sol de la Tierra; el m(í)stico Sexto Sol de los mexicanos, que se acostará en el Oriente y se levantará en el Poniente. En este Sol tendrá lugar la eternidad finita y la temporalidad eterna, la era de la energía solar y de la cultura solar. Considerando el Sol como luz inteligente o como productor de razón [. . .], en esta era de seres radiantes, de seres con la luz en la cabeza, identificados con la realidad última, el Ser, nosotros los hombres podríamos vivir en heliopolis, ciudades solares. (367)

Bibliography

Adorno, Juan Nepomuceno. "México en el año 1970." Trans. as "The Distant Future." In *Cosmos Latinos: An Anthology of Science Fiction from Latin America and Spain*. Ed. Andrea L. Bell and Yolanda Molina-Gavilán. Middletown, CT: Wesleyan U, 2003. 23–35.

A.I. Artificial Intelligence. Dir. Steven Spielberg. Universal Studios, 2001.

Alarcón, Norma. "Traduttora, Traditora: A Paradigmatic Figure of Chicana Feminism." *Cultural Critique* 13 (1989): 57–87.

Alberro, Solange. *Del gachupín al criollo o de cómo los españoles dejaron de serlo*. Mexico City: Colegio de México, 1992.

Alchon, Suzanne Austin. *A Pest in the Land: New World Epidemics in a Global Perspective*. Albuquerque: U of New Mexico P, 2003.

Aldridge, Alexandra. *The Scientific World View in Dystopia*. Ann Arbor: UMI Research, 1984.

Alonso, Alejandro. *Ceroniverso*. Mexico City: Planeta, 2000.

Alonso, Carlos J. *The Burden of Modernity: The Rhetoric of Cultural Discourse in Spanish America*. New York: Oxford UP, 1998.

Anzaldo González, Demetrio. "Recordar a pesar del olvido, la alienación en *Cielos de la tierra*." *Acercamientos a Carmen Boullosa: Actas del Simposio "Conjugarse en infinitivo—la escritora Carmen Boullosa*." Ed. Barbara Dröscher and Carlos Rincón. Berlin: Frey, 1999. 210–20.

Anzaldúa, Gloria. *Borderlands / La frontera*. 1987. San Francisco: Aunt Lute, 1999.

Appadurai, Arjun. *Modernity at Large: Cultural Dimensions of Globalization*. Minneapolis: U of Minnesota P, 1996.

Arens, W[illiam]. *The Man-Eating Myth: Anthropology and Anthropophagy*. New York: Oxford UP, 1979.

Aridjis, Homero. *1492: The Life and Times of Juan Cabezón of Castile*. Trans. Betty Ferber. New York: Plume, 1992.

———. *1492: Vida y tiempos de Juan Cabezón de Castilla*. Mexico City: Diana, 1985.

———. *Antes del reino*. Mexico City: Era, 1963.

———. *Apocalipsis con figuras*. Mexico City: Taurus, 1997.

———. *¿En quién piensas cuando haces el amor?* Mexico City: Alfaguara, 1996.

Aridjis, Homero. *Los espacios azules.* Mexico City: Joaquín Mortiz, 1968.

———. *Los espacios azules / Blue Spaces; Selected Poems of Homero Aridjis.* Trans. and ed. Kenneth Rexroth. New York: Seabury, 1974.

———. *Espectáculo del año dos mil.* Mexico City: Joaquín Mortiz, 1981.

———. *Gran teatro del fin del mundo.* Mexico City: Joaquín Mortiz, 1989.

———. *Imágenes para el fin del milenio y Nueva expulsión del paraíso.* Mexico City: Joaquín Mortiz, 1990.

———. *La leyenda de los soles.* Mexico City: Alfaguara, 1993.

———. *The Lord of the Last Days: Visions of the Year 1000.* Trans. Betty Ferber. New York: Morrow, 1995.

———. *Memorias del Nuevo Mundo.* Mexico City: Diana, 1988.

———. *La montaña de las mariposas.* Mexico City: Alfaguara, 1999.

———. *Perséfone.* Mexico City: Joaquín Mortiz, 1967.

———. *Persephone.* Trans. Betty Ferber. New York: Vintage, 1986.

———. *El poeta niño.* Mexico City: Fondo de Cultura Ecónomica, 1971.

———. *Quemar las naves.* Mexico City: Joaquín Mortiz, 1975.

———. *El señor de los últimos días: visiones del año mil.* Mexico City: Alfaguara, 1994.

———. *Vivir para ver.* Mexico City: Joaquín Mortiz, 1977.

———. *La zona del silencio.* Mexico City: Alfaguara, 2002.

Aridjis, Homero, and Fernando C. Césarman. *Artistas e intelectuales contra el ecocidio urbano.* Mexico City: Consejo de la Crónica de la Ciudad de México, 1989.

Arnold, David. *Colonizing the Body.* Berkeley: U of California P, 1995.

Artaud, Antonin. *Viaje al país de los tarahumaras.* Mexico City: Secretaría de Educación Pública, 1975.

Ashcroft, Bill, Gareth Griffiths, and Helen Tiffin. *The Empire Writes Back: Theory and Practice in Post-colonial Literature.* New York: Routledge, 1989.

Atwood, Margaret. *The Handmaid's Tale.* Boston: Houghton, 1986.

Bacon, Francis. *New Atlantis.* 1626. Chicago: Encyclopaedia Britannica, 1952.

Bakhtin, M[ikhail] M. *The Dialogic Imagination.* Trans. Caryl Emerson and Michael Holquist. Austin: U of Texas P, 1981.

Balbuena, Bernardo de. *Grandeza mexicana*. 1603. Mexico City: Porrúa, 1964.

Barr, Marlene S., and Carl Freeman, eds. "Science Fiction and Literary Studies: The Next Millennium." Spec. issue of *PMLA: Publications of the Modern Language Association of America* 119.3 (May 2004): 429–546.

Bartkowski, Frances. *Feminist Utopias*. Lincoln: U of Nebraska P, 1989.

Bartra, Roger. *Blood, Ink, and Culture: Miseries and Splendors of the Post-Mexican Condition*. Trans. Mark Alan Healey. Durham: Duke UP, 2002.

———. *La sangre y la tinta: ensayos sobre la condición postmexicana*. Mexico City: Océano, 1999.

Baudot, Georges. *Utopia and the History of Mexico: The First Chroniclers of Mexican Civilization (1520–1569)*. Trans. Bernard R. Ortiz de Montellano and Thelma Ortiz de Montellano. Niwot, CO: UP of Colorado, 1995.

Baudrillard, Jean. *The Consumer Society: Myths and Structures*. Thousand Oaks, CA: Sage, 1998.

Bell, Andrea L., and Yolanda Molina-Gavilán. *Cosmos Latinos: An Anthology of Science Fiction from Latin America and Spain*. Middletown: Wesleyan UP, 2003.

Belli, Gioconda. *Waslala: memorial del futuro*. Managua, Nicaragua: Anamá Ediciones Centroamericanas, 1996.

Ben-Tov, Sharona. *The Artificial Paradise: Science Fiction and American Reality*. Ann Arbor: U of Michigan P, 1995.

Benítez, Fernando. *Los indios de México*. Mexico City: Era, 1967.

———. *Lázaro Cárdenas y la Revolución Mexicana*. Mexico City: Fondo de Cultura Económica, 1977.

Benjamin, Thomas. *La Revolución: Mexico's Great Revolution as Memory, Myth, and History*. Austin: U of Texas P, 2000.

Bhabha, Homi. *The Location of Culture*. New York: Routledge, 1995.

Blade Runner. Dir. Ridley Scott. Warner Studios, 1982.

Bleys, Rudi C. *The Geography of Perversion: Male-to-Male Sexual Behavior outside the West and the Ethnographic Imagination, 1750–1918*. New York: New York UP, 1995.

Bloch, Ernst. *The Utopian Function of Art and Literature*. Trans. Jack Zipes and Frank Mecklenburg. Cambridge, MA: MIT P, 1988.

Bonfil [Batalla], Guillermo. "Del indigenismo de la revolución a la antro-pología crítica." *De eso que llaman antropología mexicana.* Ed. Arturo Warman et al. Mexico City: Nuestro Tiempo, 1970. 39–65.

———. *México profundo.* Mexico City: Conaculta, 1987.

Borah, Woodrow, and S[herbourne] F. Cook. *The Population of Central Mexico in 1548: An Analysis of the Suma de visitas de pueblos.* Berkeley: U of California P, 1960.

Borges, Jorge Luis. "El inmortal." *Aleph.* Madrid: Alianza/Emecé, 1971. 7–28.

Botallico, Michele. "Illness in Alejandro Morales's *The Rag Doll Plagues.*" *Cuadernos de literatura inglesa y norteamericana* 5.1–2 (2002): 64–73.

Boullosa, Carmen. *Cielos de la tierra.* Mexico City: Alfaguara, 1997.

———. *Cleopatra Dismounts.* Trans. Geoff Hargreaves. New York: Grove, 2003.

———. *De un salto desmonta la reina.* Madrid: Alfaguara, 2002.

———. *Duerme.* Mexico City: Alfaguara, 1994.

———. *Leaving Tabasco.* Trans. Geoff Hargreaves. New York: Grove, 2001.

———. *Llanto: novelas imposibles.* Mexico City: Era, 1992.

———. *El médico de los piratas.* Mexico City: Siruela, 1992.

———. *The Miracle-Worker.* London: Jonathan Cape, 1984.

———. *Son vacas, somos puercos.* Mexico City: Era, 1991.

———. *They're Cows, We're Pigs.* Trans. Leland H. Chambers. New York: Grove, 1997.

———. *Treinta años.* Mexico City: Alfaguara, 1999.

Bradbury, Ray. *Fahrenheit 451.* New York: Simon and Schuster, 1953.

Brading, D. A. *The Origins of Mexican Nationalism.* Cambridge: U of Cambridge P, 1985.

Buell, Lawrence. *The Environmental Imagination: Thoreau, Nature Writing, and the Formation of American Culture.* Cambridge, MA: Harvard UP, 1995.

Callenbach, Ernest. *Ecotopia: The Notebooks and Reports of William Weston.* Berkeley: Banyan, 1975.

———. *Ecotopia Emerging.* New York: Bantam, 1979.

Cameron, Maxwell A., and Brian W. Tomlin. *The Making of NAFTA: How the Deal Was Done.* Ithaca: Cornell UP, 2000.

Campanella, Tommaso. *La città del sole / Civitas Solis.* Ed. and trans. John Donno. Berkeley: U of California P, 1981.

Castañeda, Jorge G. *La utopía desarmada*. Mexico City: Joaquín Mortiz, 1993.

Castellanos, Rosario. *Balún Canán*. Mexico City: Fondo de Cultura Económica, 1957.

———. *Oficio de Tinieblas*. Mexico City: Joaquín Mortiz, 1962.

Castillo, Debra A. "Fantastic Arabesques in Fuentes's *Cristóbal Nonato*." *Revista de Estudios Hispánicos* 25.3 (1991): 1–14.

———. "Fuentes fronterizo." *Arizona Journal of Hispanic Cultural Studies* 4 (2000): 159–74.

Castro, Juan E. de. "Richard Rodriguez in 'Borderland': The Ambiguity of Hybridity." *Aztlán* 26.1 (2001): 101–26.

Castro-Gómez, Santiago. "The Social Sciences, Epistemic Violence, and the Problem of the 'Invention of the Other.'" *Nepantla: Views from the South* 3.2 (2002): 269–85.

Chamberlin, J. Edward, and Sander L. Gilman, eds. *Degeneration: The Dark Side of Progress*. New York: Columbia UP, 1985.

Charnas, Suzy McKee. *Walk to the End of the World*. New York: Ballantine, 1974.

Chávez Castañeda, Ricardo. *El día del Hurón*. Mexico City: Nueva Imagen, 1997.

Chorba, Carrie C. *From Mestizo to Multicultural: National Identity and Recent Representations of the Conquest*. Nashville: Vanderbilt UP, 2007.

Cohen, Sandro. *Lejos del Paraíso*. Mexico City: Sansores y Aljure, 1997.

Comte, Auguste. *Introduction to Positive Philosophy*. Ed. and trans. Frederick Ferre. Indianapolis: Bobbs-Merrill, 1970.

Cook, Noble David. *Born to Die: Disease and New World Conquest, 1492–1650*. Cambridge: Cambridge UP, 1998.

Cooper, Donald B. *Epidemic Disease in Mexico City, 1761–1813: An Administrative, Social, and Medical Study*. Austin: U of Texas P, 1965.

Cornejo, Gerardo. *Al norte del milenio*. Mexico City: Leega, 1989.

———. *Juan Justino Judicial*. Mexico City: Selector, 1996.

Cornejo-Polar, Antonio. *Sobre literatura y crítica latinoamericanas*. Caracas: Universidad Central de Venezuela, 1982.

Cornelius, Wayne, and Ann L. Craig. *Mexican Politics in Transition: The Breakdown of a One-party Dominant Regime*. La Jolla: Center for U.S.-Mexican Studies, U of California, San Diego, 1991.

Cortés, Hernán. *Cartas de relación*. 1522. Mexico City: Porrúa, 1988.

Creed, Barbara. *The Monstrous-Feminine*. London: Routledge, 1993.

Cro, Stelio. *The American Foundation of the Hispanic Utopia*. Tallahassee: DeSoto, 1994.

Crosby, Alfred. *Ecological Imperialism: The Biological Expansion of Europe 900–1900*. New York: Cambridge UP, 1986.

Crosthwaite, Luis Humberto. *La luna siempre será un amor difícil*. Mexico City: Eco, 1994.

———. *The Moon Will Forever Be a Distant Love*. Trans. Debbie Nathan and Willivaldo Delgadillo. El Paso: Cinco Puntos, 1997.

Cypess, Sandra Messinger. *La Malinche in Mexican Literature: From History to Myth*. Austin: U of Texas P, 1991.

The Day after Tomorow. Dir. Roland Emmerich. 20th Century Fox, 2004.

Debroise, Olivier. *Crónica de las destrucciones*. Mexico City: Era, 1998.

De la Maza, Francisco. *El guadalupanismo mexicano*. Mexico City: Fondo de Cultura Económica, 1953.

Díaz del Castillo, Bernal. *Historia verdadera de la conquista de la Nueva España*. Mexico City: Porrúa, 1963.

Dick, Philip K. *Do Androids Dream of Electric Sheep?* 1968. New York: Del Rey, 1975.

Domínguez Michael, Christopher. "*Cielos de la tierra*: nuevo 'criollismo.'" *Acercamientos a Carmen Boullosa: Actas del Simposio "Conjugarse en infinitivo—la escritora Carmen Boullosa."* Ed. Barbara Dröscher and Carlos Rincón. Berlin: Frey, 1999. 37–42.

Durán, Javier. "Utopia, Heterotopia, and Memory in Carmen Boullosa's *Cielos de la tierra*." *Studies in the Literary Imagination* 33.1 (2000): 51–64.

Dussel, Enrique. *The Invention of the Americas: Eclipse of "the Other" and the Myth of Modernity*. Trans. Michael D. Barber. London: Continuum, 1995.

Eaubonne, Françoise D'. *Le féminisme ou la mort*. Paris: P. Horay, 1974.

Elliot, J. H. *Spain and Its World (1500–1700)*. New Haven: Yale UP, 1989.

Fays, Hélène de. "Neo-Luddism in a Mexican Novel: *¿En quién piensas cuando haces el amor?* by Homero Aridjis." *Cyberletras* 4 (2001): n.pag. (www.lehman.edu/cyberletras).

———. "From *1984* to *Sueños digitales*: The Dystopian Novel in the Age of Globalization." Diss. U of North Carolina, Chapel Hill, 2004.

Fernández Delgado, Miguel Ángel. *Visiones periféricas: antología de la ciencia ficción mexicana.* Mexico City: Grupo Editorial Lumen, 2001.

Foucault, Michel. *Discipline and Punish: The Birth of the Prison.* Trans. Alan Sheridan. New York: Vintage, 1977.

———. "What Is Enlightenment?" *The Foucault Reader.* Ed. Paul Rabinow. New York: Pantheon, 1984. 32–50.

Franco, Dean. "Working through the Archive: Trauma and History in Alejandro Morales's *The Rag Doll Plagues.*" *PMLA: Publications of the Modern Language Association of America* 120.2 (2005): 375–87.

Fuentes, Carlos. *Las buenas conciencias.* Mexico City: Fondo de Cultura Económica, 1959.

———. *Cambio de piel.* Mexico City: Joaquín Mortiz, 1967.

———. *Cervantes o la crítica de la lectura.* Mexico City: Grijalbo, 1976.

———. *A Change of Skin.* Trans. Sam Hileman. London: Jonathan Cape, 1968.

———. *Christopher Unborn.* Trans. Alfred J. MacAdam and Carlos Fuentes. New York: Farrar, 1989.

———. *Cristóbal Nonato.* Mexico City: Fondo de Cultura Económica, 1987.

———. *The Crystal Frontier.* Trans. Alfred J. MacAdam. San Diego: Harcourt, 1995.

———. *The Death of Artemio Cruz.* Trans. Sam Hileman. New York: Farrar, 1964.

———. *Los días enmascarados.* Mexico City: Los Presentes, 1954.

———. *La frontera de cristal.* Mexico City: Alfaguara, 1995.

———. *The Good Conscience.* Trans. Sam Hileman. New York: Farrar, 1989.

———. *La muerte de Artemio Cruz.* Mexico City: Fondo de Cultura Económica, 1962.

———. *El naranjo, o los círculos del tiempo.* Mexico City: Alfaguara, 1993.

———. *A New Time for Mexico.* Trans. Marina Gutman Castañeda and Carlos Fuentes. 1996. Berkeley: U of California P, 1997.

———. *Nuevo tiempo mexicano.* Mexico City: Aguilar, 1994.

———. *The Orange Tree.* Trans. Alfred J. MacAdam. New York: Farrar, 1994.

Fuentes, Carlos. *La región más transparente*. Mexico City: Fondo de Cultura Económica, 1958.

———. *Terra nostra*. Mexico City: Joaquín Mortiz, 1975.

———. *Terra Nostra*. Trans. Margaret Sayers Peden. New York: Farrar, 1976.

———. *This I Believe*. Trans. Kristina Cordero. New York: Random, 2005.

———. *Tiempo mexicano*. Mexico City: Joaquín Mortiz, 1971.

Gamio, Manuel. *Forjando patria*. 1916. Mexico City: Porrúa, 1964.

García Bergua, Ana. *El umbral: Travels and Adventures*. Mexico City: Era, 1993.

García Canclini, Néstor. *Consumers and Citizens: Globalization and Multicultural Conflicts*. Trans. Geroge Yúdice. Minneapolis: U of Minnesota P, 2001.

———. *Consumidores y ciudadanos: conflictos multiculturales de la globalización*. Mexico City: Grijalbo, 1995.

———. "Cultural Reconversion." *On Edge*. Ed. George Yúdice, Jean Franco, and Juan Flores. Minneapolis: U of Minnesota P, 1992. 29–43.

———. *Culturas híbridas*. Mexico City: Grijalbo, 1990.

———. *Las culturas populares en el capitalismo*. Rev. 6th ed. Mexico City: Grijalbo, 2002.

———. *La globalización imaginada*. Buenos Aires: Paidós, 1999.

———. *Hybrid Cultures: Strategies for Entering and Leaving Modernity*. Trans. Christopher L. Chiappari and Silvia L. Lopez. Minneapolis: U of Minnesota P, 1995.

———. *Transforming Modernity*. Trans. Lydia Lozano. Austin: U of Texas P, 1993.

García Márquez, Gabriel. *Cien años de soledad*. Buenos Aires: Sudamericana, 1967.

———. *One Hundred Years of Solitude*. Trans. Gregory Rabassa. New York: Avon, 1971.

Garibay K., Ángel María. *Historia de la literatura náhuatl*. Mexico City: Porrúa, 1954.

Garreau, Joel. *The Nine Nations of North America*. Boston: Houghton, 1981.

Giddens, Anthony. *The Consequences of Modernity*. Palo Alto: Stanford UP, 1990.

Gilman, Charlotte Perkins. *Herland.* New York: Pantheon, 1979.

Gilman, Sander L. *The Jew's Body.* New York: Routledge, 1991.

Glantz, Margo. *La Malinche, sus padres y sus hijos.* Mexico City: UNAM, 1994.

Glotfelty, Cheryll, and Harold Fromm. *Ecocriticism Reader: Landmarks in Literary Ecology.* Athens: U of Georgia P, 1996.

Ginway, M. Elizabeth. *Brazilian Science Fiction: Cultural Myths and Nationhood in the Land of the Future.* Lewisburg: Bucknell UP, 2004.

Gómez Canedo, Lino. *La educación de los marginados durante la época colonial.* Mexico City: Porrúa, 1982.

Gonzalbo Aizpuru, Pilar. *Historia de la educación en la época colonial: el mundo indígena.* Mexico City: Colegio de México, 1990.

González Echevarría, Roberto. *Myth and Archive.* Durham: Duke UP, 1990.

Greene, Graham. *Another Mexico.* New York: Viking, 1939.

———. *The Power and the Glory.* New York: Viking, 1940.

Greenleaf, Richard E. *Zumárraga and the Mexican Inquisition, 1536–1543.* Washington, DC: Academy of American Franciscan History, 1962.

Gruzinski, Serge. *The Conquest of Mexico: The Incorporation of Indian Societies into the Western World, 16th–18th Centuries.* London: Polity, 1993.

———. *Images at War.* Trans. Heather MacLean. Durham: Duke UP, 2001.

Guerra, Francisco. *The Pre-Columbian Mind.* London: Seminar, 1971.

Gutiérrez Mouat, Ricardo. "Postmodernity and Postmodernism in Latin America: Carlos Fuentes's *Christopher Unborn.*" *Critical Theory, Cultural Politics, and Latin American Narrative.* Ed. Steven Bell et al. London: U of Notre Dame P, 1993. 153–79.

Habermas, Jürgen. *The Philosophical Discourse of Modernity.* Trans. Frederick Lawrence. Cambridge, MA: MIT P, 1987

———. *Die Postnationale Konstellation.* Frankfurt am Main: Suhrkamp, 1998.

Hamnett, Brian. *A Concise History of Mexico.* New York: Cambridge UP, 1999.

Haraway, Donna. "A Manifesto for Cyborgs: Science, Technology, and Socialist Feminism in the 1980s." *Feminism/Postmodernism.* Ed. Linda Hutcheon. New York: Routledge, 1990. 190–233.

Harvey, David. *The Condition of Postmodernity.* Oxford: Basil Blackwell, 1989.

Harvey, Neil. *The Chiapas Rebellion: The Struggle for Land and Democracy.* Durham: Duke UP, 1998.

Hernández, Jorge. *Carlos Fuentes: Territorios del tiempo.* Mexico City: Fondo de Cultura Económica, 1999.

Herrera-Sobek, María. "Epidemics, Epistemophilia, and Racism: Ecological Literary Criticism and *The Rag Doll Plagues.*" *Alejandro Morales: Fiction, Past, Present, Future Perfect.* Ed. José Antonio Gurpegui. Tempe: Bilingual/Bilingüe, 1996. 99–108.

Hiriart, Hugo. *La destrucción de las cosas.* Mexico City: Era, 1992.

Hoeg, Jerry. *Science, Technology, and Latin American Narrative in the Twentieth Century and Beyond.* Cranbury, MA: Associated U Presses, 2000.

Homer. *The Odyssey.* Trans. A. T. Murray. Cambridge, MA: Harvard UP, 1919.

Huacuja del Toro, Malú. *Un dios para Cordelia.* Mexico City: Océano, 1995.

———. *Herejía contra el ciberespacio o los destinos del Desertor.* Mexico City: Océano, 1999.

Huxley, Aldous. *Brave New World.* London: Chatto and Windus, 1932.

Huyssen, Andreas. *After the Great Divide.* Bloomington: Indiana UP, 1986.

I, Robot. Dir. Alex Proyas. Twentieth Century Fox, 2004.

Isaacs, Jorge. *María.* 1867. Mexico City: Porrúa, 1966.

Jameson, Fredric. *Archaeologies of the Future: The Desire Called Utopia and Other Science Fictions.* London and New York: Verso, 2005.

Juan-Navarro, Santiago. *Archival Reflections: Postmodern Fiction of the Americas (Self-Reflexivity, Historical Revisionism, Utopia).* Lewisburg: Bucknell UP, 2000.

———. "En busca de la utopía: la novela como alegoría de la nación en *Cristóbal Nonato* de Carlos Fuentes." *Explicación de Textos Literarios* 20.1 (1991–92): 24–46.

Klaic, Dragan. *The Plot of the Future: Utopia and Dystopia in Modern Drama.* Ann Arbor: U of Michigan P, 1991.

Knight, Alan. "Racism, Revolution, and *Indigenismo*: Mexico, 1910–1940." *The Idea of Race in Latin America (1870–1940).* Ed. Richard Graham. Austin: U of Texas P, 1990. 71–113.

Krauze, Enrique. *Mexico: Biography of Power: A History of Modern Mexico, 1810–1996*. New York: Harper, 1997.

Kumar, Krishan. *Utopia and Anti-Utopia in Modern Times*. New York: Blackwell, 1987.

Lacan, Jacques. "The Mirror Stage as Formative of the Function of the 'I' as Revealed in Psychoanalytic Experience." *Écrits*. Trans. Alan Sheridan. New York: Tavistock, 1966. 1–7.

Lafaye, Jacques. *Quetzalcoatl and Guadalupe: The Formation of Mexican National Consciousness, 1531–1813*. Trans. Benjamin Keen. Foreword Octavio Paz. Chicago: U of Chicago P, 1986.

Lanning, John Tate. *The Royal Protomedicato: The Regulation of the Medical Profession in the Spanish Empire*. Ed. John Jay TePaske. Durham: Duke UP, 1985.

Larson, Ross. *Fantasy and Imagination in the Mexican Narrative*. Tempe: Arizona State UP, 1977.

Lawrence, D. H. *The Plumed Serpent*. New York: Knopf, 1926.

Leal, Luis. "Historia y ficción en la narrativa de Alejandro Morales." *Alejandro Morales: Fiction, Past, Present, Future Perfect*. Ed. José Antonio Gurpegui. Tempe: Bilingual/Bilingüe, 1996. 31–42.

LeGuin, Ursula K. *The Dispossessed: An Ambiguous Utopia*. New York: Harper. 1974.

León-Portilla, Miguel. *Los antiguos mexicanos a tráves de sus crónicas*. Mexico City: Fondo de Cultura Económica, 1961.

———. *La filosofía náhuatl*. Mexico City: Universidad Nacional Autónoma de México, 1993.

———. *La visión de los vencidos*. Mexico City: Universidad Nacional Autónoma de México, 1959.

Lewis, Bart L. *The Miraculous Lie: Lope de Aguirre and the Search for El Dorado in the Latin American Historical Novel*. Lanham, MD: Lexington, 2003.

Lienhard, Martin. *La voz y su huella*. Hanover, NH: Ediciones del Norte, 1991.

Lomnitz, Claudio. *Exits from the Labyrinth: Culture and Ideology in Mexican National Space*. Los Angeles: U of California P, 1995.

———. *Deep Mexico, Silent Mexico: An Anthropology of Nationalism*. Minneapolis: U of Minnesota P, 2001.

López, James Joseph. *Eden in the Age of the Fifth Sun: The Narrative Work of Homero Aridjis*. Diss. Florida International U, 2000.

López, James Joseph. "Homero Aridjis: *La leyenda de los soles.*" *Revista de Literatura Mexicana Contemporánea* 3.5 (1997): 48–56.

López, Kimberle S. *Latin American Novels of the Conquest: Reinventing the New World.* Columbia: U of Missouri P, 2002.

López Austin, Alfredo. *La educación de los antiguos Nahuas.* Mexico City: Secretaría de Educación Pública, 1985.

López y Fuentes, Gregorio. *El indio.* 1935. Mexico City: Porrúa, 1975.

López-Lozano, Miguel. "The Politics of Blood: Miscegenation and Degeneration in Alejandro Morales's *The Rag Doll Plagues.*" *Aztlán: A Journal of Chicano Studies* 28.1 (2003): 39–74.

López Velarde, Ramón. "Suave patria." *Suave patria y otros poemas.* Mexico City: Fondo de Cultura Económica, 1983. 156–60.

Lovelock, J. E. *The Ages of Gaia: A Biography of Our Living Earth.* New York: Oxford UP, 1988.

Lowry, Malcolm. *Under the Volcano.* New York: Reynal and Hitchcock, 1947.

Lugo, Luis Alonso. "Remittances are Mexico's Biggest Source of Income, Says Fox." Associated Press, 24 Sept. 2003. (www.signosandiego.com/news/200030924-2051-us-mexico.html).

Malchow, H. L. *Gothic Images of Race in Nineteenth-Century Britain.* Palo Alto: Stanford UP, 1996.

Manuel, Frank E., and Fritzie P. Manuel. *Utopian Thought in the Western World.* Cambridge, MA: Harvard UP, 1979.

Márquez, Antonio C. "The Use and Abuse of History in Alejandro Morales's *The Brick People* and *The Rag Doll Plagues.*" *Alejandro Morales: Fiction, Past, Present, Future Perfect.* Ed. José Antonio Gurpegui. Tempe: Bilingual/Bilingüe, 1996. 76–85.

Martín-Rodríguez, Manuel M. "The Global Border: Transnationalism and Cultural Hybridism in Alejandro Morales's *The Rag Doll Plagues.*" *Alejandro Morales: Fiction, Past, Present, Future Perfect.* Ed. José Antonio Gurpegui. Tempe: Bilingual/Bilingüe, 1996. 86–98.

Martré, Gonzalo. *La ciencia ficción en México: hasta el año 2002.* Mexico City: Instituto Politécnico Nacional, 2004.

Marx, Leo. *The Machine in the Garden: Technology and the Pastoral Ideal in America.* New York: Oxford UP, 1964.

The Matrix. Dir. Andy and Larry Wachowski. Warner, 1999.

Menton, Seymour. *Latin America's New Historical Novel.* Austin: U of Texas P, 1993.

Merchant, Carolyn. *The Death of Nature: Women, Ecology and the Scientific Revolution*. San Francisco: Harper, 1980.

Metropolis. Dir. Fritz Lang. Screenplay Thea von Harbou. 1926. Kino International, restored authorized ed., 2002.

Meyer, Michael C., William L. Sherman, and Susan M. Deeds. *The Course of Mexican History*. Durham: Duke UP, 2003.

Middlebrook, Kevin. *The Paradox of the Revolution: Labor, the State and Authoritarianism in Mexico*. Baltimore: Johns Hopkins UP, 1995.

Mignolo, Walter. "La colonización de la memoria y la escritura de la historia." *De la crónica a la nueva narrativa mexicana*. Ed. Merlin H. Foster and Julio Ortega. Mexico City: Oasis, 1986. 13–28.

——. *The Dark Side of the Renaissance*. Ann Arbor: U of Michigan P, 1995.

Miller, Mary, and Karl Taube. *The Gods and Symbols of Ancient Mexico and the Maya*. London: Thames and Hudson, 1993.

Molina, Mauricio. *Mantis religiosa*. Mexico City: Aldus, 1996.

——. *Tiempo lunar*. Mexico City: Corunda, 1993.

Molina, Silvia. *Ascensión Tun*. Mexico City: Joaquín Mortiz, 1979.

Molina Enríquez, Andrés. *Los grandes problemas nacionales*. Mexico City: Carranza, 1909.

Monsiváis, Carlos. "De la cultura mexicana en vísperas del Tratado de Libre Comercio." *La educación y la cultura ante el Tratado de Libre Comercio*. Ed. Gilberto Guevara Niebla and Néstor García Canclini. Mexico City: Nueva Imagen, 1992. 179–209.

——. *Mexican Postcards*. Ed. and trans. John Kraniauskas. London: Verso, 1997.

——. *Los rituales del caos*. Mexico City: Era, 1995.

Monsiváis, Carlos, and Julio Scherer García. *Parte de guerra*. Mexico City: Aguilar, 1999.

Montrose, Louis. "The Work of Gender in the Discourse of Discovery." *New World Encounters*. Ed. Stephen Greenblatt. Berkeley: U of California P, 1993. 177–217.

Moraga, Cherríe. *The Last Generation: Prose and Poetry*. Boston: South End, 1993.

Morales, Alejandro. *Barrio on the Edge*. Trans. Francisco Lomelí. Tempe: Bilingual/Bilingüe, 1996.

——. *The Brick People*. Houston: Arte Público, 1988.

Morales, Alejandro. *Caras viejas y vino nuevo*. Mexico City: Joaquín Mortiz, 1975.

———. *"Cielos de la tierra* por Carmen Boullosa: escribiendo la utopía mexicana a través del eterno apocalipsis mexicano." *Acercamientos a Carmen Boullosa: Actas del Simposio "Conjugarse en infinitivo—la escritora Carmen Boullosa."* Ed. Barbara Dröscher and Carlos Rincón. Berlin: Frey, 1999. 193–201.

———. *Death of an Anglo*. Trans. Judith Ginsberg. Tempe: Bilingual/ Bilingüe, 1988.

———. "Dynamic Identities in Heterotopia." *Alejandro Morales: Fiction, Past, Present, Future Perfect*. Ed. José Antonio Gurpegui. Tempe: Bilingual/Bilingüe, 1996. 14–27.

———. *Old Faces and New Wine*. Trans. Max Martínez. San Diego: Maize, 1981.

———. *The Rag Doll Plagues*. Houston: Arte Público, 1994.

———. *Reto en el paraíso*. Mexico City: Grijalbo, 1993.

———. *La verdad sin voz*. Mexico City: Joaquín Mortiz, 1979.

———. *Waiting to Happen*. Los Angeles: Chusma, 2002.

More, Thomas. *Utopia*. 1516. Ed. Clarence H. Miller. New Haven: Yale UP, 2001.

Morison, Samuel Eliot. *Journals and Other Documents on the Life and Voyages of Christopher Columbus*. New York: Heritage, 1963.

Morson, Gary Saul. *The Boundaries of Genre*. Austin: U of Texas P, 1981.

Moylan, Tom. *Demand the Impossible: Science Fiction and the Utopian Imagination*. New York and London: Methuen, 1986.

———. *Scraps of the Untainted Sky: Science Fiction, Utopia, Dystopia*. Boulder: Westview, 2000.

Mumford, Lewis. *The City in History: Its Origins, Its Transformations, and Its Prospects*. New York: Harcourt, 1961.

———. "Utopia, the City, and the Machine." *Utopias and Utopian Thought*. Ed. Frank Manuel. London: Souvenir, 1973. 3–24.

Murphy, Patrick. *Literature, Nature, and Other: Ecofeminist Critiques*. Albany: State U of New York P, 1995.

Nervo, Amado. *Almas que pasan: últimas prosas de Amado Nervo*. Madrid: Tip. de la Revista de Archivos, 1906.

Nolasco Armas, Margarita. "La antropología aplicada en México y su destino final: el indigenismo." *De eso que llaman antropología mexicana*. Ed. Arturo Warman et al. Mexico City: Nuestro Tiempo, 1970. 94–118.

O'Gorman, Edmundo. *La invención de América*. Mexico City: Fondo de Cultura Económica, 1958.

———. *The Invention of America: An Inquiry into the Historical Nature of the New World and the Meaning of Its History*. Bloomington: Indiana UP, 1961.

Ortiz, Fernando. *Contrapunteo cubano del tabaco y el azúcar*. Havana: José Montero, 1940.

Ortner, Sherry B. "Is Female to Male as Nature Is to Culture?" *Women, Culture and Society*. Ed. Michele Zimbalist Rosaldo and Louise Lamphere. Palo Alto: Stanford UP, 1974. 67–87.

Orwell, George. *Animal Farm*. London: Signet, 1946.

———. *Nineteen Eighty-Four*. London: Secker and Warburg, 1949.

Pacheco, Cristina. *La última noche del tigre*. Mexico City: Océano, 1987.

Padilla, Ignacio. *Si volviesen sus majestades*. Mexico City: Nueva Imagen, 1996.

Palau, Pedro Ángel. *Memoria de los días*. Mexico City: Joaquín Mortiz, 1995.

Pastor, Beatriz. *El jardín y el peregrino*. Mexico City: Universidad Nacional Autónoma de México, 1999.

Paz, Octavio. *El laberinto de la soledad*. Mexico City: Fondo de Cultura Económica, 1950.

———. *The Labyrinth of Solitude*. 1950. Trans. Lysander Kemp. New York: Grove, 1985.

Pérez, Luciano. *Cuentos fantásticos de la ciudad de México, o, Aventuras en Mexicópolis*. Mexico City: Praxis, 2002.

Pérez Montfort, Ricardo. *Estampas de nacionalismo popular mexicano*. Mexico City: CIESAS, 1994.

Piedra, José. "Nationalizing Sissies." *¿Entiendes?: Queer Readings, Hispanic Writings*. Ed. Emilie L. Bergmann and Paul Julian Smith. Durham: Duke UP, 1995. 370–409.

Piercy, Marge. *Woman at the Edge of Time*. New York: Knopf, 1976.

———. *He, She, and It*. New York: Knopf; dist. Random, 1991.

Plato. *Republic*. 380 B.C. Trans. G. M. A Grube. Indianapolis, IN, and Cambridge, MA: Hackett, 1992.

Plumwood, Val. *Feminism and the Mastery of Nature*. New York: Routledge, 1993.

Poniatowska, Elena. *Massacre in Mexico.* Trans. Helen R. Lane. New York: Viking, 1975.

———. *La noche de Tlatelolco; testimonios de historia oral.* Mexico City: Era, 1971.

Prado, Gloria M. "En el amplio espacio de los márgenes: *Cielos de la tierra* de Carmen Boullosa." *Acercamientos a Carmen Boullosa: Actas del Simposio "Conjugarse en infinitivo—la escritora Carmen Boullosa.*" Ed. Barbara Dröscher and Carlos Rincón. Berlin: Frey, 1999. 202–09.

Pratt, Mary Louise. *Imperial Eyes.* New York: Routledge, 1992.

Priewe, Marc. "Bio-Politics and the ContamiNation of the Body in Alejandro Morales's *The Rag Doll Plagues.*" *MELUS: The Journal of the Society for the Study of the Multi-Ethnic Literature of the United States* 29.3–4 (2004): 397–412.

Quijano, Aníbal. *Modernidad, identidad y utopía en América Latina.* Quito: El Conejo, 1990.

———. "Modernity, Identity, and Utopia in Latin America." *The Postmodernism Debate in Latin America.* Ed. John Beverley, Michael Aronna, and José Miguel Oviedo. Durham: Duke UP, 1995. 201–16.

Rabasa, José. *Inventing A-M-E-R-I-C-A.* Norman: U of Oklahoma P, 1993.

Rama, Ángel. *Transculturación narrativa en América Latina.* Mexico City: Siglo Veintiuno, 1982.

Raudzens, George. *Technology, Disease, and Colonial Conquest.* London: Brill, 2001.

Reid, Anna. "The Operation of Orality and Memory in Carmen Boullosa's Fiction." *Acercamientos a Carmen Boullosa: Actas del Simposio "Conjugarse en infinitivo—la escritora Carmen Boullosa.*" Ed. Barbara Dröscher and Carlos Rincón. Berlin: Frey, 1999. 181–92.

Reyes-Tatinclaux, Leticia. "*Cristóbal Nonato,* ¿Descubrimiento o clausura del Nuevo Mundo?" *Revista de Crítica Literaria Latinoamericana* 15.30 (1989): 99–104.

Robinson, Kim Stanley. *The Gold Coast.* New York: St. Martin's, 1988.

Rodriguez, Richard. *Brown: The Last Discovery of America.* New York: Penguin, 2002.

Rowe, William, and Vivian Schelling. *Memory and Modernity in Latin America.* London: Verso, 1991.

Rueckert, William. "Literature and Ecology: An Experiment in Ecocriticism." *Iowa Review* 9 (1978): 71–86.

Rushdie, Salman. *The Satanic Verses.* 1988. New York: Viking, 1989.

Russ, Joanna. *The Female Man.* Boston: Beacon, 1975.

Sahagún, Bernardino de. *Historia de las cosas de la Nueva España.* 1557. Ed. Ángel María Garibay. Mexico City: Porrúa, 1986.

Saldaña-Portillo, Josefina. "Who Is the Indian in Aztlán? Re-Writing *Mestizaje*, Indianism, and Chicanismo from the Lacandón." *The Latin American Subaltern Studies Reader.* Ed. Ileana Rodríguez. Durham: Duke UP, 2001. 402–23.

Salles-Reese, Verónica. "Colonizando a la colonia: versiones postcoloniales de las crónicas." *Revista Canadiense de Estudios Hispánicos* 26.1–2 (2001): 141–53.

Samperio, Guillermo. *Gente de la ciudad.* Mexico City: Fondo de Cultura Económica, 1986.

Saona, Margarita. "Do We Still Need the Family to Imagine the Nation?" *Disciplines on the Line: Feminist Research on Spanish, Latin American, and U.S. Latina Women.* Ed. Anne J. Cruz, Rosalie Hernández-Pecoraro, and Joyce Tolliver. Newark: Juan de la Cuesta, 2003. 220–31.

Sargent, Lyman Tower, and Gregory Claeys. *The Utopia Reader.* New York: New York UP, 1999.

Schaffler, Federico. *Más allá de lo imaginado.* Mexico City. Consejo Nacional para la Cultura y las Artes, 1991.

Schneider, Luis Mario. "Artaud y México." *Viaje al país de los tarahumaras.* By Antonin Artaud. Mexico City: Secretaría de Educación Pública, 1975. 5–82.

Shelley, Mary Wollstonecraft. *Frankenstein, or, the New Prometheus.* 1818. New York: Modern Library, 1993.

Sheridan, Guillermo. *El dedo de oro.* Mexico City: Alfaguara, 1996.

Sigüenza y Góngora, Carlos de. "Alboroto y motín de los indios de México." 1693. *Teatro de virtudes políticas. Alboroto y motín de los indios de México.* Mexico City: Porrúa, 1986. 149–217.

Solares, Ignacio. *Nen, la inútil.* Mexico City: Alfaguara, 1994.

Sommer, Doris. *Foundational Fictions.* Berkeley and Los Angeles: U of California P, 1991.

Sontag, Susan. *AIDS and Its Metaphors.* New York: Farrar, 1989.

———. *Illness as Metaphor.* New York: Farrar, 1978.

Soylent Green. Dir. Richard Fleischer. Warner, 1973.

Stavans, Ilán. "Carlos Fuentes and the Future." *Science Fiction Studies* 20.61 (1993): 409–13.

Stavans, Ilán "Tristram Shandy regresa de nuevo." *Quimera* 68 (1987): 50–51.

Sterne, Laurence. *The Life and Opinions of Tristram Shandy, Gentleman.* 1759–67. New York: Penguin, 1967.

Story, Dale. *The Mexican Ruling Party: Stability and Authority.* New York: Praeger, 1986.

Taibo, Paco Ignacio II. *Máscara azteca y el doctor niebla (después del golpe).* Mexico City: Alfaguara, 1996.

Taylor, Claire. "Cities, Codes and Cyborgs in Carmen Boullosa's *Cielos de la tierra.*" *Bulletin of Hispanic Studies* 80.4 (2003): 479–92.

Taylor, Peter J. *Modernities: A Geohistorical Interpretation.* Minneapolis: U of Minnesota P, 1999.

Todorov, Tzvetan. *The Conquest of America: The Question of the Other.* Trans. Richard Howard. New York: Harper, 1984.

Torgovnick, Marianna. *Gone Primitive.* Chicago: U of Chicago P, 1990.

Torrez, Everardo. *Narco.* Houston: Arte Público, 2004.

Treichler, Paula A. *How to Have Theory in an Epidemic: Cultural Chronicles of AIDS.* Durham: Duke UP, 1999.

Trejo, Mario. *La ciencia ficción en México.* Mexico City: Insituto Politécnico Nacional, 2004.

Trejo Fuentes, Ignacio. "En búsqueda de la mexicanidad." *Quimera* 68 (1987): 28–33.

Trexler, Richard C. *Sex and Conquest.* Ithaca: Cornell UP, 1995.

Trujillo Muñoz, Gabriel. *Biografías del futuro: la ciencia ficción mexicana y sus autores.* Mexicali: Universidad Autónoma de Baja California, 2000.

———. *Confines: crónica de la ciencia ficción mexicana.* Mexico City: Vid, 1999.

———. *El futuro en llamas: cuentos clásicos de la ciencia ficción mexicana.* Mexico City: Vid, 1997.

Urroz, Eloy. *Las Rémoras.* Mexico City: Nueva Imagen, 1996.

Van Delden, Maarten. *Carlos Fuentes, Mexico, and Modernity.* Nashville: Vanderbilt UP, 1998.

Vasconcelos, José. *La raza cósmica.* Mexico City: Espasa-Calpe, 1948.

Verne, Jules. *Works of Jules Verne.* Ed. Charles F. Horne. New York: Parke, 1911.

Villalobos, José Pablo. "Border Real, Border Metaphor: Altering Boundaries in Miguel Méndez and Alejandro Morales." *Arizona Journal of Cultural Studies* 4 (2000): 131–40.

Volpi, Jorge. *El temperamento melancólico.* Mexico City: Nueva Imagen, 1996.

Warman, Arturo. "Todos santos y todos difuntos: crítica histórica de la antropología mexicana." *De eso que llaman antropología mexicana.* Arturo Warman et al. Mexico City: Nuestro Tiempo, 1970. 9–38.

Wegner, Phillip E. *Imaginary Communities: Utopia, the Nation, and the Spatial Histories of Modernity.* Berkeley: U of California P, 2002.

Wells, H. G. *The Shape of Things to Come.* London: Hutchinson, 1933. 9–94.

———. *The Time Machine.* 1895. *The H. G. Wells Reader.* Philadelphia: Courage, 1996.

White, Hayden. *Tropics of Discourse: Essays in Cultural Criticism.* Baltimore: Johns Hopkins UP, 1978.

Wittig, Monique. *Les Guerrillères.* 1969. Trans. David Le Vay. London: Owen, 1971.

Womack, John. *Zapata and the Mexican Revolution.* New York: Vintage, 1968.

Young, Robert C. *Colonial Desire: Hybridity in Theory, Culture, and Race.* New York: Routledge, 1995.

Yúdice, George. "Postmodernity and Transnational Capitalism in Latin America." *On Edge.* Ed. George Yúdice, Jean Franco, and Juan Flores. Minneapolis: U of Minnesota P, 1992. 1–28.

Zamora, Lois Parkinson. *The Usable Past: The Imagination of History in Recent Fiction of the Americas.* New York: Cambridge UP, 1997.

———. *Writing the Apocalypse: Historical Vision in Contemporary U.S. and Latin American Fiction.* New York: Cambridge UP, 1989.

Zamyatin, Yevgeny. *We.* (1920) 1924. Trans. Mirra Ginsburg. New York: Avon, 1972.

Index

About the Author

Miguel López-Lozano, University of New Mexico, teaches Latin American narrative and Border Studies. His research focuses on Mexican women indigenist writers, and on utopia, apocalypse, and globalization in the Mexican and Chicano novel. His articles have appeared in Mexico, the United States, and Germany.